Studying Appalachian Studies

Studying Appalachian Studies

Making the Path by Walking

Edited by
**CHAD BERRY, PHILLIP J. OBERMILLER,
AND SHAUNNA L. SCOTT**

UNIVERSITY OF ILLINOIS PRESS
Urbana, Chicago, and Springfield

Library of Congress Cataloging-in-Publication Data
Studying Appalachian studies: making the path by walking /
edited by Chad Berry, Phillip J. Obermiller, and Shaunna L. Scott.
pages cm
Includes bibliographical references and index.
ISBN 978-0-252-03929-4 (cloth : alk. paper)
ISBN 978-0-252-08083-8 (pbk. : alk. paper)
ISBN 978-0-252-09734-8 (e-book)
1. Appalachian Region—Study and teaching. 2. Appalachian
Region—Civilization.
I. Berry, Chad, 1963– editor. II. Obermiller, Phillip J., editor.
III. Scott, Shaunna L., 1960– editor.
F106.S93   2015
974—dc23   2014046097

Traveller, there is no path,
The path is made by walking.
By walking you make a path,
And turning, you look back
At a way you will never tread again.

—Antonio Machado, *Border of a Dream: Selected Poems*,
   translated by Willis Barnstone

This book is dedicated to all those walking
the Appalachian studies path.

To President West,

To a person who loves
the mountains and its
wonderful people.

Chad Berry
October 2019

Contents

Acknowledgments

Many folks have cleared the path for this journey, and we are grateful for their support. A special note of appreciation to Brent Hutchinson, Holly Baldridge, and Rita Ritchie at Hindman Settlement School for the place and the space; Susan Vaughn in the Office of the Academic Vice President at Berea College for her administrative backup; Laurie Matheson at the University of Illinois Press for her confidence and encouragement; Betsy Taylor, Emily Satterwhite, and Steve Fisher for their detailed and helpful comments; the contributors for their trust and patience; and our colleagues in Appalachian studies for their advice and insight (you know who you are).

Studying Appalachian Studies

Introduction

We began making our path for this book in 2008, a year and a half after the thirtieth anniversary of the Appalachian Studies Association, when former association presidents Chad Berry and Phil Obermiller convened some two dozen "Appalachianists" at Berea College to reflect on this collective endeavor. When compared to other interdisciplinary fields of study that emerged in response to social movements in the 1960s (e.g., women's studies and African American studies), Appalachian studies had been slower to produce a critical self-assessment. A consensus soon emerged that a critical consideration of the field was in order.

This book is not just about keeping up with the area-study Joneses, however. Nor is it intended only for an Appalachian studies audience. Although it will introduce readers to the field and possibly encourage new scholarship on the region, this examination of Appalachian studies has much to offer anyone interested in interdisciplinary research and practice. Those who challenge the intellectual blind spots of disciplinary balkanization and are place-committed to democratization, engagement, and participatory research centered on social justice should find the following essays of interest. The volume seeks to provide insights into how interdisciplinary fields of study emerge, organize, and institutionalize themselves and how they engage with local and global intellectual, political, and economic forces.

Our volume is not entirely without precedents, as is made clear in chapter 1. While some scholars in the Appalachian studies community have taken time to assess specific aspects of its work (Banks, Billings, and Tice 2002; Billings 2007; Brown et al. 2003; Cunningham 2003; Maggard 1986; Smith

1998; Tucker 2003; Walls and Billings 1977), to date the field has not produced a more systematic, comprehensive review of the field compared to other interdisciplinary fields such as women's studies and African American studies (Brown 1997; Butler and Walters 1991; Ginsberg 2008; Karenga 1993; Rojas 2007; Rooks 2006).

To rectify this, those who gathered in Berea in 2008 identified the topics addressed in this volume. Fundamental questions were posed: Exactly what *is* the field of Appalachian studies? What is its purpose? Whom does it serve? What has it done well? What has it not done well? Where should the field have gone? Where is it going? In an attempt to transcend the boundaries of the field, additional questions were posed: How does Appalachian studies compare with other fields of interdisciplinary studies? How does Appalachian studies interact with academic, social, and regional enterprises and institutions? How has the field defined legitimate "know-ers" and knowledge, and what are the pitfalls and misrepresentations of that process? What factors were important in creating the field of Appalachian studies? How did macro- and micro-level political factors and other contextual concerns affect the development of Appalachian studies, its content, the questions it asks, and the methods it employs? These are a few of the questions that the essays in this volume address.

Over time the group also constructed a book outline and brainstormed lists of authors who could write competently and even provocatively on the selected topics, with the goal of including the perspectives of established, experienced people in Appalachian studies, as well as young, emerging thinkers. Our work occurred in a series of phone and email conversations that occurred throughout the spring of 2009, when Shaunna Scott joined the editorial team. She took advantage of a sabbatical leave in New Zealand to interview students and faculty involved in Pacific Islands studies, using this opportunity to observe the parallels and differences between various types of place-based interdisciplinary studies. Phillip Obermiller and Chad Berry reviewed books and essays on related interdisciplinary fields, and all three drew upon their own experiences in and understandings of Appalachian studies, women's studies, and black/African American studies.

Interestingly, a book that was initially envisioned as a critical assessment, in part as a basis for passing the torch to a new generation, actually became the means by which the torch was passed to a new generation. This volume includes experienced contributors, such as Barbara Ellen Smith and Phillip Obermiller; people in midcareer, such as Chris Baker, Chad Berry, Donald Davis, Chris Green, Michael Samers, and Shaunna Scott; and a rising generation, such as Erica Abrams Locklear, Douglas Reichert Powell, and Amanda Fickey (who cowrote her chapter while still a doctoral student at the University of Kentucky).

The long gestation of this work was the result of a strong commitment to following the Appalachian studies tradition of making its projects democratic endeavors. The field, as will become apparent in the following chapters, has long placed a high value on participatory, engaged, and democratic processes, from writing to organizing conferences to community-based participatory research. This volume has been true to that commitment. It has been a collaborative effort, from planning to identifying contributors and even to the content of chapter 6, based, in part, on interviews with a diverse group of people involved in Appalachian studies. That said, we must acknowledge that this volume remains firmly lodged in the academic wing of Appalachian studies; we did not solicit input or invite contributions from academics working outside of Appalachian studies.

Apart from the process, what is the substance of this volume? The following summaries provide a sense of the vibrancy and tensions inherent in Appalachian studies and in interdisciplinary area studies at large.

Editors Shaunna Scott, Phillip Obermiller, and Chad Berry open the volume in chapter 1 by analyzing Appalachian studies in comparison to four other interdisciplinary fields that focus on either regional geography or identity and oppression, such as gender, race, and class: women's studies, African American studies, New West studies, and Pacific Islands studies. The histories and politics of a variety of interdisciplinary projects reveal the problems and potentials of Appalachian studies and interdisciplinary area studies generally. The chapter concludes with a specific examination of the history and development of Appalachian studies to provide a context for the subsequent essays.

Barbara Ellen Smith's contribution in chapter 2 uses feminist theory as a lens to examine the interaction of gender, sexuality, class, and race with identifying and being identified as Appalachian. After exploring the prevailing paradigms in Appalachian studies, each of which tends to homogenize a richly diverse region, Smith points to new and promising trends in the field. For her, Appalachian studies and women's studies "together point toward that knife-edge of tension between the impossibility of apprehending the full social complexity of Appalachia and the urgent necessity of making the attempt."

In chapter 3 Chris Green and Erica Abrams Locklear appraise developments in Appalachian literature, including fiction, folklore, poetry, and drama, since the nineteenth century. Finding both bright examples and obscure lacunae along the way, they provide an overview of Native American, African American, and women's contributions to Appalachian literature. In doing so they address problems of both geographic location (are regional boundaries important?) and psychological location (is there such a thing as a master Appalachian identity, or, given the diversity in the region, is a blended personal identity more likely?).

Donald Davis and Chris Baker in chapter 4 provide a "summary and analysis of the most well-known attempts at solving the problems of inadequate education, poverty, and economic development in Appalachia." After examining efforts to "fix" the region by organized religion, such as settlement schools, and the federal government, such as the Tennessee Valley Authority and the Appalachian Regional Commission, they describe the achievements of several successful community-based organizations, such as Save Our Cumberland Mountains (SOCM) and Kentuckians for the Commonwealth (KFTC) as effective grassroots strategies for addressing regional problems.

Based on evidence that many development efforts in Appalachia have failed, chapter 5 by Amanda Fickey and Michael Samers considers how development has been defined in the past and the ways those involved in Appalachian studies might redefine development. The authors use *Appalachia: A Report by the President's Appalachian Regional Commission, 1964*, as a case study, then present alternative economic development models being implemented internationally. They conclude by stressing the importance of teachers understanding these models so that they can share them with students and local communities.

In chapter 6 Phillip Obermiller and Shaunna Scott marshal both the relevant literature and the voices of those involved in the field to examine the accomplishments and shortcomings of Appalachian studies. The topics discussed include, but are not limited to, globalization, poststructuralism, community, diversity, quality of scholarship, community-based participatory research, theoretical orientations, social change, disciplinary blind spots, and the future of the field.

Douglas Reichert Powell offers alternative ways of thinking about and seeing the region in chapter 7. In this essay, Reichert Powell invites the reader to travel with him to Scottsboro, Alabama, site of the racially biased trial of the "Scottsboro Boys"; then to the arts-and-crafts center Tamarack, an economic development effort in West Virginia; and finally to the Cumberland Gap at the intersection of Virginia, Tennessee, and Kentucky. Throughout this journey, the author shares alternative ways of seeing these Appalachian landscapes, encouraging the reader to use these examples to reinterpret other elements of the region and develop new ways of thinking, writing, and teaching about Appalachia.

We close the volume by providing a brief overview of the emergence of higher education and its foundational disciplinary fields, discussing the connection Appalachian studies has to knowledge making since the Middle Ages. We offer some questions and some possible directions, and we focus attention on several biases and blind spots by those who teach and learn about the Appalachian region.

At least seven themes tie these essays together. One is the vibrancy and tension inherent in fields such as Appalachian studies. When inclusiveness is a core value in terms of academic disciplines, community participation, research methodologies, theoretical orientations, economic development strategies, or suitable areas of inquiry, to name only a few, tension is a given. The full range, from vigorous community discussions to rigorous academic disputation, is an occasionally untidy yet necessary aspect of area studies.

Another theme emerging from the essays is the need for both vertical and horizontal integration. Appalachian studies has kindred spirits in other interdisciplinary fields such as African American, women's, American, and southern studies. Each has much to offer the other in terms of insight and support, yet little integration has occurred, at least at the institutional level. In some instances, direct opposition is encountered, as has been the case with the wary acceptance by southern studies of Appalachian studies. The other vector of integration called for in the essays is vertical—from the regional, to the national, to the international. Appalachian studies, for instance, has made progress in globalizing its perspective, but much is left to be done in this area. The potential synergies involved in horizontal and vertical integration are remarkable.

A third theme is the need to go beyond the established memes, tropes, and stereotypes that adhere to the region and the people who study it. Popular and academic cultures have deeply embedded preconceptions about the region and the field of Appalachian studies, ranging from simply inaccurate to dismissive, an unfortunate circumstance that also affects other areas of interdisciplinary studies. The contributors to this volume advocate for and provide examples of a more sophisticated second level of observation leading to a more accurate understanding of both area studies and their subjects.

A strong desire for social change is the fourth theme running through these essays. It must be acknowledged that interdisciplinary fields such as Appalachian studies can and do attract academic careerists (hopefully at a lower rate than traditional disciplines). Nonetheless, in the roots of Appalachian studies and its cognate fields can be found movements for social justice, roots that provide both the historical basis and contemporary motivation for many involved in area studies. While the focus of each interdisciplinary field may vary, those involved most often are united by a shared sense of commitment and dedication to social change.

Another theme found throughout this volume is the diversity and heterogeneity of the subject matter in area studies. In the case of Appalachian studies, for instance, regional realities are complex, complicated, and not amenable to the "elegant" analyses admired in academia or the simplistic interpretations demanded by mass media. Conversely, the manifold and interrelated aspects of the subjects of area studies are precisely why an interdisciplinary approach is most effective. Put simply, the contributors agree that a multifaceted understanding of the messy reality found on Appalachia's uneven ground is simultaneously the only and best option.

A sixth common thread among the essays is a commitment to conducting applied, participatory action, or community-based research. When research is done in a democratic, participatory fashion—when communities are involved in formulating research topics and questions and then collecting and analyzing information—that research is more likely to be useful to the communities we serve. The assumption here is that knowledge is not solely the province of experts, that deep local knowledge comes from the grassroots, and that the most accurate (and powerful) insights are produced when campus and community collaborate.

A final theme can be expressed in the negative: what is not found across these essays are *them/us*, *insider/outsider* dichotomies. The more sophisticated analyses in interdisciplinary fields, including Appalachian studies, see identifying and vilifying Others as counterproductive to addressing larger structural concerns. Groups that collaborate to address social and political issues are more effective than those that are divided by surface differences.

Taken together, then, the essays presented here offer insights not only into Appalachian studies but also into interdisciplinary studies' potential, as well as the obstacles they face in the social and institutional construction of knowledge and the social change they hope to achieve.

CTB
PJO
SLS
At the Forks of Troublesome Creek
Hindman, Kentucky
2014

Works Cited

Banks, Alan, Dwight Billings, and Karen Tice. 2002. "Appalachian Studies, Resistance and Postmodernism." In *Appalachia: Social Context Past and Present*, 5th ed., edited by Phillip Obermiller and Michael Maloney, chap. 3. Dubuque, Iowa: Kendall/Hunt Publishers.

Billings, Dwight B. 2007. "Appalachian Studies and the Sociology of Appalachia." In *21st-Century Sociology: A Reference Handbook*, vol. 2, edited by Clifton D. Bryant and Dennis L. Peck, 390–96. Thousand Oaks, Calif.: Sage Publications.

Brown, Logan, Theresa Burchett-Anderson, Donavan Cain, and Jinny Turman Deal, with Howard Dorgan. 2003. "Where Have We Been? Where Are We Going? A History of the Appalachian Studies Association." *Appalachian Journal* 31(Fall): 30–92.

Brown, Wendy. 1997. "The Impossibility of Women's Studies." *Differences: A Journal of Feminist Women's Studies* 9(3): 79–101.

Butler, Johnella, and John Walters. 1991. *Transforming the Curriculum: Ethnic Studies and Women's Studies*. Albany: State University of New York Press.

Cunningham, Rodger. 2003. "Appalachian Studies among the Posts." *Journal of Appalachian Studies* 9(2): 377–86.

Ginsberg, Alice E., ed. 2008. *The Evolution of American Women's Studies: Reflections on Triumphs, Controversies, and Change*. New York: Palgrave Macmillan.

Karenga, Maulana. 1993. *Introduction to Black Studies*. Los Angeles: University of Sankore Press.

Maggard, Sally Ward. 1986. "Class and Gender: New Theoretical Priorities in Appalachian Studies." In *The Impact of Institutions in Appalachia (Proceedings of the Annual Appalachian Studies Conference 8)*, edited by Jim Lloyd and Anne G. Campbell, 100–113. Boone, N.C.: Appalachian Consortium Press.

Rojas, Fabio. 2007. *From Black Power to Black Studies: How a Radical Social Movement Became an Academic Discipline*. Baltimore, Md.: Johns Hopkins University Press.

Rooks, Noliwe M. 2006. *White Money/Black Power*. Boston: Beacon Press.

Smith, Barbara Ellen. 1998. "Walk-Ons in the Third Act: Women in Appalachian Historiography." *Journal of Appalachian Studies* 4(1): 1–23.

Tucker, Bruce. 2003. "Harry Caudill and the Problem of the Past." *Journal of Appalachian Studies* 9(1): 114–46.

Walls, David S., and Dwight B. Billings. 1977. "The Sociology of Southern Appalachia." *Appalachian Journal* 5(1): 125–28.

1

Making Appalachia

Interdisciplinary Fields and Appalachian Studies

SHAUNNA L. SCOTT, PHILLIP J. OBERMILLER,

AND CHAD BERRY

Our metaphor of "pathway" highlights how five interdisciplinary fields, women's, African American, New West, Pacific Islands, and Appalachian studies, though situated differently, nevertheless negotiate shared political terrains and seem to be headed in the same (or at least similar) directions. While the comparative method provides a clearer understanding of each of these fields, the chapter's primary focus is on the development of Appalachian studies. Having established this context, the chapter ends with a critical observation of the paths Appalachian studies has taken—as well as those it has overlooked.

For the sake of brevity, the term "area studies" will be used going forward in order to refer to interdisciplinary fields that focus not only upon regions or places, such as Appalachia and the Pacific Islands, but also upon social groups and forces, such as gender and race or ethnicity. In contemporary U.S. educational institutions, especially larger research universities, one can find a variety of area studies: Hispanic studies, working-class studies, southern studies, Asian studies, central Eurasian studies, and border studies, to name a few. The cases discussed here are representative, but not exhaustive, of the relevant possibilities. The founding and growth of each field is described, as are the points of contention and debate within each, along with the ways these points connect and depart from those of Appalachian studies.

Four Comparative Examples

WOMEN'S STUDIES

One of the most pervasive fields in area studies is women's studies (also currently known as women's and gender studies, gender studies, or gender and sexuality). In 1970 the first official women's studies program was founded at San Diego State University. The political impetus for the creation of women's studies programs was provided by the women's movement in the 1960s and 1970s and, more specifically and directly, from two pieces of federal legislation: Title IX in 1972, which prohibited discrimination against women in educational institutions that receive federal funding, and the Women's Educational Equity Act of 1974, which provided funding to institutions to help them comply with Title IX. Women's studies programs also received funding from the National Institute for Education, the Fund for the Improvement of Post-secondary Education (FIPSE), and general government revenues earmarked for education. In 1979 the National Women's Studies Association organized its first annual meeting, and today there are over eight hundred women's or gender studies programs in U.S. higher education (Ginsberg 2008). In addition, there are at least thirty-five journals focusing on gender and women's studies, including interdisciplinary journals such as *Frontiers*, *Signs*, *Women's Studies Quarterly*, and *Women's Studies: An Interdisciplinary Journal*, as well as disciplinary journals such as *Hypatia* (philosophy), *Gender and Society* (sociology), and *Psychology of Women Quarterly* (psychology) (Association of College and Research Libraries 2012).

Over recent decades, women's studies has expanded and become increasingly diverse. It has also been characterized by contentious debates about key issues, including whether biology provides an essential unity to women and forms the basis for fundamental differences between women and men (Martin 1997); whether the category of "woman" is variable, enacted, and defined by context rather than monolithic and causative (Auslander 1997); whether women's studies and the women's movement, dominated historically by white, educated women, could or should transform themselves to incorporate racial, ethnic, religious, and sexual diversity; whether and how to relate to studies of men and masculinity; how the academic field of women's studies should relate to interdisciplinary fields organized around other axes of differentiation; the political costs of institutional legitimation; the relationship between theory and practice (Bouchard 2012, 56–58); and whether women's studies should constitute a separate field of study or be integrated into traditional disciplines, or both (Brown 1997). The question of whether women's studies requires a broad epistemological break from traditional androcentric disciplines or requires new languages, conceptual structures, research methods, and practices based upon women's experiences and perspectives is far from settled. If, as Audre Lorde suggests, "the master's tools will never dismantle the master's house" (1984, 110), is it possible to forge a new set of tools that reflects the diversity incorporated into the category of "woman" or, for that matter, "man," "African American," or "Appalachian"?

Regardless of the political pressure to establish women's studies programs and the federal mandate and funding to do so, higher education's disciplinary and administrative willingness to integrate women and women's studies into the curriculum changed slowly. Initially, women's studies was thought to lack "objectivity" and be overly politicized; furthermore, the field's data sources, methods, analyses, and pedagogy were regarded as suspect. In many cases, faculty who became actively involved in women's studies were regarded as abandoning their main purpose and the rigor of disciplinary work; often work in women's studies was considered as a "sideline" to a primary mission of disciplinary research and education (Ginsberg 2008).

AFRICAN AMERICAN STUDIES

The Association for the Study of Negro Life and History was founded in 1915 by Jesse E. Moorland and Berea College alumnus Carter G. Woodson (Association for the Study of Negro Life and History 2010). However, when the civil rights movement gave rise to the Black Power movement in the late 1960s, both movements challenged higher education to revise the curriculum in a more inclusive and radical direction (Henderson 1971; Rojas 2007, 1–21). Student riots at San Francisco State College during the 1968–69 academic year resulted in the formation there of the first African American studies program in the country. Funding from the Ford Foundation fostered the growth of some five hundred campus-based African American (also known as black, Afro-American, or Africana) studies departments, programs, and institutes across the nation between 1968 and 1971 (Rojas 2007, 130–57; Rooks 2006, 93–105). Not surprisingly, black students, activists, academic institutions, the Ford Foundation, and the nation at large did not agree that such programs were needed and, even if they were, what purposes they should serve. The students, and later some program faculty, saw African American studies as a means to lay the groundwork for broader campaigns of social justice and to serve the needs and interests of African Americans. From this perspective, African American studies programs should challenge both the academic and the social status quo. By and large, higher education institutions took a pragmatic attitude, hoping to attract and co-opt black students and faculty into research careers, new curricula, intellectual debate, and reform-oriented civic engagement rather than confrontational political activism (Rojas 2007, 172–210). The Ford Foundation likewise saw African American studies as a way of promoting racial integration, first on campus and then in society at large. As a result, the foundation rejected funding proposals based on the tenets of Black Power, black nationalism, or revolutionary viewpoints (Rooks 2006, 106–22). As the black student population increased as a result of the GI Bill and still further after the Higher Education Act of 1965 and the Basic Educational Opportunity Program of 1972, critics saw African American studies as an illegitimate endeavor, a way of providing underprepared and unqualified students with a means to obtain a college degree (Rooks 2006; Rojas 2007).

In 1977 the National Council of Black Studies was founded. The University of Illinois at Champaign Library currently lists fifty-nine academic journals under the category of "black studies," including interdisciplinary journals such as *Journal of Black Studies* and *Black Scholar*, as well as disciplinary venues such as *Black Sociologist* and *Journal of African American History*. By 2012 there were roughly 200 programs and 45 departments in African American studies in U.S. colleges and universities; 146 institutions offer BAs, 15 offer MAs, and 15 offer PhDs in African American studies (Akalumat et al. 2013; Small 2012, 662).

Similar to women's studies, African American studies has grown dramatically since its establishment in the 1970s (Karenga 1993). It also has had many contentious debates about how to define the object of its study: Is there unity within racial/ethnic categories and, if so, on what basis? Who is African American, who is not, and why? What is the relationship between race and ethnicity? Can the field include sexual minorities and others? How should the academic field of African American studies relate to political activism and various movements for liberation (Rojas 2007; Rooks 2006)? Should African American studies constitute a separate discipline, "Africology," with an Afro-centered epistemology and methodology, also known as the "Temple University model," or should it be integrated into traditional disciplines, commonly referred to as the "Harvard University model" (Small 1999, 665)? Related to these questions of identity, epistemology, and political alliance, what should the field be called? Black studies, Afro-American studies, African American studies, or Africana studies (Small 1999)? How should it relate to theories and studies of whiteness, a racial/ethnic category against which "blackness" is defined and judged? Such questions remain.

NEW WEST STUDIES

Unlike women's and African American studies, New West studies has no direct relationship to social movements or governmental policies. However, it does trace its roots to the "new social history" in the 1960s and 1970s, an intellectual movement that sought to document the ignored and silenced histories of common citizens. Arising in the same decade as women's and African American studies and powerfully influenced by the New Left, new social history was an academic response to social movements of the twentieth century, particularly the labor, civil rights, Black Power, and women's movements, and a reflection of the academy's increasing emphasis on democratization and public service. A 1989 conference on the history of the American West laid the groundwork for a paradigm shift when, instead of discussing the traditional routes of pioneer settlement across the frontier, participants urged a critical rethinking of the concepts of "pioneer," "settlement," and "frontier" (Limerick, Milner, and Rankin 1991; White 1991; see also Limerick 1996, 2000). New western historians pointed out that the category of "pioneer" should not be restricted to European Americans but should also include Hispanic, Asian, and African Americans. Key concepts within western studies, such as "settlement," "frontier," and "civilization," were problematized as ethnocentric, power-laden terms obscuring the processes of colonialism and exploitation and the oppression that reinforced dominant political ideologies (Limerick 2000).

Critics of New West studies acknowledge that the field has produced some excellent work, particularly in recovering the history of women in the West; but they accuse its practitioners of failing to acknowledge its intellectual debt to predecessors such as Frederick Jackson Turner and his intellectual followers in the progressive school of western history (Allen 1994). New West studies emphasize the importance of interdisciplinary scholarship and the study of the environment, critics charge, while failing to acknowledge Turner's interdisciplinary and environmental studies advocacy (Allen 1994, 203). Critics also maintain that the emphasis on processes of colonialism is nothing new; the progressive school had long conceptualized the western economy as a colonial one in which western business owners and workers were exploited by eastern capital (Allen 1994, 205). In addition, New West studies, they argue, have traded one form of selectivity and exclusion for another. While their predecessors emphasized ethnic and class diversity among European "settlers," New West scholars regard Europeans as a monolithic whole, instead preferring to focus on Native, Hispanic, and Asian populations (Allen 1994, 203). Finally, they accuse New West studies of being overly politicized. Some accuse it of "presentism"—that is, using history to wage contemporary political battles (Allen 1994, 206–7); others view it as an attempt to enforce "political correctness" and advance a neo-Marxist political agenda (Allen 1994, 202; Nash 1993; Thompson 1993).

Compared to women's and African American studies, area studies focusing on the American West are not widely institutionalized as separate academic programs and departments. Much of the scholarship in this area occurs in history departments and American studies programs and through informal and temporary interdisciplinary collaboration in history, literature, environmental studies, and the social sciences. The University of Colorado at Boulder's Center of the American West offers an undergraduate studies certificate in western American studies, while Central Wyoming College and Wyoming's community colleges offer associate of arts degrees in western American studies. Regional and state history journals such as *Western Historical Quarterly*, *Great Plains Quarterly*, *California History*, and *Journal of Mormon History* are common publishing venues for New West researchers. New West scholarship is also published in history journals such as the *American Historical Review* and the *Historian*, in literary and arts journals, and in interdisciplinary journals in American studies, environmental studies, and planning and public policy journals.

PACIFIC ISLANDS STUDIES

This field takes on the challenging task of studying the nations and territories of the Pacific Ocean, including 25,000 islands spread over 65.3 million square miles, one-third of the earth's surface. On these islands, 125 languages are spoken by approximately 10 million people (PIPSA 2010). Pacific Islands studies traces its roots to amateur ethnographies and travel writing from the seventeenth century and to articles published in *Oceania* and the *Journal of the Polynesian Society* in the late nineteenth century. In 1946 the Australian National University founded the Research School of Pacific Studies. In 1950 the University of Hawaii established the Pacific Islands Studies Program, which evolved into the Center for Pacific Island Studies by 1973 (Teaiwa 2001, 348). Interest in Pacific Islands studies boomed as the islands decolonized in the 1970s. Interestingly, centers for Pacific Islands studies are located in Hawaii and Australia but not at Fiji's University of the South Pacific, which is owned by several nations with a large Pacific Islander population (Teaiwa 2001, 348).

By the end of the twentieth century, Asian studies had emerged and was either viewed as a rival to or incorporated in Pacific Islands studies as Pacific,

Pacific Rim, or Asia-Pacific studies (Wesley-Smith 1995, 121–23). There are currently hundreds of Asia Pacific centers and programs at universities and colleges in the United States, Australia, New Zealand, China, Japan, Canada, the United Kingdom, and elsewhere. Scholars interested in the Pacific find their homes in professional associations, such as the Pacific Science Association (1920), the Pacific Islands Political Studies Association (1987), the Pacific Islands Political Association (1987), and the recent Asia Pacific Studies Association. Also, the International Studies Association and various disciplinary associations have sections devoted to the Pacific and Asia. Major journals related to this area include *Oceania, Pacific Science, Pacific Studies, Journal of Pacific Studies, Contemporary Pacific, Journal of Asia and Pacific Studies, International Journal of Asia Pacific Studies,* and *Asia Pacific World.*

The discipline of anthropology has been centrally engaged in the study of the Pacific since Bronisław Malinowski was stranded there during World War I and, as a result, studied indigenous trade, society, and culture in the Trobriand Islands (see Malinowski [1922] 1984). Historians, social scientists, and literary/cultural studies scholars have also played an important role in the field (White and Tengan 2001, 384). Interdisciplinary integration has been more "on paper" than in fact, according to self-critical Pacific Island studies scholars (Wesley-Smith 1995; Whimp 2008), though the most common interdisciplinary collaborations occur between anthropology and history and in the field of political economy (Wesley-Smith 1995, 128).

A factor in the emergence of Pacific Islands studies was the region's strategic importance during World War II and the subsequent Cold War. As a consequence, much of the early scholarship on the Pacific was done by nonnative representatives of the nation-states and militaries that sought control of this territory for strategic purposes. According to Wesley-Smith (1995), the pragmatic focus of Pacific Islands studies has been particularly evident at the University of Hawaii and the Australian National University and in New Zealand. The Australian model, also employed by New Zealand, maintained traditional disciplinary boundaries in an effort to educate professionals with career interests in former island colonies. The U.S. model emphasized more interdisciplinary collaboration because it assumed that a variety of disciplines and tools were necessary to protect the variety of U.S. interests in the region.

In addition to scholars engaged in service to security interests, others were drawn to the Pacific Islands as "laboratories" for research and experimentation (Wesley-Smith 1995, 121). Like the pragmatically motivated researchers, those employing the "laboratory" model assumed that it was "possible to understand other societies and even whole regions in their totality, that there are certain essential characteristics that, once grasped, will lead to an adequate understanding of the whole" (117–18). Wesley-Smith's list of conceptual problems with traditional pragmatic and laboratory studies of the Pacific is similar to the list of problems associated with Appalachian studies and the other area studies reviewed above. First, the regional unit of analysis is arbitrary and based upon historic constructs of strategic political-economic interests. When geographic boundaries dictate a field of study, as they do for Pacific, New West, and Appalachian studies, the region becomes reified. As a consequence, there is a tendency to overemphasize assumed continuities and to ignore both variation and context, particularly linkages to other places. This, ultimately, creates both an insider-outsider dichotomy that distracts from the complexity of spatially organized social relations (120–21) and an exclusionary "insider identity" that marginalizes some within the region (Teaiwa 2001, 347).

Just as the 1960s proved to be a transformational era for studies of the U.S. West, women, and African Americans, a new rationale and purpose for Pacific studies emerged in this era as well: the empowerment rationale (Wesley-Smith 1995). The emergence of this orientation coincides with decolonization in the Pacific in the 1960s and 1970s; not coincidentally, the field sought to reorient itself to serve the needs and interests of the Pacific Islands rather than the nations that once colonized them (124–25). While indigenization of the academy is integral to this approach (Hau'ofa 1975; Harrison [1991] 1997), some have argued that merely introducing more native Pacific Islanders to universities is not sufficient. In order to change Pacific Islands studies, one must challenge its Western epistemological and methodological roots and create "systemized bodies of knowledge" based upon indigenous histories, beliefs, and practices (Wesley-Smith 1995, 126; Teaiwa 2001), a project that echoes Lorde's (1984) challenge to women's studies and to the Temple University model of African American studies (Small 1999, 663–65). A concern in this process is that the indigenization of Pacific studies could evolve into a "reverse orientalism" (Said 1991, 24) that excludes or devalues work done by nonindigenous scholars while reinforcing insider/outsider dichotomies. Finally, critics note that the "Pacific Islands" have a limited utility as a unit of analysis for scholarship because of the heterogeneity and spatial dispersion of these islands. Wesley-Smith advocates, instead, that Pacific Islands studies "move toward more solid, much smaller spatial categories" (1995, 127) so as to transition from the study of the history and politics *of* Pacific Islands to an examination of history and politics *in* the Pacific Islands (an approach similar to the argument regarding Appalachia made in Scott 2002).

Appalachian Studies

The Appalachian region includes the Allegheny, Blue Ridge, and Smoky Mountains and the Cumberland Plateau, as well as the roughly twenty-five million people who live amid these mountains and valleys. In addition, Appalachian studies also embraces the millions of people who have migrated from the region but whose heritage has deep roots in the region. The migrants and their descendants, often called "urban Appalachians," form an interesting middle position in the perceived dichotomy between studies of social groups (black studies, women's studies) and those based on geographical areas (New West studies, Pacific Islands studies). Urban Appalachians are people who live away from the region yet still feel connected to the region; as such, they invite Appalachian studies to ask questions similar to those posed in other fields of study about group membership, place-based identity, and diaspora (Alexander and Berry 2010; Obermiller 2004).

Similar to Pacific Islands and New West studies, Appalachian studies draws upon a much longer history that precedes its institution as an interdisciplinary academic enterprise in the 1970s. The field of Appalachian studies can trace its origins to the home missionary movement of the eighteenth and nineteenth centuries, which aimed to spread Christianity to frontier areas; to the local color writers who wrote travel logs and fictional stories set in the mountains during the late nineteenth century; to the settlement school movements of the Progressive Era (1890–1920), which sometimes sought to educate and assimilate rural mountaineers to adopt urban, middle- and upper-middle-class norms, values, and behaviors; and to the rural handicraft and Danish folk school movements, which sought to reinvigorate craftsmanship and teach practical, mechanical, agricultural, and citizenship skills to rural working people. Two institutions, the Conference of Southern Mountain Workers (later named the Council of the Southern Mountains in 1954) and the Highlander Folk School, both influenced by the Danish folk school movement, were key precursors to and influences on Appalachian studies.

THE COUNCIL OF THE SOUTHERN MOUNTAINS AND THE APPALACHIAN VOLUNTEERS

The settlement schools, many mountain colleges such as Berea College, and some components of the Council of the Southern Mountains focused on defining, "preserving," teaching, and marketing regional arts and crafts (Becker 1998; Whisnant 1983). In reaction to the alienating and exploitive effects of industrialization and to a large influx of immigrants to this country, participants in this folk movement often ignored the cultural traditions and products of non-Celtic and non-Anglo ethnic groups in the mountains in a search for a "pure" and "nostalgic" British whiteness (Satterwhite 2011; Whisnant 1983). Established in 1913, the Conference of Southern Mountain Workers was composed largely of Appalachian academics, agricultural extension workers, home mission board members, settlement school administrators, and participants in the rural handicraft and folk school movements. Funded by the Russell Sage Foundation and based in Berea, Kentucky, the Conference of Southern Mountain Workers held annual conferences and special commission meetings where its membership discussed health, education, religion, and crafts in Appalachia.

In 1954 the group changed its name to the Council of the Southern Mountains (CSM) and remained in operation until 1989.[1] From 1925 to 1989 the CSM published a quarterly magazine called *Mountain Life and Work* that included poetry, essays, photographs, cartoons, and news articles. In the 1950s and 1960s Chicago insurance magnate W. Clement Stone and the Ford Foundation funded the CSM to develop programs and centers to assist Appalachian out-migrants adjust to urban life in the Midwest (Obermiller and Wagner 2000; Berry 2000). This funding also allowed the CSM to hold summer workshops for educating urban and rural social workers and teachers about Appalachians and to organize college student volunteers to do community development and education in the region (Whisnant 1980, 3–39). The Appalachian Volunteer (AV) program received funding from the federal Office of Economic Opportunity (OEO) and was a precursor to the national program, Volunteers in Service to America (VISTA).

Tensions emerged between the CSM's more conservative, reform-oriented approach to community and economic development and the more radical, confrontational approach adopted by the young AVs in the 1960s. In 1966 the AVs broke away from the CSM, incorporated as an independent nonprofit, and moved their headquarters out of Berea, taking OEO funding with them (Kiffmeyer 2008). But this move did not resolve the conflict between the reform and radical forces within the CSM. At the 1969 and 1970 CSM conferences, held in North Carolina, various motions were passed that resulted in the withdrawal of Ford Foundation funding, the resignation of the CSM's executive director, and the exodus of many longtime CSM members who charged that the organization had been taken over by radical outside agitators. These motions included a proposal that low-income people compose at least 51 percent of the CSM board of directors, as well as resolutions opposing the Vietnam War and strip mining and favoring a living wage. In 1972 a reorganized CSM moved its headquarters to Clintwood, Virginia, and focused on such issues as welfare, women's and workers' rights, mine health and safety, opposition to strip mining, environmentalism, and alternative economic development. The CSM disbanded in 1989.

The AVs, in contrast, had ceased operation in 1969 after the organization was accused of being "un-American" (i.e., Communist). Because the AVs, along with other OEO community development programs, had come under attack from conservative lawmakers, federal funding for this initiative was eliminated. Before dissolving, the AVs transferred workforce training projects to the Commission on Religion in Appalachia (CORA), an ecumenical antipoverty organization that operated from 1965 to 2006 (West Virginia Council of Churches 2013). It also transferred advocacy projects to the Appalachian Research and Defense Fund (now AppalReD Legal Aid; see AppalReD 2013), which is still in operation.

THE HIGHLANDER CENTER

Inspired by the Danish folk school movement, Myles Horton, Don West, and James Dombrowski established the Highlander Center in 1932, taking it in a more overtly political and activist direction than the CSM—a direction that recognized and resisted class, race/ethnicity, and gender oppression. During the 1930s through the 1960s, Highlander played a fundamental role in labor organizing and racial integration in the mountains and the South. Its workshops and training sessions, attended by Rosa Parks, Ralph Abernathy, John Lewis, and Martin Luther King, Jr., among others, played a part in the Montgomery bus boycott, the Student Nonviolent Coordinating Committee (SNCC), and the provision of literacy education to assist African Americans to qualify to vote in the Jim Crow South. "Long before we started sitting in, long before we'd been on the freedom rides, some of us got our foundation . . . at Highlander," reported Georgia congressman John Lewis (Cornish 2007). Lewis, organizer of the lunch counter protests in Nashville and chairman of the SNCC, visited Highlander as a college student. Accused of being Communist, Highlander's charter was revoked, and its Monteagle, Tennessee, properties were seized in 1961; the school immediately reopened in Knoxville as the Highlander Research and Education Center. In 1972 it moved to its current location in New Market, Tennessee, where it continues to support grassroots struggles of all kinds (Highlander Research and Education Center 2013). Highlander programs have continued to evolve in response to regional and global transformation, now focusing on immigration, bilingual labor organizing, environmental issues, sexuality, local economic development, and youth leadership training.

Highlander also played a key role in the landmark Appalachian Land Ownership Study (Appalachian Land Ownership Task Force 1983), a community-based, participatory research project involving academics, activists, students, and citizens funded by the Appalachian Regional Commission in 1979–80. The landownership study is still cited as one of the transformative experiences in the field of Appalachian studies (Scott 2008); it also set a standard for evaluating later Appalachian studies collaborative initiatives. The study's renown is not simply the result of many policy reports and scholarly publications. Rather, the study was most noteworthy because it emerged from the grassroots efforts of the Appalachian Alliance, formed in response to major flooding in 1977. The alliance, in turn, provided the impetus for the creation of several new community-based organizations—most notably, Kentuckians for the Commonwealth (Scott 2009).

APPALSHOP

Another important precursor to and ongoing element of Appalachian studies more generally is the arts and media cooperative Appalshop. Founded in 1969 as an OEO project during the War on Poverty, Appalshop sought to train young people in media production so that they might learn valuable, marketable skills while at the same time telling the story of their region and communities and working to solve social problems. As the only rural initiative funded by the OEO and the only such project still in operation, Appalshop has become a nationally and internationally known arts and media cooperative. Though it is best known for its documentary films, which are routinely aired on public television, screened at film festivals, and used in classrooms throughout the world, Appalshop also runs a community radio station; produces storytelling, theater, and public arts projects; and provides filmmaking and media training to youth and community organizations throughout the region. Appalshop has managed to integrate two strains of the Appalachian studies movement, using its film, theater, radio, musical, and other productions to document and celebrate regional arts, cultures, and traditions while at the same time using these tools to tackle difficult social issues and political conflicts affecting the region. In addition, Appalshop regularly sponsors international cultural exchanges with filmmakers, storytellers, artists, and musicians throughout the world. It has received funding from both public sources and private foundations (Appalshop 2013). Elements of the Appalshop model of community-based and public arts and media production have spread beyond the Appalachian context to other rural regions in the United States and the world.

THE APPALACHIAN STUDIES ASSOCIATION

The interdisciplinary academic field of Appalachian studies was launched in the 1970s. The first conference at Clinch Valley College in 1970, the brainchild of the CSM Educational Commission, was held in the year following the creation of Appalshop, an obviously transformative time for the region. The inaugural conference included "college professors, graduate students, undergraduate students, community organizers, community activists, Community Action program staff, National Education Association staff, and representatives from religious groups" (Best 2011, 56). The gathering was cancelled during its second day due to disagreements over the academic versus the social goals of the meeting. Following that, the *Appalachian Journal* was established in 1972 at Appalachian State University in Boone, North Carolina (Brown et al. 2003, 31).

In 1978 Richard Drake convened an organizational meeting at Berea College to outline the goals of what would become the annual Appalachian Studies Conference (Brown et al. 2003, 35). The primary goal of this conference was to provide a space for diverse participants to present their work and engage in dialogue; this would include activists, artists, and scholars interested in and committed to the Appalachian region. Undeterred by the bitter cold at the 1979 conference, held at a 4-H Camp in Jackson Mill, West Virginia, or the 1982 snowstorm that chased attendees away from the Blue Ridge Assembly on Black Mountain, North Carolina, the annual conferences persisted and grew, from 250 attendees at the 1978 meeting to 789 at the 2014 conference.

Over time the conferences not only succeeded in terms of membership growth but also played a central role in various other initiatives throughout the region. As conference chair Richard Drake noted in preparation for the 1985 conference, the annual gathering had supported the 1979 Appalachian Land Ownership Study and given birth to the Appalachian Writers Association in addition to providing a forum for Appalachian scholarship, music, art, and activism.[2] He observed that the conference had included "its own harshest critics who have accused Appalachian Studies of being both self-serving and irrelevant" (Drake 1984, 1). Quoting Jim Wayne Miller, who said that debates in Appalachian studies had captured the "intellectual situation interior to the region," Drake concluded, "If indeed we have talked meaningfully about Appalachia in all its complexity and diversity, we have accomplished a great deal already" (1).

APPALACHIAN STUDIES CENTERS

During the 1970s, Appalachian studies as an academic field was institution-alized beyond the Appalachian Studies Association (ASA) through Appa-lachian studies centers in regional universities, colleges, and community colleges, including Appalachian State University, Berea College, East Ten-nessee State University, Eastern Kentucky University, North Georgia Col-lege and State University, Sinclair Community College, Radford University, Southeast Kentucky Community and Technical College, and the University of Kentucky, as well as regional studies centers at Mars Hill College, West Virginia University, and Western Carolina University (Appalachian Stud-ies Association 2013b). Thirty-six private four-year liberal arts institutions spread across the central Appalachian Mountains are members of the Ap-palachian College Association, which was created in 1980 with funding from the Andrew W. Mellon Foundation to share ideas and resources and promote collaborative efforts to serve the region and its people (Appalachian College Association 2013a, 2013b). Some of these colleges offer individual-ized undergraduate majors, official minors, or certificate programs in Ap-palachian studies; most receive the bulk of their students from within or at least near the Appalachian region. Generally, Appalachian studies students earn degrees within a traditional discipline, such as history or geography, and then pursue a specialization in the region, though in some cases mas-ter's degrees can be earned in Appalachian studies. Appalachian studies scholarship is published in such journals as the *Appalachian Journal, Journal of Appalachian Studies, Now & Then*, and *Appalachian Heritage*, as well as disciplinary and subregional journals such as *West Virginia History, North Carolina Historical Review*, and *Tennessee Folklore Society Bulletin*, among others (Appalachian Studies Association 2013b). In addition, some Appa-lachian studies scholarship finds a home in disciplinary, American, and southern studies journals.

CRITICAL COMMENTARY

Though there have been conflicts between the radical and reform camps in Appalachian studies, both have shared an enduring commitment to collabo-rate in order to address significant issues facing the region. To this end, the ASA provides scholarships for citizens and community activists to attend the conference. These initiatives receive financial support from the ASA mem-bership and the Appalachian Regional Commission. Citizens and activists are sometimes integrated into Appalachian studies research, into posters and presentations, and also into publications (Appalachian Land Ownership Task

Force 1983; Fisher 1993; Fisher and Smith 2012; Hinsdale, Lewis, and Waller 1995; McSpirit, Faltraco, and Bailey 2012). Appalachian centers at institutions of higher learning, along with the Highlander Center, Appalshop, and other institutions throughout the region, have played an important role in supporting this effort through community-based participatory research, leadership training, and service-learning initiatives. The *Journal of Appalachian Studies* regularly features "Teaching" or "Community Notes" columns that describe collaborations between researchers, students, activists, and residents to document the past, inventory local knowledge and assets, and promote community empowerment and sustainable development.

This is not to say that all Appalachian studies scholarship uses community-based, participatory research methods. Nevertheless, a case can be made that Appalachian studies places a high value on local and regional knowledge, dialogical scholarship and writing, and a critique of how authority (including technocratic/scholarly authority) delegitimates and dismisses local knowledge, thereby disempowering communities, families, and individuals in the region (Appalachian Land Ownership Task Force 1983; Cable 2012; Fisher 1993; Gaventa 1982; Hinsdale, Lewis, and Waller 1995; Hufford 1998, 2000; Keefe 2009; Puckett et al. 2012; Reid and Taylor 2010; McSpirit, Faltraco, and Bailey 2012; Spatig and Amerikaner 2014). Maintaining this tension-filled yet productive partnership, however, remains a challenge in contemporary Appalachian studies.

It is important to acknowledge that a great deal of applied and theoretical knowledge about Appalachia and its people has occurred, and continues to occur, outside the domain of academic Appalachian studies, such as the Appalachian Studies Association and Appalachian centers and studies programs. This work includes investigative journalism, documentary films, contract research for the Appalachian Regional Commission (ARC) and other government agencies, community-based participatory research addressing local and regional issues, and academic research conducted by disinterested scholars who simply use the region as a convenient unit of analysis. In other words, much knowledge about Appalachia and many representations of the region have been produced outside of the institutional confines of Appalachian studies as represented by the ASA and Appalachian studies centers and programs throughout the region.

In addition to its commitment to participatory research and community engagement, Appalachian studies provides an example of the push-and-pull tension between disciplinary-based inquiry and interdisciplinary endeavors. The field holds an annual interdisciplinary conference each spring sponsored by the ASA, with support from various Appalachian studies centers and the

Appalachian Regional Commission. However, there are a number of other types of conferences and institutions that take a less holistic approach, focusing on various aspects of the region or on groups or communities in Appalachia or, in at least one case, choosing a disciplinary perspective over an interdisciplinary one. Those who write about the region convene at the Appalachian Writers' Workshop and the Southern Appalachian Writers Cooperative; in crafts, music, and dance, the John C. Campbell Folk School, Augusta Heritage Center, Arrowmont School of Arts and Crafts, and the Southern Highland Craft Guild are a few of the regionally focused institutions that offer a space to work and interact. The Women of Appalachia Conference is held annually in Ohio.

The Society for Appalachian Historians (SAH) represents a disciplinary approach to the study of Appalachia. Founded in 2009 by a caucus of historians who met during the annual meetings of the Southern Historical Association, the SAH began as a working group in which senior scholars mentored young scholars who were interested in Appalachian history. It now holds annual meetings of forty to fifty attendees who convene in sequential sessions to discuss preposted papers. This format allows the members of the group to retain a focus on mentorship. The founding document of the SAH demonstrates the disciplinary solidarity that often threatens to pull apart interdisciplinary endeavors: "While the Appalachian Studies Association remains a flagship conference [*sic*], historians seem to have taken a bit of a backseat to other disciplines at the annual meeting" (Richard Starnes, pers. comm., November 9, 2009, in which he proposed "a new organization" and an "inaugural conference").[3] Although they have been concerned that history was not getting enough attention at the Appalachian studies conference, SAH and other specialized groups can more positively be viewed as a part of the maturation of the field. Just as the Appalachian studies bibliography has grown and diversified to include works on regional history, literature, poetry, and social conditions, it is not surprising that there are now books, programs, workshops, and working groups with a particular disciplinary focus within the field of Appalachian studies.

An early preoccupation of Appalachian studies was to document, historically, ethnographically, and journalistically, Appalachian cultures, traditions, music, stories, crafts, language, skills, and creative arts—all of which were thought to be disappearing in the wake of the region's obvious and systematic incorporation into industrialized capitalism and the homogenization that attends this transformation. Building upon American pragmatism, populism, radical, and/or Marxian social history traditions, some academics have also spent a great deal of effort documenting exploitation, class conflict, and politics in the central Appalachian coalfields (e.g., Corbin 1981; Eller 1982; Hennen 1996; Hevener [1978] 2002; Lewis 1998; Portelli 2010; Scott 1995; Smith 1987). Stephen Fisher (1993) and his work with Barbara Ellen Smith (2012) have documented Appalachian social movements and other practices of political resistance and social transformation. Social scientists and demographers have documented migration "out from" and "back to" the region, with an emphasis on investigating how kinship and community ties organize migratory patterns and the impact of migration on economic well-being (Berry 2000; Halperin 1990; Ludke and Obermiller 2014; Obermiller, Wagner, and Tucker 2000; Schwarzweller, Brown, and Mangalam 1971), the construction of Appalachian regional/ethnic identities (Batteau 1990; Billings, Norman, and Ledford 1999; Hsuing 1997; Obermiller 1981), and the discrimination and inequities faced by Appalachian families who have left the region (Berry 2000; Gitlin and Hollander 1970; Hartigan 1999; Obermiller and Philliber 1987).

Over the past decade and a half, environmental, social justice, and other movements have displaced class conflict and unions as the cutting edge of regional dissent and social movements and, therefore, have taken a greater share of academic and literary/artistic attention in the field of Appalachian studies (Bell 2013; Bell and York 2010; Burns 2007; Davis 2000; Engelhardt 2003; Foster 1988; Fritsch and Johannsen 2004; House and Howard 2009; Howell 2002; Keefe 2009; McNeil 2011; McSpirit, Faltraco, and Bailey 2012; Montrie 2003; Morrone and Buckley 2011; Reece 2006; Reece and Krupa 2013; Scott 2010). Those who study central Appalachia have much to contribute to contemporary environmental studies and the political ecology literature by virtue of the central role the region has played in energy industries and in water quality. Central Appalachia is a major coal producer and the scene of major coal-related disasters (coal waste spill, flooding, mine explosions, landslides, land subsidence, acid rain, groundwater and stream contamination), health problems (cancer, respiratory diseases), and highly destructive forms of mining practices (mountaintop removal). As such, it is relevant to some of the major issues facing the planet today: greenhouse gas production, decreased biodiversity, air and water pollution, the production of toxic and carcinogenic waste products, and global climate change. The region is also host to natural gas production, processing, and piping, including the controversial practice of hydraulic fracturing (fracking). Fracking has been associated with water contamination, cancer, increased methane release, and, most recently, increased earthquakes. The application of new technologies to natural gas extraction has resulted in cheaper natural gas, which is currently out-competing coal on the energy market (Gold 2014). This, along with exhaustion of the region's easily accessible coal seams and concerns about coal's impact on global climate change and public health, has resulted in a decline in the region's coal industry. The central Appalachian coalfields, therefore, are facing dire economic challenges and the need to transition to a more diverse and sustainable postcoal economy.

Poverty and economic development have long been a central focus of research on Appalachia. This is not surprising, given the region's definition as a poverty "problem area" in the 1960s (Eller 2008; Kiffmeyer 2008; Whisnant 1980; see also Fickey and Samers in this volume). The "growth center" economic development strategy adopted by the ARC in the 1960s and 1970s encouraged investment of financial resources in urban centers and the transportation networks between them. This strategy was criticized by regional leaders, activists, and academics for its propensity to concentrate money in cities located on the periphery of the region and also for its implicit assumption that depopulation of the region and urbanization were the key to economic "progress" (Eller 2008, 180–85). From this perspective, Appalachian lands seemed destined to serve two purposes: the central part of the mountains could provide an environmental "sacrifice" zone for energy production through strip mining and mountaintop removal and serve as a site to dump garbage and toxic waste, while the southern section could offer a wilderness preserve and national recreational playground for (wealthy) urban dwellers in the Great Smoky Mountains National Park, Blue Ridge, and Shenandoah Valley. Both scenarios showed little regard for the people residing in the region who, like the Cherokee before them, were expected to clear the way for economic "growth" and profit generation. Appalachian studies activists, students, and researchers have resisted this dominant trend with various initiatives to challenge environmentally destructive economic development driven solely by profit motive (McSpirit, Faltraco, and Bailey 2012) and to promote local community planning to imagine different economic futures for the region (Fritsch and Johannsen 2004; Howell 2002; Keefe 2009; Seitz 1995). Here Appalachian studies is building on its traditional roots as embodied by the Highlander Center and those inspired by the Danish folk school movement. However, Appalachian studies could make more of an effort to connect to critical and sustainable economic development research and vice versa (Escobar 1992; Shet 1987; Shiva 1989).

Appalachian studies scholarship has not necessarily been progressive and inclusive. Despite early attention to resistance and creating alternatives to capitalism and through the Highlander Center's early progressive attitudes toward civil rights and racial justice, Appalachian studies has often privileged the white male heterosexual coal miner and farmer over other Appalachian demographic groups. It has failed to incorporate fully the insights of feminist, postcolonial, critical race, poststructural, and queer theory. Sally Maggard (1986) was among the first to argue for an integration of gender as a theoretical priority in Appalachian studies, and while studies incorporating women and explaining gendered social processes have followed (Anglin 1993, 1995, 2002; Barney 2000; Bell 2013; Dunaway 2003, 2008; Hall 1986; Maggard 2001; Morris 2008; Scott 2010; Scott 1994, 1995, 1996a, 1996b; Seitz 1995; Spatig and Amerikaner 2014; Yarrow 1991), progress has been slow (Smith 1998).

While early precursors to Appalachian studies, particularly "local color writers" and folk music collectors, promoted the misconception that all Appalachians were white and Protestant and had descended from British pioneers, the 1980s saw Appalachian studies engage in a more concerted effort to examine and express regional racial/ethnic diversity (Lewis 1987; Trotter 1990; Turner and Cabbell 1985), though it has clearly been slow to gain momentum (Inscoe 2000; Lewis 2008; Smith 1999; Wagner and Obermiller 2004; Weiner 2006). Unsurprisingly, historical examinations of slavery and race relations in Appalachia also found their way into print relatively late as well (Billings and Blee 2000; Dunaway 2008; Inscoe 2000; Smith 1999). Currently, the reclamation of African Americans' presence in and contribution to the region is expressed by former Kentucky poet laureate Frank X Walker's term "Affrilachian," which seeks to unsettle racialized spatial constructions of Appalachia as rural white and of urban inner cities as black (see Donahue and Johnson 2008). There is room for growth in the study of the social construction of whiteness, but even here some provocative work has been done (Ferrence 2014; Hartigan 1999, 2004; Morris 2008; Smith 2004).

Recognition of LGBT Appalachians and the integration of queer theory have been even slower to impact Appalachian studies than theories of gender and race/ethnicity have been, however (Black and Rhorer 1995; Gray 2009; Mann 2005). In an attempt to change that and in response to Silas House's 2014 Appalachian Studies Association keynote presentation, which challenged the association and region to openly confront homophobia, heterosexism, heteronormativity, discrimination, and hatred in the region, the Fall 2014 issue of the *Journal of Appalachian Studies* published a symposium of essays on these topics.

Thus far, the documentation of these hitherto "invisible" and oppressed Appalachian constituencies has not resulted in a radical transformation of the field of Appalachian studies, its theories, or its methods. This is notable considering that the exclusion of women, indigenous, and nonwhite populations from Western academic disciplines provided the impetus for the rise of many area studies, including women's and black studies. Also, when new western studies emerged in 1989, its integration of women and nonwhite westerners provided the impetus for what some see as a "paradigm shift" from Turner's progressive school of western history to a neo-Marxist perspective (Allen 1994, 202; Nash 1993; Thompson 1993). Why was there no paradigm shift for Appalachian studies in the 1980s, especially after 1986, when Maggard called for new theoretical priorities and William Turner and Edward Cabbell published *Blacks in Appalachia* (1985)?

If we accept the claim that New West studies does represent a significant paradigm shift—and not everyone does (Allen 1994)—then we must explain why it occurred in this field but not in Appalachian studies. A possible explanation could be found in the timing and circumstances in which New West and Appalachian studies were created. The New West studies paradigm shift occurred relatively recently (1989) from within the discipline of history as a reaction to a dominant theoretical paradigm. Appalachian studies, in contrast, emerged earlier (1970s) from an interdisciplinary/activist engagement with political and economic development strategies that sought to explain and intervene in regional economic development. At its birth in the 1970s, Appalachian studies was influenced by the world systems theory of global capitalist development. Rather than emerging as a response to a single historical paradigm, Appalachian studies was the "academic wing" of a broader regional reaction to hegemonic government- and corporate-sponsored economic development initiatives. Though the field was (and arguably still is) androcentric, heterosexist, and racist, it was born "more radical" than western studies or, for that matter, Pacific Islands studies, which was initially based on the research of Western, mostly white academics studying colonized, nonwhite Pacific Islanders.

Somewhat ironically, Appalachian studies is quite similar to women's and black studies in its "radical" nature and social movement parentage. Furthermore, it has stayed at least somewhat connected with its social movement/community activist roots by encouraging community-based participatory research and by trying to include researchers, activists, practitioners, artists, teachers, planners, and others in its association and conferences. This nonacademic engagement has placed constraints on the ability to stray too far from the pragmatic, applied, and political-economic roots of Appalachian studies. To be sure, there have been poststructural excursions (Reichert Powell 2007; Stewart 1996) and calls for more (Banks, Billings, and Tice 2002), but these efforts tend to concentrate on the construction of the "idea" of Appalachia (Batteau 1990; Shapiro 1978) and a deconstruction of essentialized conceptions of the region and its inhabitants rather than the construction of social actors and political subjectivities or the reclamation of a democratic, generative commons (Reid and Taylor 2010).

The idea of "Appalachia" has played an important role in U.S. political discourses concerning national identity and its complicated relationship to "whiteness," Protestantism, and wealth (Batteau 1990; Shapiro 1978; Whisnant 1983). This has, in turn, fostered bifurcated understandings of the region and its people. At times, Appalachian people have been represented as the "worthy" poor: white, Anglo-Saxon, isolated, traditional frontier folk untouched by the evils of industrialization and racial/ethnic integration. At other times, Appalachians have been viewed as subhuman: a degraded, ignorant, incestuous population prone to violence and substance-abuse problems involving moonshine, methamphetamine, and prescription drugs. Reporting on the central Appalachian coal mine labor struggles of the 1920s and 1930s, American leftists represented Appalachian mining families as an exploited proletariat with revolutionary promise (National Committee on the Defense of Political Prisoners [Theodore Dreiser] 1932). In 1973 the region once again gained national attention when a Harlan County, Kentucky, coal mine strike became the subject of an Academy Award–winning documentary film (Koppel [1976] 2006). Clearly, the region and its people have been a source of periodic fascination to the rest of the world, most recently as titillating, sensationalized characters in reality television shows such as *Buckwild* (MTV), *Moonshiners* (Discovery Channel), and *Snake Salvation* (National Geographic).

Not surprisingly, interdisciplinary fields are concerned with the social construction of knowledge and how we construct the objects of our inquiry. Questions of identity, category, and helpful generalization occupy us all. For instance, Appalachia's boundaries are as arbitrary and porous as the shifting dimensions of the "Pacific"—islands, ocean, rim, and parts of Asia. Definitions of the region shift depending on the criteria one uses to delineate it, whether physiographic, geological, demographic, cultural, economic, or self-identification (Alexander and Berry 2010; Raitz and Ulack 1981), and the purposes for which such delineations are made. One dominant strategic and institutionalized regional definition comes from the U.S. government's creation of the Appalachian Regional Commission. Inspired by John F. Kennedy's campaign visits to West Virginia in 1960, an increasing national awareness of the underclass championed in *The Other America*

(1962), Thomas Ford's (1962) survey of the region, Jack Weller's *Yesterday's People*, Harry Caudill's (1963) *Night Comes to the Cumberlands*, and the 1964 report by the President's Appalachian Regional Committee, the U.S. Congress created the Appalachian Regional Commission in 1965 to support economic development in the area (Appalachian Regional Commission 2013a). In this way, Appalachia acquired a political-administrative definition tied more to the politics of federal funding allocation and planning implementation than to mountainous terrain or cultural coherence. In 2010 the commission also divided the region into five subregions for research purposes (Appalachian Regional Commission 2013b), thus acknowledging that the Appalachian region, like the Pacific, the West, "women," and "African Americans," may be too large and too heterogeneous to serve as a useful unit of analysis.

In spite of the region's arbitrary and shifting boundaries, much like the Pacific and the West, Appalachia has nevertheless served as an effective, albeit arbitrary, umbrella under which to conduct intellectual and political debates and inquiries. This umbrella may be more "ideal" and "discursive" than real in a material or physical sense, however. Throughout the twentieth century and into the twenty-first, the Appalachian region has predominantly been viewed as a social problem, an area of the United States that failed to live up to American standards of prosperity and achievement.

Because of commitments to the complicated and particular subjects of research, area studies can be prone to a parochial focus on a privileged historical thread or set of structural forces that leads to a myopic exceptionalism and a concomitant failure to make links across time and space that might result in productive comparative scholarship (Billings, Pudup, and Waller 1995). It is not useful to think of the Appalachian region as exceptional and distinctive but, rather, to scrutinize its similarity and connection to other places, a dramatic historiographic and paradigmatic shift in the face of continued and repeated cultural messages that the region is definitely different from the American mainstream in positive or negative ways. Charting a middle course between an overgeneralized universalism and an exclusionary individualism that sees everything as unique is clearly no easy task.

African American studies, like women's studies, for example, invites such questions as who is Appalachian, who is not, and why? New West scholarship inspires a continued recognition of the multiracial and multiethnic origins of Appalachia, thereby making it easier to be mindful of contemporary diversity and incoming groups. Pacific Islands studies serves as a powerful reminder of the diversity within our regions and also the ways in which regional definitions and boundaries are constructed and contested in a variety of political, economic, social, and cultural contexts. There is nothing innocent about or inherent in regionally based inquiries; such projects are inevitably strategic and based upon competing interests and values. Pacific Islands and Appalachian studies both have been regarded as isolated, microcosmic laboratories for academic research when actually both regions are connected to national and transnational commerce and geopolitical conflict. It is imperative that area studies be placed in a global context (Moseley 2009).

Similar to disciplines, interdisciplinary fields such as Appalachian studies also valorize the perspectives of some and disqualify others from consideration, although 1960s and 1970s social movement–inspired interdisciplinary fields generally reverse the direction of the traditional exclusions. Reversal of exclusions can be empowering and allow the world to be seen in a new way, both of which are productive. However, that reversal can also lead to the reification of the subject as an immutable given. This sort of essentialism can result in overgeneralization, misattributions of causality, and the demonization of the "other." In that light, Appalachian studies needs to be careful to avoid the tendency to produce an identity politics based on exclusionary "insider"/"outsider" dichotomies.

Perhaps even more than disciplines, interdisciplinary fields focusing on oppressed groups and places can inspire an obsession with stereotypes, often to the exclusion of other topics that may be more productive in improving the lives and conditions of those groups or areas, which has certainly been the case in Appalachian studies. Pacific Islands studies' apparently emancipatory and empowering move to pursue "indigenization" can be seen as an anti- or postcolonial project, one that is long overdue, but if the experience of other interdisciplinary fields is an indicator, care must be taken to avoid essentialist and exclusionary ideas and practices in a search for authenticity or insider status. Related to this is a tendency of emancipatory-based interdisciplinary endeavors to indulge themselves in an "unseemly race for victimhood" (MacMillan 2009, 59) in which groups and places compete to prove who has been the most oppressed (Limerick 2001, 22). Playing a zero-sum game to win the "most oppressed" award is not a productive way to spend time; there is more than enough oppression to go around.

In contrast to Pacific Islands studies, many key figures in the academic institutionalization of Appalachian studies were natives of the region. In this sense, Appalachian studies was "indigenized" rather early in its development. Thus, the field appears to be ahead of Pacific Islands studies in integrating "indigenous" regional viewpoints into the mainstream of its work. Those born and raised in Appalachia have played a central role in establishing the field of Appalachian studies and continue to produce much of its scholarship and art. Perhaps this is because class interacts with race, ethnicity, and indigenous status differently in Appalachia compared to the Pacific Islands. The majority of "native" Appalachianists are white and educated, and many come from middle- and upper-class backgrounds. Even though there are pockets of poverty and unemployment and low levels of educational attainment across the region, this does not mean that everyone in or from Appalachia is poor, jobless, and uneducated—Appalachian studies scholars are (by definition) not uneducated, at least, notwithstanding joblessness and poverty as realistic possibilities in today's academic job market. When Appalachianists do not conform to stereotypical constructions of Appalachians, they may be regarded as "inauthentic" or "outsiders" both by Appalachian natives and by those from outside the region.

The intersection of class, race/ethnicity, and "nativity" is as complicated in Appalachia as it is elsewhere. Because the westward expansion of European populations and the Indian Removal Act of 1830 forcibly relocated Appalachian and southern U.S. Native populations to the Southwest, the Cherokee regional presence declined so much that by the twentieth century's inception of Appalachian studies, the "native" Appalachian population was defined as "white"—more specifically, "white, Anglo-Saxon, and Protestant." As a result, Appalachian studies has paid scant attention to what remains of the Cherokee population in the region, nor do the Eastern Band Cherokee appear to self-identify as Appalachian—nor, for that matter, do many residents of urban centers in the region or African Americans residing in the region, particularly those unfamiliar with Affrilachian poets and writers.

In sum, Appalachian studies and other area studies share similar concerns, trajectories, and purposes even as they focus on particular places and people. Indeed, the parallels between these fields are quite remarkable, including their emergence in the 1970s as academic outgrowths of related social movements of the 1960s. In addition, these fields share similar institutional, intellectual, and practical concerns: dwindling institutional support and funding; indifference and resistance from the disciplines; struggles with exclusivity, exceptionalism, and counterproductive binaries; the relationship between research and action; overemphasis on representation and stereotypes; and a tendency to compete for victimization status.

Despite these similarities, it is important to be aware of the differences among these fields. For instance, although parallels can be drawn between Appalachia and "developing" postcolonial areas such as the Pacific Islands (Lewis, Johnson, and Askins 1978), Appalachia was never literally a colony of the United States. To be fair, the use of "colonial" and, more appropriately, the world-systems model to theorize Appalachian "underdevelopment" represents a radical and productive paradigm shift from midcentury modernization and "culture of poverty" theories (Ball 1968; Dunaway 1996; Lewis 1959). Although global political-economic models "birthed" Appalachian studies, by the 1980s it was clear that the colonial-based model obscured more than it illuminated. Thus, comparing Appalachia to the Pacific Islands with an actual colonial history, for instance, calls for caution. This is why more comparative research and dialogue between different interdisciplinary fields are needed. What else is needed to advance the field of Appalachian studies and similar enterprises through the rest of the twenty-first century? The following essays address that question from different perspectives.

Notes

1. See http://en.wikipedia.org/wiki/Council_of_the_Southern_Mountains.

2. From 1985 to 1993 there was an Appalachian Studies Youth Conference inspired by the Foxfire (Georgia) Youth Groups (Brown et al. 2003, 56). Financial shortfalls and low attendance resulted in the abandonment of this attempt to develop youth activists in the region.

3. This, despite the fact that the president of the ASA in 2009 was an historian, as were ten of that president's predecessors, and that over one-fifth (22 percent) of the sessions in the 2009 ASA conference program were focused on some aspect of Appalachian history.

Works Cited

Akalumat, Abdul, Ronald Bailey, Sam Byndom, Desiree McMillion, LaTasha Nesbitt, Kate Williams, and Brian Zelip. 2013. "African American Studies 2013: A National Web-Based Survey." Department of Afro-American Studies, University of Illinois at Urbana-Champaign. http://www.afro.illinois.edu/documents/BlackStudiesSurvey.pdf.

Alexander, Trent, and Chad Berry. 2010. "Who Is Appalachian? Self-Reported Appalachian Ancestry in the 2000 Census." *Appalachian Journal* 38:46–54.

Allen, Michael. 1994. "The 'New' Western History Is Stillborn." *Historian* 57(1): 201–8.

Anglin, Mary K. 1993. "Engendering the Struggle: Women's Labor and Traditions of Resistance in Rural Southern Appalachia." In *Fighting Back in Appalachia: Traditions of Resistance and Change*, edited by Stephen L. Fisher, 263–82. Philadelphia: Temple University Press.

———. 1995. "Lives on the Margin: Rediscovering the Women of Antebellum Western North Carolina." In *Appalachia in the Making: The Mountain South in the Nineteenth Century*, edited by Mary Beth Pudup, Dwight B. Billings, and Altina L. Waller, 185–209. Chapel Hill: University of North Carolina Press.

———. 2002. *Women, Power, and Dissent in the Hills of Carolina.* Urbana: University of Illinois Press.

Appalachian College Association. 2013a. "About the ACA." http://www.acaweb.org /about/.

———. 2013b. "History." http://www.acaweb.org/about/history/.

Appalachian Land Ownership Task Force. 1983. *Who Owns Appalachia? Land Ownership and Its Impact.* Lexington: University Press of Kentucky.

Appalachian Regional Commission. 2013a. "The Appalachian Region." http://www .arc.gov/about/ARCHistory.asp.

———. 2013b. "Appalachian Subregions." http://www.arc.gov/research/Mapsof Appalachia.asp?MAP_ID=31.

Appalachian Studies Association. 2008. "The Road Ahead: The Appalachian Studies Association's Plan for Action 2008–2013." http://www.appalachianstudies.org /content/policies/long-range-plan.pdf.

———. 2010. "Mission, Policies, and By-Laws." http://www.appalachianstudies.org /association/mission/.

———. 2013a. "Appalachian Research Centers." http://www.appalachianstudies.org /resources/centers/detail/index.php.

———. 2013b. "Bibliographies." http://www.appalachianstudies.org/resources /bibliographies/tedesco/index.php#Journals.

AppalReD. 2013. "About AppalReD." http://www.ardfky.org/AboutUs.aspx.

Appalshop. 2013. "History." http://appalshop.org/about/history.html.

Association for the Study of Negro Life and History. 2010. http://en.wikipedia.org /wiki/Association_for_the_Study_of_African_American_Life_and_History.

Association of College and Research Libraries. 2012. "Women and Gender Studies Section." http://www.libr.org/wgss/projects/serial.html.

Auslander, Leora. 1997. "Do Women's + Feminist's + Men's + Lesbian and Gay + Queer Studies = Gender Studies?" *Differences: A Journal of Feminist Cultural Studies* 9(3): 1–30.

Ball, Richard A. 1968. "A Poverty Case: The Analgesic Subculture of the Southern Appalachians." *American Sociological Review* 33:885–95.

Banks, Alan, Dwight Billings, and Karen Tice. 2002. "Appalachian Studies, Resistance and Postmodernism." In *Appalachia: Social Context Past and Present*, 5th ed., edited by Phillip Obermiller and Michael Maloney, 25–35. Dubuque, Iowa: Kendall/Hunt Publishers.

Barney, Sandra Lee. 2000. *Authorized to Heal: Gender, Class, and the Transformation of Medicine in Appalachia, 1880–1930.* Chapel Hill: University of North Carolina Press.

Barth, Fredrik. 1969. *Ethnic Groups and Boundaries: The Social Organization of Cultural Difference.* Boston: Little, Brown.

Batteau, Allen. 1990. *The Invention of Appalachia.* Tucson: University of Arizona Press.

Becker, Jane S. 1998. *Selling Tradition: Appalachia and the Construction of an American Folk, 1930–1940.* Chapel Hill: University of North Carolina Press.

Bell, Shannon Elizabeth. 2013. *Our Roots Run Deep as Ironweed: Appalachian Women and the Fight for Environmental Justice*. Urbana: University of Illinois Press.

Bell, Shannon Elizabeth, and Richard York. 2010. "Community Economic Identity: The Coal Industry and Ideology Construction in West Virginia." *Rural Sociology* 75(1): 111–43.

Berry, Chad. 2000. *Southern Migrants, Northern Exiles*. Urbana: University of Illinois Press.

Best, Bill. 2011. "Remembering the First Appalachian Studies Conference, October, 1970." *Now and Then* 27(1): 54–57.

Billings, Dwight B. 1974. "Culture and Poverty in Appalachia: A Theoretical Discussion and Empirical Analysis." *Social Forces* 53:315–23.

Billings, Dwight B., and Kathleen Blee. 2000. *The Road to Poverty: The Making of Wealth and Hardship in Appalachia*. Cambridge: Cambridge University Press.

Billings, Dwight B., Gurney Norman, and Katherine Ledford. 1999. *Back Talk from Appalachia: Confronting Appalachian Stereotypes*. Lexington: University Press of Kentucky.

Billings, Dwight B., Mary Beth Pudup, and Altina Waller. 1995. "Taking Exception with Exceptionalism: The Emergence and Transformation of Historical Studies of Appalachia." In *Appalachia in the Making: The Mountain South in the Nineteenth Century*, ed. Mary Beth Pudup, Dwight B. Billings, and Altina Waller, 1–24. Chapel Hill: University of North Carolina Press.

Black, Kate, and Marc Rhorer. 1995. "Out in the Mountains: Exploring Lesbian and Gay Lives." *Journal of the Appalachian Studies Association* 7:18–28.

Bouchard, Danielle. 2012. *A Community of Disagreement: Feminism in the University*. New York: Peter Lang.

Brown, Logan, Theresa Burchett-Anderson, Donavan Cain, and Jinny Turman Deal, with Howard Dorgan. 2003. "Where Have We Been? Where Are We Going? A History of the Appalachian Studies Association." *Appalachian Journal* 31(Fall): 30–92.

Brown, Wendy. 1997. "The Impossibility of Women's Studies." *Differences: A Journal of Feminist Women's Studies* 9(3): 79–101.

Burns, Shirley Stewart. 2007. *Bringing Down the Mountains: The Impact of Mountaintop Removal Surface Coal Mining on Southern West Virginia Communities, 1970–2004*. Morgantown: West Virginia University Press.

Cable, Sherry. 2012. "Confessions of the Parasitic Researcher to the Man in the Cowboy Hat." In *Confronting Ecological Crisis in Appalachia and the South*, edited by Stephanie McSpirit, Lynne Faltraco, and Conner Bailey, 21–38. Lexington: University Press of Kentucky.

Caudill, Harry M. 1963. *Night Comes to the Cumberlands: A Biography of a Depressed Region*. Boston: Little, Brown and Company.

Corbin, David Alan. 1981. *Life, Work, and Rebellion in the Coal Fields: The Southern West Virginia Miners, 1880–1922*. Urbana: University of Illinois Press.

Cornish, Audie. 2007. "Highlander Celebrates 75 Years of Social Activism." National Public Radio (NPR), September 7, http://www.npr.org/templates/story/story .php?storyId=14106495.

Davis, Donald E. 2000. *Where There Are Mountains: An Environmental History of the Southern Appalachians*. Athens: University of Georgia Press.

Donahue, Jean, and Fred Johnson. 2008. *Coal Black Voices*. Media Working Group. Kentucky Educational Television.

Drake, Richard. 1984. "A Note from the Chair." *Appalink* 7(4): 1.

Dunaway, Wilma A. 1996. *The First American Frontier: Transition to Capitalism in Southern Appalachia, 1700–1860*. Chapel Hill: University of North Carolina Press.

———. 2003. *Slavery in the American Mountain South*. Cambridge: Cambridge University Press.

———. 2008. *Women, Work and Family in the Antebellum Mountain South*. Cambridge: Cambridge University Press.

Dunn, Durwood. 1988. *Cades Cove: The Life and Death of a Southern Appalachian Community, 1818–1937*. Knoxville: University of Tennessee Press.

Eller, Ronald D. 1982. *Miners, Millhands, and Mountaineers: The Modernization of the Appalachian South, 1880–1930*. Knoxville: University of Tennessee Press.

———. 2008. *Uneven Ground: Appalachia since 1945*. Lexington: University Press of Kentucky.

Engelhardt, Elizabeth S. D. 2003. *The Tangled Roots of Feminism, Environmentalism, and Appalachian Literature*. Athens: Ohio University Press.

Escobar, Arturo. 1992. "Reflections on 'Development': Grassroots Approaches and Alternative Politics in the Third World." *Futures* 24(5): 411–36.

Feller, Irwin. 2002. "New Organizations, Old Cultures: Strategy and Implementation of Interdisciplinary Programs." *Research Evaluation* 11:109–16.

Ferrence, Matthew J. 2014. *All-American Redneck: Variations on an Icon, from James Fenimore Cooper to the Dixie Chicks*. Knoxville: University of Tennessee Press.

Fisher, Stephen L., ed. 1993. *Fighting Back in Appalachia: Traditions of Resistance and Change*. Philadelphia: Temple University Press.

Fisher, Stephen L., Patti Church, Bennett M. Judkins, Shaunna L. Scott, and Chris Weiss. 2003. "The Politics of Change in Appalachia." In *Handbook of Appalachia*, edited by Grace Toney Edwards, JoAnn A. Asbury, and Ricky L. Cox, 85–100. Knoxville: University of Tennessee Press.

Fisher, Stephen L., and Barbara Ellen Smith, eds. 2012. *Transforming Places: Lessons from Appalachia*. Urbana: University of Illinois Press.

Ford, Thomas R. 1962. *The Southern Appalachian Region: A Survey*. Lexington: University of Kentucky Press.

Foster, Stephen William. 1988. *The Past Is Another Country: Representation, Historical Consciousness, and Resistance in the Blue Ridge*. Berkeley: University of California Press.

Fritsch, Al, and Kristin Johannsen. 2004. *Ecotourism in Appalachia: Marketing the Mountains.* Lexington: University Press of Kentucky.

Gaventa, John. 1982. *Power and Powerlessness: Quiescence and Rebellion in an Appalachian Valley.* Urbana: University of Illinois Press.

Ginsberg, Alice E. 2008. "Triumphs, Controversies, and Change: Women's Studies 1970s to the Twenty-First Century." In *The Evolution of American Women's Studies: Reflections on Triumphs, Controversies, and Change,* edited by Alice E. Ginsberg, 9–37. New York: Palgrave Macmillan.

Gitlin, Todd, and Nancy Hollander. 1970. *Uptown: Poor Whites in Chicago.* Chicago: Harper & Row.

Gold, Russell. 2014. *The Boom: How Fracking Ignited the American Energy Revolution and Changed the World.* New York: Simon and Schuster.

Gray, Mary L. 2009. *Out in the Country: Youth, Media, and Queer Visibility in Rural America.* New York: New York University Press.

Hall, Jacqueline Dowd. 1986. "Disorderly Women: Gender and Labor Militancy in the Appalachian South." *Journal of American History* (September):354–62.

Halperin, Rhoda. 1990. *The Livelihood of Kin: Making Ends Meet the Kentucky Way.* Austin: University of Texas Press.

Harrison, Faye V. (1991) 1997. *Decolonizing Anthropology: Moving Further toward an Anthropology for Liberation.* Arlington: Association of Black Anthropologists, American Anthropological Association.

Hartigan, John, Jr. 1999. *Racial Situations: Class Predicaments of Whiteness in Detroit.* Princeton, N.J.: Princeton University Press.

———. 2004. "Whiteness and Appalachian Studies: What's the Connection?" *Journal of Appalachian Studies* 10(1&2): 58–72.

Hau'ofa, Epeli. 1975. "Anthropology and Pacific Islanders." Discussion Paper 8. Port Moresby: Institute of Papua New Guinea Studies.

———. 1994. "Our Sea of Islands." *Contemporary Pacific* 6:148–61.

Henderson, Donald. 1971. "What Direction Black Studies?" In *Topics in Afro-American Studies,* edited by Henry J. Richards, 9–26. Buffalo, N.Y.: Black Academy Press.

Hennen, John C. 1996. *The Americanization of West Virginia: Creating a Modern Industrial State, 1916–1925.* Lexington: University Press of Kentucky.

Hevener, John. (1978) 2002. *Which Side Are You On? The Harlan County Coal Miners, 1930–1939.* Urbana: University of Illinois Press.

Highlander Research and Education Center. 2013. "Timeline." http://highlandercenter.org/media/timeline/.

Hinsdale, Mary Ellen, Helen M. Lewis, and S. Maxine Waller. 1995. *It Comes from the People: Community Development and Local Theology.* Philadelphia: Temple University Press.

House, Silas, and Jason Howard. 2009. *Something's Rising: Appalachians Fighting Mountaintop Removal.* Lexington: University Press of Kentucky.

Howell, Benita J. 2002. *Culture, Environment, and Conservation in the Appalachian South.* Urbana: University of Illinois Press.

Hsuing, David C. 1997. *Two Worlds in the Tennessee Mountains: Exploring the Origins of Appalachian Stereotypes*. Lexington: University Press of Kentucky.

Hufford, Mary. 1998. "Tending the Commons: Ramp Suppers, Biodiversity, and the Integrity of the 'Mountains.'" *Folk Life Center News* 20(4): 3–11.

———. 2000. "Building the Commons: Folklore, Citizen Science, and the Ecological Imagination." *Indian Folklife* 1(3): 15–16.

Humphreys, Macartan, Jeffrey Sachs, and Joseph E. Stiglitz. 2007. *Escaping the Resource Curse*. New York: Columbia University Press.

Inscoe, John C., ed. 2000. *Appalachians and Race: The Mountain South from Slavery to Segregation*. Lexington: University Press of Kentucky.

Karenga, Maulana. 1993. *Introduction to Black Studies*. Los Angeles: University of Sankore Press.

Keefe, Susan E., ed. 2009. *Participatory Development in Appalachia: Cultural Identity, Community, and Sustainability*. Knoxville: University of Tennessee Press.

Kiffmeyer, Thomas. 2008. *Reformers to Radicals: The Appalachian Volunteers and the War on Poverty*. Lexington: University Press of Kentucky.

Koppel, Barbara. (1976) 2006. *Harlan County, U.S.A.* Cabin Creek Films.

Lewis, Helen M., Linda Johnson, and Donald Askins. 1978. *Colonialism in Modern America: The Appalachian Case*. Boone, N.C.: Appalachian Consortium Press.

Lewis, Oscar. 1959. *Five Families: Mexican Case Studies in the Culture of Poverty*. New York: Basic Books.

Lewis, Ronald L. 1987. *Black Coal Miners in America: Race, Class, and Community Conflict, 1780–1980*. Lexington: University Press of Kentucky.

———. 1998. *Transforming the Appalachian Countryside: Railroads, Deforestation, and Social Change in West Virginia, 1880–1920*. Chapel Hill: University of North Carolina Press.

———. 2008. *Welsh Americans: A History of Assimilation in the Coalfields*. Chapel Hill: University of North Carolina Press.

Limerick, Patricia Nelson. 1996. "Region and Reason." In *All Over the Map: Rethinking American Regions*, edited by Edward L. Ayers, Patricia Nelson Limerick, Stephen Nissenbaum, and Peter S. Onuf, 83–128. Baltimore, Md.: Johns Hopkins University Press.

———. 2000. *Something in the Soil: Legacies and Reckonings in the New West*. New York: W. W. Norton.

———. 2001. "Going West and Ending Up Global." *Western History Quarterly* 32(1): 4–23.

Limerick, Patricia Nelson, Clyde Milner II, and Charles E. Rankin, eds. 1991. *Trails: Toward a New Western History*. Lawrence: University Press of Kansas.

Lorde, Audre. 1984. "The Master's Tools Will Never Dismantle the Master's House." In *Sister Outsider*, 110–13. Berkeley: Crossing Press.

Ludke, Robert L., and Phillip J. Obermiller. 2014. "Recent Trends in Appalachian Migration." *Journal of Appalachian Studies* 20(1): 24–42.

MacMillan, Margaret. 2009. *Dangerous Games: The Uses and Abuses of History*. New York: Modern Library.

Maggard, Sally Ward. 1986. "Class and Gender: New Theoretical Priorities in Appalachian Studies." In *The Impact of Institutions in Appalachia (Proceedings of the Annual Appalachian Studies Conference 8)*, edited by Jim Lloyd and Anne G. Campbell, 100–113. Boone, N.C.: Appalachian Consortium Press.

———. 2001. "Coalfield Women Making History." In *Confronting Appalachian Stereotypes: Back Talk from an American Region*, edited by Dwight B. Billings, Gurney Norman, and Katherine Ledford, 228–50. Lexington: University Press of Kentucky.

Malinowski, Bronisław. (1922) 1984. *Argonauts of the Western Pacific*. Prospect Heights: Waveland Press.

Mann, Jeff. 2005. *Loving Mountains, Loving Men*. Athens: Ohio University Press.

Martin, Biddy. 1997. "Success and Its Failures." *Differences: A Journal of Feminist Cultural Studies* 9(3): 102–31.

McNeil, Bryan T. 2011. *Combating Mountaintop Removal: New Directions in the Fight against Big Coal*. Urbana: University of Illinois Press.

McSpirit, Stephanie, Lynne Faltraco, and Conner Bailey, eds. 2012. *Confronting Ecological Crisis in Appalachia and the South*. Lexington: University Press of Kentucky.

McSpirit, Stephanie, Shaunna L. Scott, Sharon Hardesty, and Robert Welch. 2005. "EPA Actions in Post-disaster Martin County, Kentucky: An Analysis of Bureaucratic Slippage and Agency Recreancy." *Journal of Appalachian Studies* 11(1&2): 30–58.

Montrie, Chad. 2003. *To Save the Land and People: A History of the Opposition to Surface Coal Mining in Appalachia: University and Community Partnerships*. Chapel Hill: University of North Carolina Press.

Morris, Edward. 2008. "'Rednecks,' 'Rutters,' and ''Rithmetic': Social Class, Masculinity, and Schooling in a Rural Context." *Gender and Society* 22:728–51.

Morrone, Michelle, and Geoffrey L. Buckley, eds. 2011. *Mountains of Injustice: Social and Environmental Injustice in Appalachia*. Athens: Ohio University Press.

Moseley, William G. 2009. "Area Studies in a Global Context." *Chronicle Review*, December 4.

Nash, Gerald D. 1993. "Point of View: One Hundred Years of Western History." *Journal of the West* 32:3–4.

National Committee on the Defense of Political Prisoners [Theodore Dreiser]. 1932. *Harlan Miners Speak: A Report on Terrorism in the Kentucky Coal Fields*. New York: Harcourt-Brace.

Obermiller, Phillip J. 1981. "Labeling Urban Appalachians: The Role of Stereotypes in the Formation of Appalachian Ethnic Group Identity." Ph.D. diss., Union Graduate School.

———. 2004. "Migration." In *High Mountains Rising: Appalachia in Time and Place*, edited by Richard A. Straw and H. Tyler Blethen, 88–100. Urbana: University of Illinois Press.

Obermiller, Phillip J., and William W. Philliber, eds. 1987. *Too Few Tomorrows: Urban Appalachians in the 1980s*. Boone, N.C.: Appalachian Consortium Press.

Obermiller, Phillip J., and Thomas E. Wagner. 2000. "Hands across the Ohio: The Urban Initiatives of the Council of Southern Mountains, 1954–1971." In *Appalachian Odyssey: Historical Perspectives on the Great Migration*, edited by Phillip J. Obermiller, Thomas E. Wagner, and E. Bruce Tucker, 121–40. Westport, Conn.: Praeger.

Obermiller, Phillip J., Thomas E. Wagner, and E. Bruce Tucker, eds. 2000. *Appalachian Odyssey: Historical Perspectives on the Great Migration*. Westport, Conn.: Praeger.

PIPSA. 2010. "Pacific Islands Political Studies Association." http://pipsa2014 .wordpress.com/about-pipsa/.

Portelli, Alessandro. 2010. *They Say in Harlan County: An Oral History*. Oxford: Oxford University Press.

President's Appalachian Regional Committee. 1964. *Appalachia: A Report*. Washington, D.C.: U.S. Government Printing Office.

Puckett, Anita, Elizabeth Fine, Mary Hufford, Ann Kingsolver, and Betsy Taylor. 2012. "Who Knows? Who Tells? Creating a Knowledge Commons." In *Transforming Places: Lessons from Appalachia,* edited by Stephen L. Fisher and Barbara Ellen Smith, 239–51. Urbana: University of Illinois Press.

Pudup, Mary Beth, Dwight Billings, and Altina Waller, eds. 1995. *Appalachia in the Making: The Mountain South in the Nineteenth Century*. Chapel Hill: University of North Carolina Press.

Raitz, Karl, and Richard Ulack. 1981. "Appalachian Vernacular Regions." *Journal of Cultural Geography* 1(1): 106–19.

Reece, Erik. 2006. *Lost Mountain: A Year in the Vanishing Wilderness / Radical Strip Mining and the Devastation of Appalachia*. New York: Riverhead Books.

Reece, Erik, and James J. Krupa. 2013. *Embattled Wilderness: The Natural and Human History of Robinson Forest and the Fight for Its Future*. Athens: University of Georgia Press.

Reichert Powell, Douglas. 2007. *Critical Regionalism: Connecting Politics and Culture in an American Landscape*. Chapel Hill: University of North Carolina Press.

Reid, Herbert, and Betsy Taylor. 2010. *Recovering the Commons: Democracy, Place, and Global Justice*. Urbana: University of Illinois Press.

Rojas, Fabio. 2007. *From Black Power to Black Studies: How a Radical Social Movement Became an Academic Discipline*. Baltimore, Md.: Johns Hopkins University Press.

Rooks, Noliwe M. 2006. *White Money / Black Power*. Boston: Beacon Press.

Ross, Michael L. 2001. Does Oil Hinder Democracy? *World Politics* 53:325–61.

Said, Edward. 1991. "The Politics of Knowledge." *Raritan* 11 (1):17–31.

Salstrom, Paul. 1994. *Appalachia's Path to Dependency: Rethinking a Region's Economic History, 1730–1940*. Lexington: University Press of Kentucky.

Satterwhite, Emily. 2011. *Dear Appalachia: Readers, Identity, and Popular Fiction since 1878*. Lexington: University Press of Kentucky.

Scanlan, Michael J. 2014. "'Mined' for Its Citizens? Poverty, Opportunity Structure, and Appalachian Soldier Deaths in the Iraq War." *Journal of Appalachian Studies* 20(1): 43–67.

Schwarzweller, Harry K., James S. Brown, and J. J. Mangalam. 1971. *Mountain Families in Transition: A Case Study of Appalachian Migration*. University Park: Pennsylvania State University Press.

Scott, Rebecca R. 2010. *Removing Mountains: Extracting Nature and Identity in the Appalachian Coalfields*. Minneapolis: University of Minnesota Press.

Scott, Shaunna L. 1994. "'They Don't Have to Live by the Old Traditions': Saintly Men, Sinner Women and an Appalachian Pentecostal Revival." *American Ethnologist* 21(2): 227–44.

———. 1995. *Two Sides to Everything: The Cultural Construction of Class Consciousness in Harlan County, Kentucky*. Albany: State University of New York Press.

———. 1996a. "Drudges, Helpers and Team Players: Oral Historical Accounts of Farm Work in Appalachian Kentucky." *Rural Sociology* 61(2): 209–26.

———. 1996b. "Gender among Appalachian Kentucky Farm Families: The Kentucky Farm Family Oral History Project and Beyond." *Journal of Appalachian Studies* 8(3): 103–14.

———. 2002. "From Sociology *of* Appalachia to Sociology *in* Appalachia: Transforming SOC 534 into a Field Research Class." *Journal of Appalachian Studies* 8(1): 144–65.

———. 2008. "Revisiting the Appalachian Land Ownership Study: An Oral Historical Account." *Appalachian Journal* 35(2): 236–52.

———. 2009. "Discovering What the People Knew: The 1979 Appalachian Land Ownership Study." *Action Research* 7(2): 185–205.

———. 2012. "What Difference Did It Make? The Appalachian Land Ownership Study after 25 Years." In *Confronting Ecological Crisis in Appalachia and the South*, edited by Stephanie McSpirit, Lynne Faltraco, and Conner Bailey, 39–60. Lexington: University Press of Kentucky.

Seitz, Virginia Rinaldo. 1995. *Women, Development, and Communities for Empowerment in Appalachia*. Albany: State University of New York Press.

Shapiro, Henry. 1978. *Appalachia on Our Mind: The Southern Mountains and Mountaineers in the American Consciousness, 1870–1920*. Chapel Hill: University of North Carolina Press.

Shet, D. L. 1987. "Alternative Development as Political Practice." *Alternatives* 12(2): 155–71.

Shiva, Vandana. 1989. *Staying Alive: Women, Ecology and Development*. London: Zed Books.

Small, Michael L. 1999. "Department Conditions and the Emergence of New Disciplines: Two Cases in the Legitimation of African-American Studies." *Theory and Society* 28(5): 659–707.

Smith, Barbara Ellen. 1987. *Digging Our Own Graves: Coal Miners and the Struggle over Black Lung Disease*. Philadelphia: Temple University Press.

———. 1998. "Walk-Ons in the Third Act: Women in Appalachian Historiography." *Journal of Appalachian Studies* 4(1): 1–23.

———. ed. 1999. *Neither Separate nor Equal: Women, Race and Class in the South*. Philadelphia: Temple University Press.

———. 2004. "De-gradation of Whiteness: Appalachia and the Complexities of Race." *Journal of Appalachian Studies* 10(1&2): 38–57.

Spatig, Linda, and Layne Amerikaner. 2014. *Thinking Outside the Girl Box: Teaming Up with Resilient Youth in Appalachia.* Athens: Ohio University Press.

Stewart, Kathleen. 1996. *A Space by the Side of the Road: Cultural Poetics in an Other America.* Princeton, N.J.: Princeton University Press.

Teaiwa, Teresia K. 2001. "L(o)osing the Edge." *Contemporary Pacific* 13(2): 343–57.

Thompson, Gerald. 1993. "The New Western History: A Critical Analysis." *Continuity* 17:6–24.

Trotter, Joseph William, Jr. 1990. *Coal, Class, and Color: Blacks in Southern West Virginia, 1915–32.* Urbana: University of Illinois Press.

Turner, William H., and Edward G. Cabbell. 1985. *Blacks in Appalachia.* Lexington: University Press of Kentucky.

University of Illinois at Champaign Library. 2012. "Black Studies Scholarly Journals." http://www.library.illinois.edu/afx/aajournals.htm.

Wagner, Thomas E., and Phillip J. Obermiller. 2004. *African American Miners and Migrants: The Eastern Kentucky Social Club.* Urbana: University of Illinois Press.

Waller, Altina. 1988. *Feud: Hatfields, McCoys, and Social Change in Appalachia, 1860—1900.* Chapel Hill: University of North Carolina Press.

Walls, David S., and Dwight B. Billings. 1977. "The Sociology of Southern Appalachia." *Appalachian Journal* 5(1): 125–28. Special issue: A Guide to Appalachian Studies.

Weiner, Deborah. 2006. *Coalfield Jews: An Appalachian History.* Urbana: University of Illinois Press.

Weller, Jack. 1965. *Yesterday's People: Life in Contemporary Appalachia.* Lexington: University of Kentucky Press.

Wesley-Smith, Terence. 1995. "Rethinking Pacific Islands Studies." *Pacific Studies* 18(2): 115–37.

West Virginia Council of Churches. 2013. News bulletin. http://wvcc.org/?content=news07&article=76.

Whimp, Graeme. 2008. "Interdisciplinary and Pacific Studies: Roots and Routes." *Contemporary Pacific* 20(3): 397–421.

Whisnant, David E. 1980. *Modernizing the Mountaineer: People, Power and Planning in Appalachia.* New York: Burt Franklin and Company.

———. 1983. *All That Is Native and Fine: The Politics of Culture in an American Region.* Chapel Hill: University of North Carolina Press.

White, Geoffrey, and Ty Kawika Tengan. 2001. "Disappearing Worlds: Anthropology and Cultural Studies in the Pacific." *Contemporary Pacific* 13(2): 381–416.

White, Richard. 1991. *"It's Your Misfortune and None of My Own": A New History of the American West.* Norman: University of Oklahoma Press.

Yarrow, Michael. 1991. "The Gender-Specific Class Consciousness of Appalachian Coal Miners." In *Bringing Class Back In: Historical and Contemporary Perspectives*, edited by Scott McNeil, Rhonda Levine, and Rick Fantasia, 285–310. Boulder, Colo.: Westview Press.

2

Representing Appalachia

The Impossible Necessity of Appalachian Studies

BARBARA ELLEN SMITH

In 1997 Wendy Brown inflamed debates over women's studies' institutional location and intellectual direction with her essay "The Impossibility of Women's Studies." People in Appalachian studies have much to learn from her analysis of a contradiction that has both produced some of the most influential works in feminism and threatened to paralyze women's studies as an interdisciplinary field. On the one hand is the need to stabilize "women" as a uniform and universal topic in order to establish the academic legitimacy and coherence of women's studies. On the other hand, elevating the differentiating processes of gender in order to focus on women in general ineluctably, even if unintentionally, makes the primary subject of women's studies those *particular* women for whom gender represents the foremost category of identity, source of oppression, and axis of resistance: class-privileged, heterosexual, white women of the "West." To frame the dilemma in more explicitly political terms: feminist activists require a universal subject in order to claim, for example, women's rights (but does this include the right for Muslim women to wear the "veil"?); women's economic advancement (even if this means a demanding career for middle-class women who depend on working-class women of color to care for their house and children?); and women's equality (with whom? homeless men?). Social identities—and their academic representation and political transformation—are complicated.

It is telling that we have never faced a similar crisis in Appalachian studies. Despite the scholarship of nearly three generations of feminists (Anglin 1993, 1995; Barney 2000; Dunaway 2008; Engelhardt 2003; Maggard 1986, 1999; Scott 2010; Smith 1998, 1999), the fine-grained histories of different racial/ethnic/national groups (Cook 2000; Finger 2005; Fones-Wolf 2007; Fones-Wolf and Lewis 2002; Lewis 1987; Ray 2001; Weiner 2006), and the emergent attention to sexual identity (Black and Rohrer 1995; Gray 2009; Howard 1997; Mann 2005), it is still possible to speak of "Appalachians" and "mountaineers" as generic and seemingly self-evident categories.[1] As if being from the region overrides other forms of social identity. As if Appalachia were an "imagined community" of insiders, united by sameness (Anderson 1983).

This essay examines the articulation between the growing literature about women, African Americans, Native Americans, and other "minority" groups and the dominant paradigms in Appalachian studies. My premise in pursuing this line of inquiry is that any field of study requires overarching conceptual frameworks that set the terms of its scholarship. These change over time, but, as Thomas Kuhn (1970) influentially argued, not through an accretion of ever more comprehensive and accurate evidence; rather, they tend to transform dramatically, or undergo revolutions (to use Kuhn's term), in complex and sometimes oblique relationship to historically specific social processes. The emergence during the 1970s of Appalachian studies, with its broadside attacks on the tradition of condescending and victim-blaming cultural explanations for regional dispossession, was one such transformation.

Today, it seems to me that we are ripe for another paradigm shift in Appalachian studies. In accord with Kuhn and others' insights regarding the socially contingent production of knowledge, this is less because of developments internal to our academic enterprise and more because of tectonic transformations in the region and the world. When the United Mine Workers of America is disappearing from the coalfields and coal barons are managing to position themselves alongside miners as embattled "insiders" to the region through, for example, such organizations as Friends of Coal, contemporary intra- and interclass dynamics *within* Appalachia become confounding, unexplained by the unidimensional paradigm of mountaineer insiders pitted against venal "outsiders." When the traditional political economy of mining and manufacturing, complemented by a "moral economy" of masculine provisioning within heteronormative families, is being replaced by a plethora of household arrangements and an employment base of low-wage feminized jobs, past and present entanglements of gender and sexuality become less "natural," more visible and questionable. And when white working-class resentment against immigrants, "welfare" recipients, and variously racialized Others, so shrewdly mobilized by the Right, gains increasing traction in Appalachia, the operations of race become more apparent and urgent, unexplained (indeed, concealed) by class-driven portraits of heroic miners and mountaineers.

The next section briefly summarizes the major competing paradigms in Appalachian studies and argues that, despite fundamental distinctions and contradictions among them, all serve to homogenize the region in different ways. The subsequent section examines the epistemological impact of studies of women and various racial/ethnic groups, which have partially, but in my view, insufficiently, diversified the human subjects of Appalachian studies. The chapter ends with a discussion of promising new scholarship in Appalachian studies and earlier work in women's studies, which together point toward that knife-edge of tension between the impossibility of apprehending the full social complexity of Appalachia and the urgent necessity of making the attempt.

Whose Appalachia? Who Is Appalachia?

Since its inception, Appalachian studies has been fractured between scholars who favor cultural explorations and explanations of the region and those who emphasize political economy. This is in part a matter of disciplinary training and political inclination, though there are no doubt other factors at work as well. My purpose is not to recapitulate or analyze, much less reinforce, this tension. Rather, I argue that, when mobilized to generate paradigmatic conceptualizations of the region, both tendencies work, albeit unintentionally, to homogenize Appalachia and, in the case of political economy, marginalize those marked by inequalities other than, or in addition to, the exploitation of social class.

Scholars have formulated cultural paradigms of Appalachia as responses to two quite different types of questions: (1) Why is the region impoverished? and (2) What makes the region distinctive? Cultural explanations for Appalachian poverty and dispossession (Oscar Lewis's [1961] culture of poverty, Richard Ball's [1968] "analgesic subculture," and so on) were largely discredited by scholarship that arose in the movement for Appalachian studies (see Billings 1974). Nonetheless, identification and celebration of the cultural traits that presumably make Appalachia *distinctive* (rather than poor) persist. Scholars such as Loyal Jones (1994), for example, have sought to codify certain cultural beliefs and practices as "Appalachian." In the realm of formal cultural expression, fiction writers, poets, and musicians who set their creative work within Appalachia have invested the region with a broad range of cultural themes and traits, but intergenerational continuity on the land, attachment to place, and the imaginary of the homeplace are among the most powerful and recurrent.

The question of who "counts" as Appalachian is not trivial. After all, if people who arrived in the region only yesterday can be considered "Appalachian," what meaning does that term possibly convey? Our tenure and location in the region vary widely, as do our cultural practices and experiences of this place. Who, then, belongs to and in Appalachia? Out-migrants, some of whom fiercely claim and defend an identity as Appalachian, who live in cities such as Cincinnati? Second-generation children of Latino immigrants in Morristown, Tennessee, who speak English with a mountain accent? Retirees from New York who reside in western North Carolina, love the Smoky Mountains, and play the dulcimer? Those whose regional ancestry stretches back at least three generations? Six generations? Ten? How do we adjudicate in cultural terms the question of what is Appalachia? Who *are* the "insiders"?

These questions are rhetorical, designed to underscore the ultimate impossibility of identifying fixed criteria, whether cultural traits, ancestry, or place attachment, that can separate the true Appalachians from everyone else. As Obermiller and Maloney (2011) argue, specifying cultural traits as criteria for authenticity incorrectly presupposes not only that culture is static and lifeless but also that Appalachia is singular; that is, there is only one Appalachian culture (and, significantly, it tends to be depicted as rural and white). Ancestry, place attachment, and intergenerational continuity on the land—when deployed as criteria for authenticity and belonging—are also problematic in that they exclude, for example, the residents of Appalachian cities and those who have migrated frequently within or beyond the region. Moreover, in historical moments when many people, due to class, race, and/or gender, could not own property, some *were* property, and still others had prior claims to the land, intergenerational continuity on the land as marker-of-belonging serves to marginalize the stories of the dispossessed (Dunaway 1996; Smith 2012). In sum, paradigms that utilize cultural criteria to define the genuine Appalachian imagine a monolithic region; they tend to reduce its social complexity to a rural, white, place-attached mountaineer (cf. Keefe 2005).

Deplorable popular representations of hillbillies are also at work, ironically, in the steadfastness of the imagined mountaineer. Among the most powerful dynamics reinforcing simplified depictions of Appalachia are not only the tiresome repetition of hillbilly stereotypes within popular culture but also our counterassertions regarding Appalachian identity. Pejorative depictions of the region tend to call forth a righteous indignation that most commonly focuses on restoring the dignity but not fundamentally challenging the singular and simplified social identity of Appalachians. "Appalachians are stupid inbred hillbillies"; "No, Appalachians are the salt of the earth, the true Americans." Rather than challenging unilateral depictions by asserting the variability of social positions and identities within (and without) the region, the tendency is to protest the injustice of the portrait ("we are the only minority that it is permissible to . . .") and proclaim the integrity of the monolithically defined Appalachian subject. The overriding dualism of American and Appalachian, normative and deviant, is thereby maintained and, as dualisms are wont to do, complexity and difference within each side are suppressed (Harkins 2004; Smith 2004).[2]

In the scholarly realm of political economy, the internal colony perspective theorizes this dualism. It divides the world into insiders and outsiders, regional residents whose land and wealth of natural resources were stolen and the external thieves who have enriched themselves at the expense of Appalachian people ever since (Lewis, Johnson, and Askins 1978). Despite its many academic critics, this framework exerts a remarkably strong and persistent appeal, reinforced no doubt by "outsiders'" hillbilly stereotypes and by the fact that certain classics in Appalachian studies, such as Ron Eller's *Miners, Millhands, and Mountaineers* (1982) and John Gaventa's *Power and Powerlessness* (1980), utilized this approach with rich results and continue to be read by successive generations of students. Viewing Appalachia, particularly the central coalfields, as a colony also seems manifestly correct; how else to understand the daily parade of railroad cars, hump-backed with coal, clanking down the tracks to Hampton Roads, the Great Lakes, and other distant destinations?

Nevertheless, spatial differentiation has a complex and by no means straightforward relationship to social inequality, exploitation, and oppression. Not all insiders to Appalachia are social equals, much less friends of social justice, nor are all outsiders exploiters and reactionaries. Moreover, notions of insiders and outsiders dig an artificial moat around the region, separating it from the rest of the world at precisely a time when global interrelatedness has become more dense, palpable, and salient (Fisher and Smith 2012). As Dwight Billings observed, "The metaphor of Appalachia as a colony replaced that of Appalachia as a backward culture, but the mythical unity of the region and the homogeneity of its population remained largely unquestioned" (2009, 9).

Even as activists and scholars were elaborating the paradigm of Appalachia as an internal colony, indeed, in the very volume that became the most influential exposition of this effort (Lewis, Johnson, and Askins 1978), critics such as David Walls (1978) were pointing to inadequacies and oversimplifi-cations in the model. Walls and others (Dunaway 1996; Lewis 1998) argued instead for world systems theory (Wallerstein 1974, 1979), through which Appalachia may be understood as a peripheral region in the global capital-ist economy, a place where primary resource extraction, agriculture, and other economic activities produce goods that are sold on unfavorable terms to the core, where more lucrative and powerful sectors, such as finance and knowledge production, predominate. This approach retains the spatiality of the internal colony but expands it from the scale of the nation-state to that of the globe. Moreover, whereas the internal colony model emphasizes rela-tions of cultural and political domination between colonizer and colonized, world systems theory foregrounds economic domination, including class relations within both the periphery and the core, and "unequal exchange" (Emmanuel 1976) between these two zones.

Two additional paradigms for conceptualizing Appalachia, both of which downplay spatial metaphors in favor of class analysis, bear mention. Although substantial elements of Marxism may be found in all the models I am clas-sifying as political economy, there is a long lineage of explicitly, in some in-stances exclusively, class-driven approaches to Appalachia. Certain historians (Barkey 2012) and other scholars (Simon 1984), along with many left-wing activists (whether of the 1930s or the 1970s), have understandably found Marxism's analysis of class exploitation and struggle particularly persuasive in the face of protracted, violent labor struggles, such as those between coal miners and operators in the central coalfields, in many locations across the region. Within this approach, Appalachia can best be understood as a zone of intense class exploitation; it matters not whether the bosses are indigenous or external to the region, they are still capitalist. To this particular iteration of a class-focused paradigm should be added Dwight Billings's (2009) call for greater attention to Barrington Moore's (1966) more nuanced historical analysis of distinct paths to modernity. Billings argues that this model of "path dependency," wherein agrarian class relations and the struggles they engender carry lasting implications for subsequent class configurations, strategies of hegemony, forms of governance, and other systemic matters, could be profit-ably used to understand differences among subregions of Appalachia. Path dependency helps to differentiate an otherwise homogenized (and singularly theorized) Appalachia through historical examination of significant varia-tions within the region.

All of these political economy paradigms leave little room for social re-lations other than class except, at least when it articulates with class, race.

This means that the wide landscape of social life telescopes into economic activities, narrowly defined in terms of capitalist forms and institutions. To be sure, many scholars, particularly historians such as Sandra Barney (2000) and others trained by Ron Lewis (Egolf, Fones-Wolf, and Martin 2009), are investigating the interplay of cultural, economic, and political life in far more sophisticated terms than was once the case; nonetheless, the formal institutions of economics and politics remain central, and cultural identities, practices, and beliefs tend to be analyzed in relation to them. Among the many consequences are the invisibility of noncapitalist economic relations and the tendency to overlook the activities of the majority of the population of Appalachia, which is female. When the majority cannot find its past (Lerner 1979) or its present (except in literature and literary studies), something in our academic accounts is wrong.

Producing Inequality, Producing Appalachia

There is a growing body of fine scholarship about, and in some cases by, women, African Americans, Jews, immigrants, sexual minorities, and others who were not prominent or even recognized regional actors in the early years of Appalachian studies. For example, Wilma Dunaway has undertaken prodigious historical research on African Americans across the region (2003a, 2003b), while others have given us revealing biographies of individual African American leaders, such as Memphis Tennessee Garrison (Bickley and Ewen 2001), and detailed studies of community life, such as Joe Trotter's (1990) book on African Americans in southern West Virginia and Thomas E. Wagner's and Phillip J. Obermiller's (2004) work on the East Kentucky Social Club. Following the path broken by William H. Turner and Edward J. Cabell in their 1985 book, *Blacks in Appalachia*, John Inscoe's collection of essays, *Appalachians and Race* (2001), brings together historical studies of slave trading, abolitionism, postbellum educational initiatives, and other aspects of African American life in the region. Meanwhile, Affrilachian poets and writers such as Frank X Walker (2000) and Crystal Wilkinson (2002) are producing contemporary literature, indeed, a movement, that demonstrates the enduring creative contributions of people of color in Appalachia.

This is not the place to undertake a comprehensive review of this exciting, extensive scholarship and creative work by and about various "minorities" in Appalachia. My purpose lies elsewhere: How and to what extent have the epistemological assumptions that undergird scholarly representations of Appalachia and its inhabitants been transformed by this work? Are we experiencing another paradigm shift in Appalachian studies, prompted by historical transformations in the region and world and realized in the scholarship of heretofore excluded groups? How could we tell?

Answering such questions requires examining dominant conceptual paradigms not only in Appalachian studies overall but also in what I loosely (and problematically) call the "minority" scholarship about groups not originally recognized as significant to Appalachia. Just because a scholar conducts research on, for example, women in Appalachia, she or he does not necessarily challenge reigning conceptualizations of the region. The intellectual history of women's studies is relevant and illuminating. As Mari Jo Buhle, Ann Gordon, and Nancy Shrom (1971) argued some four decades ago, much of the emergent feminist scholarship in U.S. women's history was readily, though certainly not automatically, absorbed within male-dominant paradigms of U.S. history. For example, what Buhle and her coauthors called "compensatory history"—the study of prominent individual women—diversified but did not fundamentally contest the historiography of generals, presidents, inventors, and other "great men." Even "contribution history," which examines women's oppression and explicates their political organizing as feminists, trade unionists, and coal miners' wives, remained confined within conceptual frameworks defined by men's activities (see Lerner 1979).

This is not to minimize the necessity and importance of scholarship about Appalachian women in the modes of "compensatory" and "contribution" history. In a context of invisibility and erasure, restoring a history to women requires multiple strategies and the painstaking, time-consuming documentation of many women's activities. It is an incremental process. However, "the limitation of such work," in the words of Gerda Lerner, "is that it deals with women in male-defined society and tries to fit them into the categories and value systems which consider *man* the measure of significance" (1979, 149–50). What is needed is "the history of [women's] ongoing functioning in that male-defined world *on their own terms*" (148; emphasis in the original).

We do not yet have such a literature—whether about women, African Americans, Native Americans, gays and lesbians, or other groups—in Appalachian studies. As Inscoe noted in his introduction to *Appalachians and Race*, "Despite the considerable advances Appalachian scholars have made in our understanding of race relations and black highlanders, it seems that we still lag behind so much of the history of African Americans elsewhere, during and after emancipation, in that we still see that history primarily from a white perspective. Much of our understanding of race relations has to do with white actions and attitudes. Here, as elsewhere, it is white highlanders who hold center stage" (2001, 10). Pursuing scholarship from the black, female, transgender, and other margins of Appalachian studies requires extraordinary effort: conducting interview upon interview, poring through neglected archives, pursuing ephemeral traces of a historical presence, reinterpreting canonical works, reading against the grain. To be sure, there are those who have intentionally undertaken these heroic tasks; Joe Trotter's (1990) study of blacks in southern West Virginia comes to mind, as does Mary Anglin's (2002) research on female mica workers in western North Carolina. Within the imagined worlds of literature, there is even more of note, including the centrality of female characters in the novels of Silas House (2002, 2005), the interplay of class and gender in Ann Pancake's work (2007), and the previously mentioned Affrilachian literary movement. But we have yet to reach critical mass, much less a revolution.

What would be the signposts of such a revolution? Once again, those who have sought to theorize the substance and implications of women's history have relevant insights. The feminist historian Joan Kelly-Gadol argued in an influential article (1976, 809) that women's history destabilized three foundations of conventional history: periodization, the categories of social analysis, and theories of social change. Her provocative question—"Did Women Have a Renaissance?" (1977) (her answer was "no")—suggested that women's experiences might differ profoundly from men of their race and class and that the common, liberal progress narrative of history might be misplaced. She commented:

> The moment one assumes that women are a part of humanity in the fullest sense[,] the period or set of events with which we deal takes on a wholly different character or meaning from the normally accepted one. Indeed, what emerges is a fairly regular pattern of relative loss of status for women precisely in those periods of so-called progressive change. . . . For women, "progress" in Athens meant concubinage and confinement of citizen wives in the gynecaeum. In Renaissance Europe, it meant domestication of the bourgeois wife and escalation of witchcraft persecution[,] which crossed class lines. And the [French] Revolution expressly excluded women from its liberty, equality, and "fraternity." Suddenly we see these ages with a new, double vision—and each eye sees a different picture. (1976, 810–11)

Kelly-Gadol did not conclude that the existing periodization of history should be rejected—events like the French Revolution were transformative throughout the society—but she left open the possibility that additional historical periods of previously submerged significance might be identified.

Kelly-Gadol's elaboration of her second and third points—wherein she asserted that gender should be a central category of social and historical analysis and that theories of social change should incorporate gender—further illuminates the path toward feminist historiography. If "women are made, not born" (Beauvoir 1952), then through what historically specific processes does that occur? And, insofar as women are "made" as gendered humans in relation to men, then through what historical processes are men also gendered? The aim of women's history becomes uncovering not only the activities of women but also the changing character of gender as a social relation. Further, what is the history-making determinacy of gender? How, for example, do gender relations articulate with those of race and social class in specific historical moments? What does the resulting scholarship tell us about processes of social change and how they might be newly theorized?

If we take Kelly-Gadol's arguments seriously as partial criteria for evidence of a paradigm shift in Appalachian studies, surely we must conclude that that shift has not happened. To paraphrase John Inscoe, white male highlanders still hold center stage. This is in no way to fault excluded groups for such a state of affairs. Within Appalachian studies, there is no doubt ambivalence about allowing heretofore-marginalized subjects to threaten the whole enterprise with unruly questions and challenges to existing paradigms and their relatively uniform Appalachian subjects. Moreover, the understandable tendency is to greet scholarship about previously neglected groups in the spirit of multiculturalism, that is, as a welcome, even enticing, addition as long as it does not upset existing institutional arrangements, epistemologies, and power relations. This is the problem with defining such literature as "minority": it discursively reinforces the normative status of the unspecified, unexamined "majority" and thereby effects the disempowerment of "minorities" even as it offers them recognition.

So, for example, one question I was given by the editors to guide this essay reads: "How will the voices of Native Americans, blacks, Latinos, women, GLBT, others be heard?" In presupposing but not identifying the listener, this question raises another: "Heard *by whom*?" The unnamed listener implicit in the original question represents the preexisting subject of Appalachian studies, the foundational Appalachian without whom the entire enterprise of Appalachian studies risks collapsing. But who is the presumptive listener? The presumptive "Appalachian"? And what are the implications for *this* subject should Appalachian studies give way to an investigation that does not take for granted as preexisting and self-evident the human subjects of Appalachian studies?

If we in Appalachian studies are serious about grappling with the "difference that difference makes," the likelihood, indeed inevitability, that the field itself will be fundamentally transformed is among the consequences. This is not because the heterosexual white male patriarch, qua culturally distinctive mountaineer, qua economically agentic worker or businessman, will be drowned out by a cacophony of identity claims from others. Rather, the processes whereby *all* social groups within Appalachia are constituted in relationship, one with another, will become central to our scholarship. In such an undertaking, nobody gets a pass as normal, unmarked, or exclusively worthy of attention. We are all implicated.

Representations of Power and the Powers of Representation

Appalachian studies could use a little theoretical ferment. Developments on the ground—such as struggles over climate change, mountaintop removal, and the future of coal; transformations in gender and sexuality, family structures, employment, and class relations; the current neoliberal iteration of capitalist globalization and its savage destruction of place—outpace our scholarship and theorization. Debates over internal colony versus world systems, tensions between cultural aficionados and those who favor political economy, the major paradigms discussed earlier—these have all been with us since the birth of Appalachian studies; at this point, they conceal as much as they illuminate about the conditions we face.[3] We need some fresh ideas.

Innovations in many fields, such as critical geography, postcolonial studies, and critical race theory, offer relevant provocations and insights for Appalachian studies. By framing this essay in part through the intellectual trajectory of women's studies and drawing on related scholarship in this conclusion, I do not mean to imply that this is the only area of scholarship that offers valuable and pertinent theorizations; it is simply a field with which I am relatively familiar. Moreover, I in no way mean to sideline the significance of social class or other dimensions of inequality, such as race and sexuality; that we live in a society and region with multiple vectors of social relations, identity, oppression, exploitation, and resistance is precisely the viewpoint I hope to encourage.

I suggested in the introduction that Appalachian studies could learn from the productive contradiction that Wendy Brown identified in women's studies. This conclusion elaborates on what that might look like. The "impossibility of women's studies," as Brown saw it, arose in part from two epistemological challenges: first was poststructuralism, with its rejection of "totalizing" narratives that pose as universal truths, insistence on the partiality and situated nature of all knowledge, and searching analysis of discourse and representation. (For a lucid overview of poststructuralism, or postmodernism, as it pertains to Appalachian studies, see Banks, Billings, and Tice 1993.) Within feminist theory, poststructuralists repudiated notions of "essential" womanhood (for example, as nurturant and maternal), contested the binary construction of gender, and examined the terms through which women and men are represented and *produced* (and thereby regulated) as gendered subjects (Butler 1990; Butler and Scott 1992).

Academic research and activist interventions by women of color were a second major influence within women's studies. These scholars argued that the "gender-first" theories and methodologies of women's studies (Alexander 2004, 53) eclipsed their experiences and led to a narrow and exclusionary brand of feminism (Dill 1983; Dill and Baca Zinn 1996; hooks 1984). Many scholars increasingly conceptualized differences among women as relational processes of social construction in which, for example, whiteness has no meaning except in relation to blackness. The growing body of empirical research on racial/ethnic women and men, including eventually research on whites as racial subjects, exemplified in practical and convincing terms poststructuralists' philosophical and frequently highly abstract critiques of knowledge production and purportedly universal truths about women. In response to both influences, there has been a rich proliferation of scholarship about heteronormativity and queer identities (Butler 2004), race- and class-specific constructions of masculinity (Kimmel 1996), the comparative experiences of women and men in particular social contexts and historical moments (Payne 1995), and many other topics.

Within Appalachian studies, these same intellectual trends are far more muffled. Poststructuralism is evident primarily in scholarship about the historical development, literary representation, and political functions of the *idea* of Appalachia (Batteau 1982; Shapiro 1978). This has provided a powerful antidote to tendencies to essentialize the region and has undergirded fascinating accounts of "Appalachia's" functions within the American imaginary (Satterwhite 2011; Silber 1997). In a somewhat different register and possibly contradictory political valence, poststructuralism has also informed pointed critiques of elitist degradations of place attachment and of academic distancing from accountability to place, especially in such disparaged locations as Appalachia (Reichert Powell 2007).

However, other crucial insights from poststructuralist theory and the burgeoning scholarship of women of color have been largely ignored. Of foremost relevance for Appalachian studies is, in my view, the theoretical premise that we are produced as social beings through relational processes involving operations of power. By "relational processes involving operations of power," I do not mean individual psychological development or the attitudinal expression of racism, sexism, and so on; rather, it is the relational production of race, gender, class, and heteronormativity—culturally, politically, economically, and socially—that is at stake. Thanks to Marxism, those in Appalachian studies tend to be well acquainted with the assertion that class is a social relationship (between workers and their bosses, at the least) and not merely a descriptive index of an individual's socioeconomic status. But those in Appalachian studies tend to treat race, gender, and sexuality as if they were individual attributes and, even worse, only relevant when people of color, women, and LGBT are in the mix.

To put it in methodological terms, the relational construction of inequality means that, for example, in women's history, it becomes critical to explore not only women acting "on their own terms" but also the historically specific production of femininity and masculinity and the implications for the construction of both women and men as gendered subjects. Within such a framework, the intellectual and political project of Appalachian studies becomes not a matter of creating spaces in which diversely "Othered" identities might be heard, because this strategy assumes the prior existence of unequal and unjust subject positions (rather than examining their production); it thereby unintentionally reinscribes certain Appalachians as normative and others as, well, *othered*. Rather, the point is that the particularistic, power-laden, and situated status of *any* Appalachian should be interrogated and decentered if we are to explore the systematic operations of power (in the forms of race, gender, etc.) as constitutive of the region.

The challenge is even more complicated than the preceding summary indicates, since race/ethnicity, class, gender, and sexuality are not ultimately separable phenomena. They are coconstitutive, or coproduced, as many feminists, including some in Appalachian studies, have argued (Maggard 1986, 1999; Smith 1998). Racial oppression and privilege, for example, are gendered, sexualized, and class specific. The constraints, expectations, and advantages that frame the social position of black professional women in Charleston, West Virginia, in the early twenty-first century are quite different from those affecting black working-class men. Failure to recognize this means engaging in what the philosopher Elizabeth Spelman (1990) has called "pop-bead metaphysics": the addition of apparently random and otherwise disconnected inequalities to one another, which grossly distorts their mutual operation.

So, for example, we can examine class relations in the coalfields without exploring masculinity as a factor in coal miners' capacity to unionize and the various modes in which they have framed their oppositional identities and solidarities (as, regrettably, did this author [1987]; for an alternative, see Yarrow 1991).

The numerous "studies programs" (African American studies, women's studies, Appalachian studies, Chicano/a studies, and so on) that proliferated during the 1970s share a dual dilemma. How do we influence and ultimately transform the wider social relations and cultural representations that demean our subjects (as Sambos, bimbos, dumbos, tacos, etc.) and shape established academic disciplines (where we are often marginalized and discredited) while remaining open to *internal* disagreement, criticism, and transformation within our relatively young embattled fields? How can we distinguish between offensive disparagement and legitimate criticism, regardless of the source, and learn to respond with righteous indignation or self-examination, as appropriate, but above all with wisdom? Understandably, the celebratory mission of the various studies programs—to valorize and gain recognition for the hitherto denigrated group or topic—tends to mitigate self-examination and internal critique. Due in part to reasons discussed in the previous sections, this may be particularly true in Appalachian studies. But self-criticism should not be avoided.

To be sure, there have long been voices of dissent within Appalachian studies. Herbert Reid has been a prophetic advocate of theoretical innovation for decades, and his book with Betsy Taylor, *Recovering the Commons* (2010), provides a new integration of ecological and political theory of great relevance to Appalachian studies. David Whisnant's (1983) provocative approaches to Appalachia have included analyses of racism and whiteness and relentless critiques of sentimental notions of regional identity. Scholars such as Mary Anglin (2002), Dwight Billings (1990), and Steve Fisher (1993) have made sophisticated use of theoretical work from numerous fields to illuminate, among other topics, resistance in the region. Moreover, several up-and-coming scholars are redefining Appalachian studies through their fresh angles of vision: Rebecca Scott (2010) has written a deeply theorized analysis of the controversy over mountaintop removal, and Shannon Bell (2013; Bell and Braun 2010) is bringing an incisive, feminist lens to the same topic. Emily Satterwhite (2011) has examined fictional representations of Appalachia and their relationship to white nostalgia and the comforts of racial innocence during different moments of American nationhood. This list is illustrative and by no means exhaustive.

Such work gives me hope that we are developing the capacity to generate new, more inclusive paradigms for the conceptualization of Appalachia. Will our "revolution" and related debates be contentious and cranky? At times, probably so. Will they be divisive? Possibly, but less so if we can engage with civility and shed fear of disagreement. Are they necessary? Absolutely. Appalachian studies will not survive as anything relevant to an Appalachian future situated within a deteriorating American empire and increasingly interconnected globe if we remain insulated from relevant theoretical innovations in other fields. If inclusion is a sincere goal, we need to create an ethos in Appalachian studies that valorizes reflexivity and critical exchange. We may thereby better examine the power of our multiple social positions, recognize the partiality of our scholarship, and collectively pursue the impossible necessity of Appalachian studies.

Acknowledgments: I am deeply grateful to Chad Berry, Steve Fisher, and Emily Satterwhite for their careful review and insightful critique of earlier drafts of this chapter; errors, omissions, and misinterpretations are my own.

Notes

1. It is not possible in this brief chapter to cite or review all the relevant literature. The examples are illustrative but regrettably not comprehensive.

2. Admittedly, it is not necessarily feasible or effective to expound on the social complexity of Appalachia in the rapid-fire exchanges of pop culture debates. However, it is possible—and necessary—to contest the *political* functions and ramifications of pejorative stereotypes in this era of mountaintop removal coal mining and social policies destructive of the region. Stereotypes that portray Appalachians as worthless, ridiculous, and/or inconsequential define the region as unworthy of protection. Why not "trash" Appalachia? It is full of (white) trash already. This is, in my view, the most potent and important point to make (see Billings, Norman, and Ledford 1999).

3. Indeed, the arguments I am making here were put forth, albeit in broader terms, some twenty years ago by Banks, Billings, and Tice (1993).

Works Cited

Alexander, Leslie M. 2004. "The Challenge of Race: Rethinking the Position of Black Women in the Field of Women's History." *Journal of Women's History* 16(4): 50–60.

Anderson, Benedict. 1983. *Imagined Communities: Reflections on the Origin and Spread of Nationalism*. New York: Verso.

Anglin, Mary K. 1993. "Engendering the Struggle: Women's Labor and Traditions of Resistance in Rural Southern Appalachia." In *Fighting Back in Appalachia: Traditions of Resistance and Change*, edited by Stephen L. Fisher, 263–82. Philadelphia: Temple University Press.

———. 1995. "Lives on the Margin: Rediscovering the Women of Antebellum Western North Carolina." In *Appalachia in the Making: The Mountain South in the Nineteenth Century*, edited by Mary Beth Pudup, Dwight B. Billings, and Altina L. Waller, 185–209. Chapel Hill: University of North Carolina Press.

———. 2002. *Women, Power, and Dissent in the Hills of Carolina*. Urbana: University of Illinois Press.

Ball, Richard A. 1968. "A Poverty Case: The Analgesic Subculture of the Southern Appalachians." *American Sociological Review* 33(6): 884–94.

Banks, Alan, Dwight B. Billings, and Karen Tice. 1993. "Appalachian Studies, Resistance, and Postmodernism." In *Fighting Back in Appalachia: Traditions of Resistance and Change*, edited by Stephen L. Fisher, 283–301. Philadelphia: Temple University Press.

Barkey, Frederick A. 2012. *Working-Class Radicals: The Socialist Party in West Virginia, 1898–1920*. Morgantown: West Virginia University Press.

Barney, Sandra Lee. 2000. *Authorized to Heal: Gender, Class, and the Transformation of Medicine in Appalachia, 1880–1930*. Chapel Hill: University of North Carolina Press.

Batteau, Allen. 1982. *The Invention of Appalachia*. Tucson: University of Arizona Press.

Beauvoir, Simone de. 1952. *The Second Sex*. New York: Alfred A. Knopf.

Bell, Shannon Elizabeth. 2013. *Our Roots Run Deep as Ironweed: Appalachian Women and the Fight for Environmental Justice*. Urbana: University of Illinois Press.

Bell, Shannon Elizabeth, and Yvonne A. Braun. 2010. "Coal, Identity, and the Gendering of Environmental Justice Activism in Central Appalachia." *Gender & Society* 24(6): 794–813.

Bickley, Ancella, and Lynda Ann Ewen. 2001. *Memphis Tennessee Garrison: The Remarkable Story of a Black Appalachian Woman*. Athens: Ohio University Press.

Billings, Dwight B. 1974. "Culture and Poverty in Appalachia: A Theoretical Discussion and Empirical Analysis." *Social Forces* 53(2): 315–23.

———. 1990. "Religion as Opposition: A Gramscian Analysis." *American Journal of Sociology* 96: 1–31.

———. 2009. "Introduction: Writing Appalachia: Old Ways, New Ways, and WVU Ways." In *Culture, Class and Politics in Modern Appalachia: Essays in Honor of Ronald L. Lewis*, edited by Jennifer Egoff, Ken Fones-Wolf, and Louis C. Martin, 1–28. Morgantown: West Virginia University Press.

Billings, Dwight B., Gurney Norman, and Katherine Ledford, eds. 1999. *Confronting Appalachian Stereotypes: Back Talk from an American Region*. Lexington: University Press of Kentucky.

Black, Kate, and Marc A. Rohrer. 1995. "Out in the Mountains: Exploring Lesbian and Gay Lives." In *Appalachia and the Politics of Culture (Journal of the Appalachian*

Studies Association 7), edited by Elizabeth C. Fine, 18–28. Johnson City: Center for Appalachian Studies and Services, East Tennessee State University.

Brown, Wendy. 1997. "The Impossibility of Women's Studies." *differences* 9(3): 79–101.

Buhle, Mari Jo, Ann G. Gordon, and Nancy Shrom. 1971. "Women in American Society: An Historical Contribution." *Radical America* 5(4): 3–66.

Butler, Judith. 1990. *Gender Trouble: Feminism and the Subversion of Identity*. New York: Routledge.

———. 2004. *Undoing Gender*. New York: Routledge.

Butler, Judith, and Joan W. Scott, eds. 1992. *Feminists Theorize the Political*. New York: Routledge.

Cook, Samuel R. 2000. *Monacans and Miners: Native Americans and Coal Mining Communities in Appalachia*. Lincoln: University of Nebraska Press.

Dill, Bonnie Thornton. 1983. "Race, Class and Gender: Prospects for an All-Inclusive Sisterhood." *Feminist Studies* 9:131–50.

Dill, Bonnie Thornton, and Maxine Baca Zinn. 1996. "Theorizing Difference from Multi-racial Feminism." *Feminist Studies* 22(2): 321–31.

Dunaway, Wilma A. 1996. *The First American Frontier: Transition to Capitalism in Southern Appalachia, 1700–1860*. Chapel Hill: University of North Carolina Press.

———. 2003a. *The African-American Family in Slavery and Emancipation*. Cambridge: Cambridge University Press.

———. 2003b. *Slavery in the American Mountain South*. Cambridge: Cambridge University Press.

———. 2008. *Women, Work, and Family in the Antebellum Mountain South*. New York: Cambridge University Press.

Egolf, Jennifer, Ken Fones-Wolf, and Louis C. Martin, eds. 2009. *Culture, Class, and Politics in Modern Appalachia: Essays in Honor of Ronald L. Lewis*. Morgantown: West Virginia University Press.

Eller, Ronald D. 1982. *Miners, Millhands, and Mountaineers: Industrialization of the Appalachian South, 1880–1930*. Knoxville: University of Tennessee Press.

Emmanuel, Arghiri. 1976. *Unequal Exchange: Study of the Imperialism of Trade*. London: New Left Books.

Engelhardt, Elizabeth S. D. 2003. *The Tangled Roots of Feminism, Environmentalism, and Appalachian Literature*. Athens: Ohio University Press.

Finger, John R. 2005. "Cherokee Accommodation and Persistence in the Southern Appalachians." In *Appalachia in the Making: The Mountain South in the Nineteenth Century*, edited by Mary Beth Pudup, Dwight B. Billings, and Altina L. Waller, 25–49. Chapel Hill: University of North Carolina Press.

Fisher, Stephen L., ed. 1993. *Fighting Back in Appalachia: Traditions of Resistance and Change*. Philadelphia: Temple University Press.

Fisher, Stephen L., and Barbara Ellen Smith, eds. 2012. *Transforming Places: Lessons from Appalachia*. Urbana: University of Illinois Press.

Fones-Wolf, Ken. 2007. *Glass Towns: Industry, Labor, and Political Economy in Appalachia, 1890–1930s*. Chicago: University of Illinois Press.

Fones-Wolf, Ken, and Ronald L. Lewis, eds. 2002. *Transnational West Virginia: Ethnic Communities and Economic Change, 1840–1940*. Morgantown: West Virginia University Press.

Gaventa, John. 1980. *Power and Powerlessness: Quiescence and Rebellion in an Appalachian Valley*. Urbana: University of Illinois Press.

Gray, Mary L. 2009. *Out in the Country: Youth, Media, and Queer Visibility in Rural America*. New York: New York University Press.

Harkins, Anthony. 2004. *Hillbilly: A Cultural History of an American Icon*. New York: Oxford University Press.

hooks, bell. 1984. *Feminist Theory: From Margin to Center*. Cambridge, Mass.: South End Press.

House, Silas. 2002. *A Parchment of Leaves*. New York: Random House.

———. 2005. *The Coal Tattoo*. New York: Random House.

Howard, John, ed. 1997. *Carryin' On in the Lesbian and Gay South*. New York: New York University Press.

Inscoe, John C., ed. 2001. *Appalachians and Race: The Mountain South from Slavery to Segregation*. Lexington: University Press of Kentucky.

Jones, Loyal. 1994. *Appalachian Values*. Ashland, Ky.: Jesse Stuart Foundation.

Keefe, Susan. 2005. *Appalachian Cultural Competency: A Guide for Medical, Mental Health, and Social Service Professionals*. Knoxville: University of Tennessee Press.

Kelly-Gadol, Joan. 1976. "The Social Relations of the Sexes: Methodological Implications of Women's History." *Signs* 1(4): 809–23.

———. 1977. "Did Women Have a Renaissance?" In *Becoming Visible: Women in European History*, edited by Renate Bridenthal and Claudia Koonz, 137–64. Boston: Houghton Mifflin.

Kimmel, Michael. 1996. *Manhood in America: A Cultural History*. New York: Free Press.

Kuhn, Thomas S. 1970. *The Structure of Scientific Revolutions*. Chicago: University of Chicago Press.

Lerner, Gerda. 1979. *The Majority Finds Its Past: Placing Women in History*. New York: Oxford University Press.

Lewis, Helen Matthews, Linda Johnson, and Donald Askins, eds. 1978. *Colonialism in Modern America: The Appalachian Case*. Boone, N.C.: Appalachian Consortium Press.

Lewis, Oscar. 1961. *The Children of Sanchez: Autobiography of a Mexican Family*. New York: Random House.

Lewis, Ronald L. 1987. *Black Coal Miners in America: Race, Class, and Community Conflict, 1780–1980*. Lexington: University Press of Kentucky.

———. 1998. *Transforming the Appalachian Countryside: Railroads, Deforestation, and Social Change in West Virginia, 1880–1920*. Chapel Hill: University of North Carolina Press.

Maggard, Sally Ward. 1986. "Class and Gender: New Theoretical Priorities in Appalachian Studies." In *The Impact of Institutions in Appalachia (Proceedings of the Annual Appalachian Studies Conference 8)*, edited by Jim Lloyd and Anne G. Campbell, 100–113. Boone, N.C.: Appalachian Consortium Press.

———. 1994. "From Farm to Coal Camp to Back Office and McDonald's: Living in the Midst of Appalachia's Latest Transformation." In *Appalachian Adaptations to a Changing World* (*Journal of the Appalachian Studies Association* 6), edited by Norma Meyers, 14–38. Johnson City: Center for Appalachian Studies and Services, East Tennessee State University.

———. 1999. "Gender, Race, and Place: Confounding Labor Activism in Central Appalachia." In *Neither Separate nor Equal: Women, Race, and Class in the* South, edited by Barbara Ellen Smith, 185–206. Philadelphia: Temple University Press.

Mann, Jeff. 2005. *Loving Mountains, Loving Men.* Athens: Ohio University Press.

Moore, Barrington, Jr. 1966. *Social Origins of Dictatorship and Democracy: Lord and Peasant in the Making of the Modern World.* Boston: Beacon Press.

Obermiller, Phillip J., and Michael E. Maloney. 2011. "The Uses and Misuses of Appalachian Culture." Urban Appalachian Council Working Paper No. 20, Cincinnati.

Pancake, Ann. 2007. *Strange as This Weather Has Been.* Berkeley: Shoemaker & Hoard.

Payne, Charles M. 1995. *I've Got the Light of Freedom: The Organizing Tradition and the Mississippi Freedom Struggle.* Berkeley: University of California Press.

Ray, Celeste. 2001. *Scottish Americans in the American South.* Chapel Hill: University of North Carolina Press.

Reichert Powell, Douglas. 2007. *Critical Regionalism: Connecting Politics and Culture in an American Landscape.* Chapel Hill: University of North Carolina Press.

Reid, Herbert, and Betsy Taylor. 2010. *Recovering the Commons: Democracy, Place, and Global Justice.* Urbana: University of Illinois Press.

Satterwhite, Emily. 2011. *Dear Appalachia: Readers, Identity, and Popular Fiction since 1878.* Lexington: University Press of Kentucky.

Scott, Rebecca R. 2010. *Removing Mountains: Extracting Nature and Identity in the Appalachian Coalfields.* Minneapolis: University of Minnesota Press.

Shapiro, Henry D. 1978. *Appalachia on Our Mind: The Southern Mountains and Mountaineers in American Consciousness, 1870–1920.* Chapel Hill: University of North Carolina Press.

Silber, Nina. 1997. *The Romance of Reunion: Northerners and the South, 1865–1900.* Chapel Hill: University of North Carolina Press.

Simon, Richard M. 1984. "Regions and Social Relations: A Research Note." *Appalachian Journal* 11:23–31.

Smith, Barbara Ellen. 1987. *Digging Our Own Graves: Coal Miners and the Struggle over Black Lung Disease.* Philadelphia: Temple University Press.

———. 1998. "Walk-Ons in the Third Act: The Role of Women in Appalachian Historiography." *Journal of Appalachian Studies* 4 (Spring): 5–28.

———. 1999. "Beyond the Mountains: The Paradox of Women's Place in Appalachian History." *National Women's Studies Association Journal* 11(3): 1–17.

———. 2004. "Degradations of Whiteness: Appalachia and the Complexities of Race." *Journal of Appalachian Studies* 10(1–2): 38–57.

———. 2012. "The Price of the Ticket: Latino Immigrants and the Challenge of Community in Appalachia." *Appalachian Journal* 39(3–4): 234–44.

Spelman, Elizabeth. 1990. *Inessential Woman*. Boston: Beacon Press.

Trotter, Joe William, Jr. 1990. *Coal, Class, and Color: Blacks in Southern West Virginia, 1915–1932*. Chicago: University of Illinois Press.

Turner, William H., and Edward J. Cabell, eds. 1985. *Blacks in Appalachia*. Lexington: University Press of Kentucky.

Wagner, Thomas E., and Phillip J. Obermiller. 2004. *African American Miners and Migrants: The Eastern Kentucky Social Club*. Urbana: University of Illinois Press.

Walker, Frank X. 2000. *Affrilachia: Poems by Frank X Walker*. Lexington, Ky.: Old Cove Press.

Wallerstein, Immanuel. 1974. *The Modern World-System I: Capitalist Agriculture and the Origins of the European World-Economy in the Sixteenth Century*. New York: Academic Press.

———. 1979. *The Capitalist World-Economy*. Cambridge: Cambridge University Press.

Walls, David S. 1978. "Internal Colony or Internal Periphery? A Critique of Current Models and an Alternative Formulation." In *Colonialism in Modern America*, edited by Helen Matthews Lewis, Linda Johnson, and Donald Askins, 319–49.

Weiner, Deborah R. 2006. *Coalfield Jews: An Appalachian History*. Urbana: University of Illinois Press.

Weller, Jack E. 1965. *Yesterday's People: Life in Contemporary Appalachia*. Lexington: University Press of Kentucky.

Whisnant, David E. 1983. *All That Is Native and Fine: The Politics of Culture in an American Region*. Chapel Hill: University of North Carolina Press.

Wilkinson, Crystal. 2002. *Water Street*. London: Toby Press.

Yarrow, Michael. 1991. "The Gender-Specific Class Consciousness of Appalachian Coal Miners." In *Bringing Class Back In: Historical and Contemporary Perspectives*, edited by Scott McNeil, Rhonda Levine, and Rick Fantasia, 285–310. Boulder, Colo.: Westview Press.

3

Writing Appalachia

*Intersections, Missed Connections,
and Future Work*

CHRIS GREEN AND ERICA ABRAMS LOCKLEAR

As with other ethnic and identity studies movements in the last forty years, Appalachian studies has increased in scope and popularity. In particular, Appalachian literature (novels, poems, stories, plays, memoirs, etc.) has generated a huge amount of attention. In pure volume, literature is the most cited, presented, and studied subject in all of Appalachian studies. Additionally, Appalachian writers such as Lee Smith, Robert Morgan, Ron Rash, and Sharyn McCrumb have enjoyed a wide readership throughout the mountains and the nation. Likewise, the last ten years have seen an out-pouring of encyclopedic work conducted on the state and regional levels in which scholars of Appalachian literature have begun to outline its history; these pieces, however, are necessarily overviews that generally catalog names of authors and their works. One of the difficulties in compiling a history of Appalachian literature has, paradoxically, been the tendency for those who study it to focus on texts and authors.

In order to instead focus on how Appalachian literature and Appalachian studies intersect, this chapter relates how a set of evolving movements and institutions affiliated with Appalachian studies has affected the shape and direction of Appalachian literature and vice versa.[1] Rather than writing a unitary history, we map the varied paths (and dead ends) that people with very different visions of Appalachia made based on their situations. Some-times such decisions were very much part of an ideological maneuvering to affect the direction of practice and understanding; other times, decisions were responses to opportunities for people to realize their visions. In other words, the history of the relationship of Appalachian studies to Appalachian literature is a set of movements and directions—at times complementary, at times not; at times interlocked, at times separate—with diverse goals and outcomes. Yet when these are considered together, important patterns and effects emerge.

In 1990 Jim Wayne Miller spent five pages in "A People Waking Up" discussing how Appalachian authors are pressured by national presses and audiences to portray the region to suit their need to "visit" the mountains in order to witness the lives of people whom "they believe to be more stable and reliable; or, alternatively, to go slumming through the lives of people who remind them of what they are not" (1990, 61). At times Appalachian authors, readers, teachers, and presses engage in a type of defensive hagiography of said writing. Such uncritical praise has a role, but ultimately it blunts the edge of cultural study. Nevertheless, literature about one's own cultural group is tremendously validating when it recognizes and describes experiences that prior representations have excluded or misrepresented and when it affirms one's culture and sense of self on an immediate level, as well as inclusion in the larger tradition of American and Western literature and culture. When readers encounter words and images that reflect their own experiences, they are provided the means to dialogue with and about that experience and permission to undertake such projects themselves. In addition to scholars, Appalachian literature includes authors, presses, magazines, readings, audiences, and classrooms (Miller 1990, 72). As we relate this history, we touch on the consequences of directions taken and untaken and of places in need of investigation. In our conclusion we summarize Appalachian literary study's major accomplishments and absences, hypothesizing about future paths for inquiry.

The first major set of relations that came to shape Appalachian studies and Appalachian literature were non-Appalachian mountain workers who came into the mountains in the late 1800s. Publications associated with Berea College, Hindman Settlement School, and the Council of Southern Mountain Workers (CSM), as well as the journal *Mountain Life and Work*, became integral in establishing the first connections between Appalachian literature and Appalachian studies. Many of the publications from these venues were nonfiction, but there were notable exceptions, including but not limited to William Eleazar Barton's *Life in the Hills of Kentucky* (1890); Lucy Furman's *Mothering the Perilous* (1913) and *The Quare Women* (1923); poems by Ann Cobb, Amy May Rogers, Don L. West, Jesse Stuart, and James Still in *Mountain Life and Work* in the 1920s and 1930s; and reviews of Olive Tilford Dargan's (pseudonym Fielding Burke) radical novels in the same publication.

A second influence involves the interconnected development of the study of ballads, folklore, and literature. While the role of ballads and ballad collecting has been much studied as it relates to the discursive history of Appalachia, scholars have not examined how the academic study of such ballads set forth core patterns that affected the shape of Appalachian studies (Krim 2006; McCarthy 1999; Shapiro 1978; Whisnant 1983; Worthington [2009]). Many English professors helped found folklore societies and also played an important role in the emergence of Appalachian studies, including Frank C. Brown, Reed Smith, John Harrington Cox, and C. Alphonso Smith (Cuthbert 2006; Wilgus 1959). Familiarity with these roots allows us to come into critical relationship with the practices that inform the current orientation, allowing for renewal or intervention.

Considering the role that university presses have played in the connections between Appalachian literature and Appalachian studies is also essential in expanding an understanding of past, current, and potential trends in the field. Heralding the coming War on Poverty in 1965, two academic publishers—West Virginia University Library and the University Press of Kentucky—released foundational materials for Appalachian studies and literature. Perhaps reflecting the energy created on campus by the folklore classes, the West Virginia University Library press brought out twenty-six books in the 1960s. In 1966 Lloyd Davis and other faculty at West Virginia University started the *Appalachian Review*, a magazine along the lines of *Mountain Life and Work*, and the first issue united essays about Appalachia by the likes of Harry Caudill and Robert Coles with poetry by Louise McNeill and fiction by Jesse Stuart. Likewise, in 1962 Kentucky published *The Southern Appalachian Region: A Survey*, edited by Thomas R. Ford and Rupert Vance, which provided the first global update about Appalachia since the 1930s. In 1959 Willis D. Weatherford, Sr., and Wilma Dykeman coauthored an essay for *The Southern Appalachian Region* that became the landmark midcentury study of the state of Appalachian literature. That same year, Dykeman's *The Tall Woman* came out, announcing her move from a nonfiction author who championed civil rights and social justice to a novelist who transferred those values into her literary writing about Appalachia.

In coming years the University Press of Kentucky published key texts in the field, including but not limited to Jack Weller's *Yesterday's People* (1965), John B. Stephenson's *Shiloh: A Mountain Community* (1968), and a reprint of John C. Campbell's seminal 1921 text, *The Southern Highlander and His Homeland* (1969). These publications and more announced not only the interest of the press but also the new status of Appalachia on university campuses, thereby opening space for the study, writing, and publishing of Appalachian literature as part of Appalachian studies.

Other than the *Appalachian Review*, the most important venue for combining Appalachian studies and literature continued to be the CSM's *Mountain Life and Work*. From 1949 to 1961 it published more folksongs and folktales than fiction or poetry; an even heavier ratio, almost two to one, occurred in reviews. While literary works in the 1950s were coupled with folktales and songs, after 1961 publication of folktales and folksongs stopped: from 1962 to 1969 *Mountain Life and Work* doubled the number of poems per year and increased the number of stories by 80 percent. And in 1968 and 1969 Gurney Norman and Jim Wayne Miller—names essential to post-1970 Appalachian studies—published more stories and poems, respectively, than any other contributors. In *Mountain Life and Work* and the *Appalachian Review* a certain type of Appalachian literature became integral to Appalachian studies, performing an important (if different) type of cultural work as scholarship, essays, and images. After the CSM radicalized, between 1970 and 1979, stories and poems in *Mountain Life and Work* became far fewer in number, while lyrics to eight labor songs were published. Instead of James Still being the literary spirit, the magazine featured an interview, an essay, and a poem by Don West; the rest of the poems that appeared were anonymous, written by nonpoets, or were laments for tragedies such as Buffalo Creek. As *Mountain Life and Work* took up such issues, it also opened the field in the 1970s for other periodicals addressing Appalachian culture and literature, a space filled by *From the Hills*, *Appalachian Heritage*, the *Appalachian Journal*, the *Mountain Review*, and twelve other magazines, each seeding the field with their particular visions of Appalachia, action, academics, and art.

In the 1970s the Appalachian Renaissance, a term coined in 1970 by Ruel E. Foster, who chaired the English Department at West Virginia University, began building (Foster 1970). Thanks to a major National Endowment for the Humanities grant secured by Bill Weinberg at Alice Lloyd College, Albert Stewart (who formerly ran a writers' workshop at Morehead State University) was able to put together the first issues of *Appalachian Heritage*. Stewart convened an impressive set of advisory and contributing editors, including Harriette Simpson Arnow, Billy C. Clark, Jean Ritchie, James Still, and Eliot Wigginton. The first issue was published in 1973, and Stewart edited the magazine for ten years until a new college president who had little interest in Appalachian studies stopped supporting its publication in 1982.

During those years, *Appalachian Heritage* published a wide range of accessible essays, short literary pieces, reviews, and graphics that sought, as

Stewart explained, to "present" the "humanness" of "the Appalachian life-style"—an intersection of "individual ways" that somehow shared "a heritage of customs, attitudes, and manners" (Stewart 1973). The magazine wove together a vision of tradition that brought some of the first Appalachian authors into conversation with the current generation. Stewart's editorial board was published alongside names who were then new but now stand as part of the foundation of Appalachian literature, such as Betty Sellers, Bennie Lee Sinclair, Sidney Saylor Farr, George Ella Lyon, and James B. Goode (Brosi 2011). Also included were important essays that leaned toward scholarship, including work by Loyal Jones, essays on Appalachian fiction by Cratis Williams, Danny Miller's essays on Appalachian women writers, and Jim Wayne Miller's cultural-political manifesto "Appalachian Values/American Values," a five-part series running from the fall of 1977 through the spring of 1979. Yet in comparison with similar magazines in the 1970s, *Appalachian Heritage* represented a more traditionalist view.

After Stewart's retirement from Alice Lloyd in 1977, he began setting up what has become perhaps the most important nexus in all of Appalachian literature: the Appalachian Writers' Workshop at Hindman Settlement School (Kendrick and Lyon 2002; Lyon, Miller, and Norman 1993; Smith and Tuttle 2005). Since its inception, the workshop—a one-week gathering given over wholly to creative writing—has been a central gathering spot for established authors who specifically identify with Appalachia and for writers who wish to learn the art. In a 2006 interview, former Hindman Settlement School executive director Mike Mullins provided a compelling summary of the workshop's dynamics as an "egalitarian gathering" where "a core group of writers has developed a loyalty to the workshop and they encouraged others to become involved." The boundaries between established writer and newcomer dissolve because of how Mullins had structured the gathering: "You live together, you work together, you eat together, you party together! You can't hide out. It forces you to be part of the community" (Mullins 2006, 329, 330). From writers who found their beginnings at the workshop, such as Silas House, to those who came into a new relationship with Appalachia, such as Lee Smith, the Appalachian Writers' Workshop continues to be a crucial, home-built nexus for forwarding a brand of Appalachian studies as literary practice renewed each year through the visions of its participants.[2]

The years leading up to the 1970s proved to be an equally critical time for Appalachian studies in North Carolina and Tennessee, which followed lines similar to those at West Virginia University. In particular, drama became more popular, and in 1952 the Southern Appalachian Historical Association commissioned and produced Kermit Hunter's *Horn in the West* in Boone, North Carolina. Hunter had already staged the well-known outdoor drama *Unto These Hills* in Cherokee, North Carolina, in 1950, and productions of it continue today. Likewise, Willis D. Weatherford, Sr., commissioned Paul Green, who was associated with the University of North Carolina at Chapel Hill, to write *Wilderness Road*, an outdoor drama that ran at Berea College from 1955 to 1959 and was revived in the 1970s. Both Cratis Williams and Weatherford used their academic positions to cultivate outdoor drama for the specific purpose of transforming the public's relationship to Appalachia (Dykeman 1966; Weiss 2006a; Wey 1976). As of 2006, "approximately fifty outdoor dramas have been presented in Appalachia," of which "twenty-one continue to be performed," constituting "nearly half" of all such dramas in the United States (Weiss 2006b). Perhaps because Appalachian studies had become established in the 1970s, the discussion of these outdoor dramas has remained nearly absent in Appalachian studies scholarship.

At East Tennessee State University (ETSU), Thomas Burton and Ambrose Manning, both English professors, "in 1964 began taping folk songs, ballads, tales, and other types of folklore from East Tennessee and western North Carolina" (Burton n.d.). In 1968 and 1969 they published two volumes of folksongs that had been gathered in the ETSU Oral History Archives. From 1966 to 1971 Burton and Manning also coauthored a weekly column on songs and ballads; similarly, they ran the university's Folk Festival from 1966 to 1972 (Burton n.d.). The study of folklore, folksong, and English as a discipline formed a common ground of the Appalachians.

At Appalachian State University, President Herbert W. Wey had asked Cratis Williams and ASU's recently retired president Blanford Barnard Dougherty to work on developing an Appalachian studies curriculum. In the course of seeking funding, the discovery was made that other area colleges and universities (including ETSU) were seeking support for similar projects, and they banded together to make a common proposal (Wey 1976; Williams [1979]). Called together by highly respected higher-education administrators, the Appalachian Consortium was founded in 1971, forming a coalition of diverse institutions that included public universities, private colleges, federal agencies, state agencies, nonprofits, and business groups. Until its dissolution in 2004, the consortium's membership fluctuated slightly, but throughout its existence the most influential members were Appalachian State and East Tennessee State. The Appalachian Consortium founded a press, and of its sixty-nine titles, a third fell under the wide umbrella of literature, including folktales, ballads, anthologies, creative works, and literary scholarship. The book that best illustrates the insightful editing of the press is Jim Wayne Miller's iconic *The Mountains Have Come Closer*, whose long poem "The Brier Sermon" has recently begun to be recited yearly at the Appalachian Writers' Workshop. Miller's text underwent significant revision at the suggestions of Cratis Williams, Patricia Beaver, and Jerry Williamson. And after the Publications Committee met on January 19, 1979, Williams wrote to Beaver that the manuscript "has a more powerful impact in its revised form, feeds with more force into the *Brier Sermon* [*sic*], a notable achievement in poetry by itself. . . . It is about the right length to appeal vividly to a possible reader, and it will impress the reader so deeply that he/she will never be the same afterwards" (Williams 1979). In other words, editors and boards who were and are deeply informed about Appalachian studies have often brought powerful influence on those literary books that, in turn, have affected the shape and identity of Appalachian studies.

Appalachian State University was—and continues to be—integral to the relationship between Appalachian studies and Appalachian literature. Jerry Williamson edited *Appalachian Journal* from its start at Appalachian State University in 1973 through 2000, when Sandra Ballard took over. Williamson's own discipline was English, but he brought a sharp edge to both literary aesthetics and social politics. With essays and articles from a wide variety of disciplinary perspectives, the journal's goal then and now was to stay connected to the ground while also engaging in cutting-edge social and political thinking. Until the Appalachian Studies Association began publishing the *Journal of Appalachian Studies* in 1989, the *Appalachian Journal* was very much the home of Appalachian studies, with two issues—Autumn 1977 (bearing the title "A Guide to Appalachian Studies") and Winter–Spring 1982 (bearing the title "Assessing Appalachian Studies")—wholly dedicated to Appalachian studies as such. (See the whole of the *Appalachian Journal* 28[1] [2000].)

A second example from the consortium's list opened paths that are still walked and argued. In 1975 Robert J. Higgs and Ambrose N. Manning edited a 540-page anthology called *Voices from the Hills*. Perhaps the most influential collection of Appalachian literature, *Voices from the Hills* answered the call to weave together some three hundred years of writing about Appalachia and its discursive and literary traditions. Appropriately, the Autumn 1976 issue of *Appalachian Journal* included two reviews about the book, including one by C. Hugh Holman, the Kenan Professor of English at the University of North Carolina at Chapel Hill, who specialized in southern literature. In the Winter 1977 issue, the journal published the book's editors' retort. This review and Higgs and Manning's response continue to serve as a critical measure of what it meant to see Appalachian literature through the lens of Appalachian studies rather than Southern studies.

Holman leveled a wholesale critique of the anthology's "inward direction," which resulted in a "very self-conscious regionalism, a defensive attitude toward its ideals, aspirations, and goals, and a critical view of its problems" (1976, 74). Holman called his disagreement with what fiction should have been included in the anthology "a lover's quarrel," but he then detailed the collection's deficiencies, called the selection of poetry "the weakest part of the book," and noted that "the influence" of Jack Weller's *Yesterday's People* "seems pervasively present" in the essay section (76). In the next sentence, Holman stated that Jim Wayne Miller's "A Mirror for the Region" is the "most telling definition of . . . the essential attitude of the editors." Yet as Higgs and Manning pointed out in their response, they purposefully juxtaposed those essays to demonstrate "an alternative approach" to education. Miller's essay offered a way to focus education on students' cultural experience and took its inspiration from Agrarian Donald Davidson's "A Mirror for Artists," which frames the social responsibility of artists and was published in *I'll Take My Stand* (1930).

The credo of education and literature set forth by Davidson in that essay and others collected in *Attack on Leviathan* (1937) powerfully forecast the values of Appalachian studies. Although not an Appalachian and incredibly problematic due to his stands on racial segregation from 1945 until his death in 1968, Davidson was a tremendous influence on critical figures in Appalachian literature such as Jesse Stuart, Ruel Foster, and Jim Wayne Miller, the last of whom graduated from Berea College in 1958 and took seminars with Davidson while working on his doctorate in German at Vanderbilt from 1960 to 1963. How Miller found his direction influenced by his work with Davidson is a crucial example of how not just Appalachian studies networks but also southern studies networks fostered critical Appalachian literature—that is, a literature not just about or based on the region but one informed by transformative dialogue with other developing facets of Appalachian and southern studies.

In his critique of *Voices from the Hills*, Holman continued to offer three more extended "complaints" about the collection: the "tendency toward sympathetic portraiture"; the disregard of contemporary Appalachia in favor of "the withdrawn, isolated, rural world which is presented almost exclusively"; and the criticism that "the southern Appalachian mountain region cannot be marked off from the general southeastern region of the nation with the precision that the editors imply." Doing so denies that "every region of the country . . . is essentially a pluralistic society" (1976, 76–78). This final point was made against the editors' focus on the "mountains" as opposed to the Piedmont South. To separate southern Appalachia so cleanly from its role as one of the South's regions was, Holman believed, to decontextualize it from what mattered most.

The subtext of Holman's critique concerns the role (and subservience) of Appalachian literature and Appalachian studies in the newly arisen field of southern literature. Focus on that literature in the 1960s would help give rise to authors such as Lee Smith and Annie Dillard, who studied with Louis Rubin, Jr., at Hollins College, and Katherine Stripling Byer and Robert Morgan, who in 1968 completed their master of fine arts degrees at the University of North Carolina Greensboro's newly minted program, where they studied with Fred Chappell and Allen Tate (Byer 2005; Chappell 1986; Morgan 1994; Parrish 1998). The relationship between the study of southern and Appalachian literature and writing is another issue deserving of its own essay, but we would like to point out that, when seen through the light of Appalachian studies, the two are by no means the same, nor does inclusion in one preclude inclusion in the other (Clabough 2007; Cunningham 1996). This anxiety and conflict over geographic and identity relations *as territory* (to be marked, owned, explored, and harvested) replays itself time and again as a theme and trial in Appalachian history and in Appalachian studies.

Higgs and Manning's response to Holman appeared in the next issue of the *Appalachian Journal* (Winter 1977) and is best summed up in its final paragraph: "For the first time, two cultures [southern and Appalachian] are finally speaking to each other, and we personally feel like citizens of some emerging nation which has just been extended overtures for diplomatic relations by a major power" (98). But, as we have seen from Holman's review, relations were anything but diplomatic. At the start of their retort—after excusing the inability to include certain pieces due to costs or by authorial intervention (as in the case of Wendell Berry, who did not consider himself Appalachian)—Higgs and Manning met each of Holman's critiques. In addressing the difficulty of defining Appalachia as a region, they point out that Holman's preferred term of the "Piedmont South" cannot be made to include "the Valley region and the Cumberland plateau" (94). Underneath this debate about geography rests the fact that Higgs, Manning, and the Appalachian Consortium were focused on a particular area of Appalachia centered on the Blue Ridge, but their anthology also included authors from the Ohio River valley (Jesse Stuart) and the Alleghenies, which run from West Virginia into

Pennsylvania (Louise McNeill). Yet Holman's diagnosis was correct: Higgs and Manning were announcing Appalachia's secession from the South.

Regarding Holman's accusations of the editors' "patronizing" attitude, Higgs and Manning were quick to point out that they included authors such as "Harriette Arnow, Wilma Dykeman, Mildred Haun, and James Still[, who] cannot get even a mention in such works as *A Bibliographic Guide to the Study of Southern Literature* (1969), edited by Louis D. Rubin" (1977, 95). Then they hit the nail on the noggin: they explained that there were two types of "Southern and American letters in the South": one of "Allen Tate on the mountain at Sewanee" and the other of "Sherwood Anderson publishing two papers at Marion, Virginia." On the one hand was Tate's version, an exclusionary literature of high modernist aesthetics that grew out of an imaginary southern aristocratic mentality; on the other hand was Anderson's version, an inclusive literature of modernist proletarianism that grew out of an egalitarian, populist mentality that strongly reflected the bent of Appalachian cultural studies in folklore, ballad, and labor.[3] "Which," the editors asked of Holman, "has been doing the patronizing?" (95).

The editors then acknowledge and embrace the living force of the critical influences that helped shape the book, influences that Holman saw as "an inwardness, reductiveness, and simplification": Jesse Stuart, Cratis Williams, and Loyal Jones. Indeed, as explained by African American, Chicano, and postcolonial scholars who study the evolution of minority groups' cultural identity from 1960 to 1990, ethnic groups set themselves against forces opposed to their development, and early ethnic literary editors and writers sought to define their ethnic cultural identity (Pérez-Torres 1995). While *Voices from the Hills* was critiqued in the 1970s for its separatism, a paper at the 2010 Appalachian studies conference critiqued it for its essentialism (of race, gender, and locality), which limited the definitions of what it meant to be "Appalachian" (Lloyd 2010). Both miss the point: *Voices from the Hills* served to rally the movement that Ruel Foster had called "the Appalachian Literary Renaissance" in 1970, wherein the proliferation of literature by Appalachian writers was facilitated by precisely this seemingly essentializing self-definition. As Higgs and Manning acknowledge, "Our book might appear to take a backward, reductive glance at the mountaineer, partially out of an instinctive reaction to and loathing for [the] national mania for sameness, and partially because we consciously wanted to depict through a history of the evolution of literary genres the essence of an Appalachian literature, a literature that somehow persists in being romantic, backward looking, and symbolic in and of itself without any great amount of nudging from the editors" (1977,

97). Such an enunciation of essence came under critique from most scholars within Appalachian studies, leading to an effective purging of figures like Jesse Stuart and scholars who studied him (Green 2008, 98). Similar critiques continue today, but what we have yet to recognize (rather than condemn) is the particular role agrarian-Scotch-Irish-Appalachian essentializing has played (LeRoy-Frazier 2007). In other words, in the fight against the destruction of Appalachian identity (which was in the 1970s, paradoxically, just then being born), how can one recoup the past to foster awareness of current identity and cultural structures without anachronistically defining the diverse and dynamic present in terms of a static past? The speaker in Jim Wayne Miller's poem "Brier Sermon—'You Must Be Born Again'" perhaps best answers this question: "What's it like—being born again? / It's going back to what you were before / without losing what you've since become" (1980, 63).

In the 1970s, thanks in large part to Dudley Cocke and Jo Carson, community-based grassroots theater became more popular in Appalachia and certainly deserves more scholarly attention. In that same decade, small independent and academic publishers, with the Appalachian Consortium in the lead, began publishing Appalachian literature. The University of Tennessee Press republished Emma Bell Miles's *Spirit of the Mountains* (1975) and Horace Kephart's *Our Southern Highlanders* (1976) and copublished the *Bibliography of Southern Appalachia* with the consortium. The poetry series at Louisiana State University Press brought out Fred Chappell's *The World between the Eyes* (1971) and Robert Morgan's *Land Diving* (1976). But the largest amount of literary publishing happened in central Kentucky, likely in response to the newly established and well-led Appalachian Center at the University of Kentucky and to the excitement elsewhere in the state surrounding *Appalachian Heritage* and the Appalachian Writers' Workshop. Among the ten books that Gnomon Press brought out that decade that touched on Appalachia were James Still's *Pattern of a Man and Other Stories* (1976), Gurney Norman's *Kinfolks* (1977), and Robert Morgan's *Ground Work* (1979) (Greene 2005). The University Press of Kentucky established itself and Appalachia's literary canon by bringing out fiction and autobiography by Harriette Simpson Arnow, Jesse Stuart, and James Still with the 1978 republication of *River of Earth*. At the same time, Appalachian-focused study of Appalachian literature began with conferences at Morris Harvey College in 1970, the Cratis Williams symposium in 1977, and the first Appalachian studies conference in 1978. The result?

In the 1980s things got cooking. Although there was debate about the "action people" versus the "creative folk" in Appalachian studies, if the proceedings of the Appalachian Studies Conference were any sign, the activist side of Appalachian literature was in bloom (Miller 1982). The introduction to the proceedings, from the third conference in 1980, discussed Jim Wayne Miller's reading from *The Mountains Have Come Closer* at the start of the conference.[4] The papers immediately thereafter address the issue of labor, with Helen Matthews Lewis and Myles Horton at the fore. Of the two literature papers, P. J. Laska's was titled "Poetry at the Periphery: The Possibilities of People's Culture in Appalachia." Around the time same, from 1977 to 1989, Kentucky reprinted books seen as being at the foundation of Appalachian literature: novels by James Still, Jesse Stuart, John Fox, Jr., Harriette Simpson Arnow, and Elizabeth Maddox Roberts. Since 1980 most Appalachian authors, however, have had books published with small, independent presses.

As the publication of literary works set in Appalachia increased, so too did the need to index them. Ambiguous definitions of the region and the urge to catalog varied types of publications resulted in bibliographers associated with Appalachian studies having a difficult time choosing relevant publications. Such work is time consuming, never ending, heroic, essential, and underappreciated, for without it, the spread of ideas and knowledge would grind to a halt. The most important bibliographic work in the 1980s happened in association with Berea College. From 1985 to 1995, George Brosi wrote and published *Appalachian Mountain Books*. Each issue contained brief essays, summaries, and bibliographies of the foundational titles in nearly every imaginable Appalachian subject. Some issues were dedicated to specific authors and others to books for specific subjects. Many of Brosi's "write-ups" were also published in *Appalachian Heritage*, where they continued to be published after 1995. Starting in 1970, Berea's Hutchins Library published lists of the fiction about Appalachia held in the Weatherford-Hammond Collection, with 1,480 works listed in 1984. Such a list is important to consult because it shows those titles that the college believed might fall under its understanding of "Appalachia" as opposed to the one thousand or so titles listed in the *Bibliography of Southern Appalachia* (1976) or the almost five hundred annotated titles in Lorise Boger's *The Southern Mountaineer in Literature* (1963). The only recent such bibliography is *Appalachian Children's Literature: An Annotated Bibliography* (2007), by Roberta Herrin, Sheila Quinn Oliver, and George Ella Lyon, with over two thousand entries. More global bibliographies are needed.

These numbers are large compared to the titles whose Library of Congress (LOC) subject headings identify them as "Appalachian" that appear in global databases such as Worldcat. The differences occur because books found in the Weatherford-Hammond Collection often appear in LOC subject headings by state, do not include geographic subjects at all, and exclude Appalachian authors writing books with non-Appalachian subjects. Nevertheless, the last forty-five years have shown a decided increase in the number of fiction titles whose subject heading includes "Appalachia."

If we compare and compile such bibliographies, we can begin to apprehend important trends with regard to the scope and focus of Appalachian literature, such as the fact that over half of the cataloged fiction entries in Worldcat that mention both Appalachia and a state involve Kentucky (with a significant increase from North Carolina). This association reflects the presence of institutions such as Hindman Settlement School, Berea College, and the University Press of Kentucky along with journals such as *Mountain Life and Work* and *Appalachian Heritage*.

As a discipline of action and thought that transcends academic boundaries, Appalachian studies needs to conduct a careful study of community-based magazines that were and continue to be central mechanisms in its rise. A list of such magazines includes *Wind* (Kentucky, 1970–2005), *Mountain Call* (West Virginia, 1973–78), *Appalachian Notes* (Kentucky, 1973–85), *Mountain Review* (Kentucky, 1974–81), *Pudding Stone* (Tennessee, 1974–77), *Plow* (Virginia, 1975–79), *Small Farm* (Tennessee, 1975–80), *Hill and Valley* (West Virginia, 1977–85), *Illustrated Appalachian Intelligencer* (West Virginia, 1977–82), *Touchstone* (Tennessee, 1977–80), *Unrealist* (West Virginia, 1978–82), *Katuah Journal: A Bioregional Journal of the Southern Appalachians* (North Carolina, 1983–93), *Pine Mountain Sand & Gravel* (Kentucky, 1986–), *The Appalachian Connection* (Ohio, 1998–2009), and *Still: The Journal* (Kentucky, 2009–).

Thus far we have focused primarily on scholarship gaps related to publication histories writ large, but certainly there are specific exclusions that have yet to be thoroughly considered. Perhaps some of the most understudied Appalachian writers are those who fall outside the Anglo-Saxon myth that has so long plagued Appalachia and the study of it. Looking back at the work of Appalachian literary studies with contemporary Native American authors and communities, one finds surprisingly sporadic discussion. When such work occurs it is almost always about the Eastern Band of Cherokee or Marilou Awiakta, with no mention of the Shawnee, Muscogee, and Lenape, all of whom continue to inhabit the Appalachian region but without official recognition.[5] However, rather than being a sparse representation, the focus on the Eastern Band is quite remarkable, because only about one of every ten Native Americans in the region defined by the Appalachian Regional Commission is from this band, which has 13,562 members (Hayden 2004; U.S. Department of the Interior 2005).

Only two publications affiliated with Appalachian studies have substantive collections about literature by members of the Eastern Band. The first, *The Cherokee Perspective: Written by Eastern Cherokees,* edited by Laurence French and Jim Hornbuckle (Appalachian Consortium Press, 1981), includes sixty-one poems as part of its 270 pages of narrative about Cherokee life in the Qualla Boundary. The second came in the Fall 2009 issue of *Appalachian Heritage.* Why such a gap, when even the Appalachian Studies Association held its 2004 annual conference in Cherokee, North Carolina? We don't have easy answers but can offer some speculations.

While the Qualla Boundary is the only federally recognized reservation in southern Appalachia, the size of the Eastern Band is only 5 percent as large as the Cherokee Nation in Oklahoma, authors from which have published widely in both Native American studies and the literary mainstream. In addition, although these two groups show a similar distribution of educational achievement (an average of 76.5 percent high school graduates, 15.2 percent undergraduates, and 6 percent with master's or professional degrees), a much higher proportion of the Eastern Band lives on its reservation in Cherokee, North Carolina, with relatively limited access to venues of higher education, as opposed to the Cherokee Nation, which has a university located within it. One important shift has been in Western Carolina University, at which Robert J. Conley (a member of the Cherokee Nation who has published over eighty books) is the Sequoyah Distinguished Professor of Cherokee Studies.

The literary and cultural networks around Native American studies have also formed a route for publication and action that have often distanced Native authors and Appalachian scholars. For instance, Maryjo Moore has edited important anthologies of Native American writing for Thundermouth Press, has led workshops on the Qualla Boundary, and has edited a collection of writings by members of the Eastern Band called *Returning to the Homeland: Cherokee Poetry and Short Stories* (1994). However, Moore's name is almost unmentioned in Appalachian studies.[6] It would seem that many Native American authors see themselves and their work in terms of being Native American rather than in relationship to Appalachia. In addition to identity, another difficulty is recognizing "literature," an issue of prime importance to Native American peoples: if one opens up Cherokee literature to storytelling, one might include the many books that Barbara Duncan edited and published with the University of North Carolina Press, but such work now seems to fall outside of the focus of those working with and in Appalachian literature and, all too often, Appalachian studies (Acoose et al. 2008; Weaver, Womack, and Warrior 2006).

Issues of identity, inclusion, exclusion, and choice are integral to ethnic studies but are perhaps more ambiguous with regard to whether and how someone is Appalachian. If, on the one hand, we find few Native Americans being recognized in Appalachian literature, remarkable strides have been made with regard to African Americans.

Literary critics are beginning to explore the wealth of literature being produced by the Affrilachian writers, as indicated by *Appalachian Heritage*'s special issue on African American Appalachian authors published in 2008 and edited by William H. Turner. In the introduction to that issue, Chad Berry explained that the material readers will encounter is a follow-up to an issue previously published seventeen years prior, and he advised readers not to "read [the material] silently to [themselves]," because "this material needs to be read aloud. No, it needs to be shouted" in an effort to "build awareness of true diversity in Appalachia" (Berry 2008). Certainly more shouting from readers and literary critics alike is in order (Burriss 2005; Dyer 1998; Locklear 2009; Miller 2003; Newberry 2000).

Although based on the term *Appalachia*, the term *Affrilachia* is not synonymous with "people of color from Appalachia." Several poets who identify themselves as Affrilachian poets are not African American, nor do they necessarily have Appalachian roots or live (or have ever lived) in the region. For instance, Nikky Finney grew up on the northern coast of South Carolina and lived in Lexington, Kentucky, where she taught at the University of Kentucky from 1990 to 2013, when she began teaching at the University of South Carolina. Ricardo Nazario y Colón was born in the South Bronx and now lives in Morehead, Kentucky. Some scholars assert that this kind of inclusivity exhibits literary theorist Werner Sollors's notion of ethnicity by consent instead of descent (Locklear 2009). Yet such self-definition is also a redefinition—in this case potentially including the broad range of African American culture throughout Appalachia but focusing on urban regions in central Kentucky, as pointed out by William H. Turner in his essay "*Affrilachia* as a Brand" in the Fall 2011 issue of *Appalachian Heritage*. Turner looked back to the seminal 1985 collection of essays, titled *Blacks in Appalachia*, that he and Edward Cabbell edited and that inaugurated greater scholarly attention on the black experience in Appalachia. He called the Affrilachian poets to look back into their *Appalachian* literary and social heritage as others have done.

Specifically, Turner pointed to Kentucky poet Effie Waller Smith, an African American woman born in 1879 near Pikeville, Kentucky. In 1991 Oxford University Press published *The Collected Works of Effie Waller Smith* as part of the Schomburg Library of Nineteenth-Century Black Women Writers. The volume came about because of the passion and interest by the author of its introduction, David Deskins, a lay literary scholar, recently retired circuit court clerk in Pikeville, and chairman of the board of directors of the Big Sandy Heritage Center. Since that time, only one scholar has thoroughly undertaken the task of considering Smith's poems: in *The Tangled Roots of Feminism, Environmentalism, and Appalachian Literature*, Elizabeth Engelhardt firmly placed Smith's work within an Appalachian context, commenting that "Effie Waller Smith expands the meaning of the terms 'woman' and 'Appalachian' at the turn of the past century, by insisting on a complex and dynamic interplay between African American, Appalachian, and woman writer" (2003, 120). By categorizing Smith's work with other feminist, environmentalist, and Appalachian writers from the early twentieth century (think Mary Noailles Murfree), Engelhardt makes a significant contribution to recognizing the diversity of Appalachian literature.

Another African American woman author to whom Appalachian studies scholars sometimes do not pay critical homage is Nikki Giovanni.[7] As with the majority of the criticism available on Smith, much of what is written about Giovanni focuses on her race, her gender, or perhaps her southernness. Rarely does it also account for her Appalachian roots in Knoxville, Tennessee, her life as a professor at Virginia Tech since 1987, her work with Appalachian authors and people, or how she might fit into the larger scope of writing in and about Appalachia (Fowler 2008). Despite the rising focus in Appalachian studies on African Americans in Appalachia, the complex analysis of race in Appalachian literature and support of publication by Appalachians of color are fields where important work remains to be done.

As with any attempt to categorize writers and the works they produce, our attempt to do so is problematic, since race, gender, class, and sexuality never function separately from one another. To consider another example of such intersectionality, Dorothy Allison's work depicts the struggles of those living in poverty on the fringe of Appalachia (Greenville, South Carolina), but her work also champions lesbian characters who rail against the patriarchal norm that defines the time and place in which they live. Yet despite the multifaceted themes present in writing by women from Appalachia, literary critics and Appalachian studies scholars alike have started tracing a distinctly woman-centered—if not always feminist—theme in Appalachian literature.

Since the 1990s literary critics have begun to devote much greater attention to women's contributions to Appalachian literature. Such treatments include Danny Miller's *Wingless Flights: Appalachian Women in Fiction* (1996);

Joyce Dyer's edited collection *Bloodroot: Reflections on Place by Appalachian Women Writers* (1998); Felicia Mitchell's edited collection *Her Words: Diverse Voices in Contemporary Appalachian Women's Poetry* (2002); Engelhardt's *Tangled Roots of Feminism* (2003) and her edited collection *Beyond Hill and Hollow: Original Readings in Appalachian Women's Studies* (2005); and Sandra Ballard's and Patricia Hudson's anthology *Listen Here: Women Writing in Appalachia* (2003). Haeja K. Chung has published a collection of critical essays about the work of Arnow; Kathy Cantley Ackerman has a monograph about Olive Tilford Dargan's (also known as Fielding Burke) work; and Nancy Parrish has published a book on the Hollins Group (Lee Smith, Annie Dillard, Lucinda McKeathen, and Anne Goodwyn Jones). But the work of many Appalachian women writers—like Wilma Dykeman—has not yet received book-length treatments. Additionally, an increasing number of doctoral students are writing dissertations on topics related to women in Appalachian literature. In some cases critical treatments of southern women's writing include Appalachian writers, as does *The History of Southern Women's Literature* (2002), which has a selection on Appalachian writers written by Parks Lanier, Jr., and sections on individual writers like Mary Noailles Murfree. To see this kind of scholarly focus on Appalachian women writers by both Appalachian and southern literary critics alike is exciting, but in what ways can Appalachian studies scholars broaden and support this growing interest in mountain women's writing?

One way to do so is by drawing from the interdisciplinary focus that characterizes Appalachian studies. For example, in recent years literacy scholars have become increasingly interested in the literacy practices of Appalachian people generally and Appalachian women in particular. The New Opportunity School for Women, founded by Jane Stephenson, is designed to improve the "educational, financial, and personal circumstances of low-income, middle-aged women in the Appalachian region in Kentucky," and the students read works of Appalachian literature as part of their course of study (Mission Statement). In 1995 Stephenson published *Courageous Paths: Stories of Nine Appalachian Women*, a book that not only chronicles the stories of graduates of the program but also includes sections written by Stephenson, Rudy Abramson, and Gurney Norman (who teaches in the program). Women read works like Wilma Dykeman's *The Tall Woman* (1962) and Norman's *Kinfolks* (1977), and one woman named Crystal explains the effect that such reading had on her self-esteem: "Here I was, ashamed of who I was and where I come from, and here he is teaching classes on the same people from the same background—people that I was ashamed of being part of. After awhile,

I felt proud—and not ashamed of where I come from" (Stephenson 1995, 47). Certainly this phenomenon can—and does—happen with both male and female writers and readers, but in a program geared specifically for women, reading works like *The Tall Woman* can have a lasting impact on a woman's sense of self, one that deserves scholarly recognition and exploration.

Another burgeoning topic in Appalachian studies is mountaintop removal, about which numerous publications—too many to list here—have appeared. These range from sociological studies to statements about environmental impact to fictional representations of an environmental issue that is a lived experience for many Appalachians. Novels such as Ann Pancake's *Strange as This Weather Has Been* (2007) and Carter Sickels's *The Evening Hour* (2012), as well as collections of poetry, including *Coal: A Poetry Anthology* (2006), edited by Chris Green, portray a practice that is embroiled in controversy, but literary scholars have yet to fully explore the impact of these fictional representations of a detrimental reality.

Certainly literary writers and critics alike are working hard to address the gaps this chapter has pointed out. In 2009 Marianne Worthington, Richard Hague, Chris Holbrook, Jeff Mann, and Frank X Walker came together in a roundtable called "The Future of Appalachian Literature" that was moderated by Laura Sutton, then the acquisitions editor for the University Press of Kentucky (Hague et al. 2010). The discussion was held at Northern Kentucky University as the inaugural event of a gathering called "Voices from the Hills: A Celebration of Appalachian Writers, in Honor of Danny Miller (1949–2008)." These authors represent both the establishment (the youngest being over forty) and the edge (a woman poet who had been publishing for only ten years); a poet and high school teacher from Appalachian Ohio; an eastern Kentucky short-story writer who went to Alice Lloyd, then attended the Iowa Writers' Workshop, and returned to teach creative writing in eastern Kentucky; a gay poet from West Virginia who teaches creative writing at Virginia Tech; and an African American poet and editor who grew up in Danville, Kentucky, and taught creative writing to students around Kentucky (and who, as of 2013–14, was Kentucky's poet laureate and associate professor in English, African American, and Africana studies at the University of Kentucky).

That list very much demonstrates the future of Appalachian literature that Jim Wayne Miller called for eighteen years before. Taking stock of their circumstances and thinking about what is to come, the group went on to recognize the continued growth of writing about Appalachia with "less . . . nostalgia and romanticizing of the past and more a depiction of contemporary lives" (Hague et al. 2010, 144). They also noted that Appalachian literature contains diversity "because the region itself is amorphous and it's changing, it's shifting, not only geographically and culturally but politically and in many other ways, so . . . it's a tremendously rich time when you have cultural shifts like that" (144). The doors to Appalachian experience continue to open when taking into consideration the point of view of African Americans, immigrant, and urban populations who are now seeking to explore the region (see Walker on page 150). The panel also recognized the act of holding one another's writing accountable to the hard truths even as writers shared resources and provided encouragement. Speaking of the past, they recognized that most Appalachian writers have "not just a sense of the depth of the past, the personal past, the communal past, but also the geologic past" about the region to which they feel an "obligation" to teach about the faults of misleading literary portrayals of Appalachia (such as the 1993 *Kentucky Cycle*) and the "responsibility to look at the truth [of realities about such issues of drug abuse and poverty] and put that in our writing" (see Mann on page 148; Holbrook on pages 149 and 152; and Worthington on page 153). Looking to the future, the authors noted the outpouring of students and younger writers bringing in new visions and renewing the field, the breaking of whose century-old ground this essay has charted.

Central to the great outpouring of *good* literature (that goes well beyond Appalachian studies) stands the community of writers and activists and scholars who work together in locales that we consider part of Appalachian studies. In many ways, such people have felt like outsiders to prescribed identities, for they do not fit well into the roles their race, gender, class, sexuality, religion, or locality have given them. But when discussing the future of Appalachian literature, Jeff Mann shared Rita Riddle's insight into identities in tension with one another: "It's not 'or,' it's 'and,' 'and,' 'and'" (Hague et al. 2010, 149). Dick Hague also shared his thinking about what makes writers in the Southern Appalachian Writers Cooperative tick, an insight we think could well be applied to those in this chapter: "And so we've had a vast array of folks, who all, in a sense become adoptive Appalachians if they aren't, and whose awareness is raised and whose activism becomes part of what they do. There's a tolerance for 'and, and, and' in the best sense. . . . And I think it's probably because Appalachia has always been synthesizing and digesting folks" (149). And what they discover, having left home to find each other, is the welcome, love, and wisdom of a group of people like themselves—people fighting to make room in the mountains for all who love justice, equality, and Appalachia.

Over the last fifty years, an outpouring of Appalachian literature and scholarship has occurred. We have seen particular success in the areas of promoting women authors, of publishing creative works, of the amount of scholarship, and of Appalachian-author activism. Lines of heritage have continued to give rise to new authors, and important steps have been made toward bringing minorities into the mix. And scholars of Appalachian literature are beginning to develop a sense of its history, if not their own (Miller, Hatfield, and Norman 2005).

Looking back at that history, important absences show themselves, particularly in terms of geography (e.g., Pennsylvania and Alabama), race (e.g., interracial authors, urban authors, the influx of Latinos, Southeast Asians, and residents from the Middle East), and genre and form (e.g., drama, "postmodern" verse and prose, and closer evaluation of Appalachian cultural forms). While Appalachian literary history since 1880 has begun to be fleshed out, little work by literary scholars associated with Appalachian studies has been done to assess the writing about the Appalachian region before that time, especially in terms of poetry, a field no less rich than fiction and nonfiction.

In terms of education and literature, we have powerful models of what is possible, but greater assessment and coordination are needed at all levels. From preschool through college, from the National Council of the Teachers of English to state departments of education, we need to discern what teachers are doing and students are learning so people can learn from each other and promote Appalachian literature and culture in Appalachian schools (Clark and Howard 2013; Sampson and Herrin 2007). Following the lead of Jane Stephenson at the New Opportunity School for Women, those interested in Appalachian literature need to go into public schools and local communities to lead workshops and teach classes that empower girls and young women: with them there is a need to discuss gender, power, and possibility through the reading and creation of Appalachian literature by and about women. Similar work is surely needed with boys and young men as well.

While the last thirty years have seen a nearly geometric escalation in the number of theses and dissertations written on Appalachian literature, in doctoral institutions such scholarship mainly occurs because of the vim of individual students and faculty.[8] More faculty lines, scholarships, and even programs need to be established. Appalachian literary criticism started with recognition, moved to justification and appreciation, and has occasionally set out to investigate and debate definitions, uses, methods, issues, topics, and means. In terms of criticism, scholarship, and theory, the work in Appalachian literature pales beside the impassioned, extensive work done in African American, American Indian, and Latino(a) studies. Similarly, rather than running from the South, let us all understand texts regularly claimed as such as being the intercultural creations they are, much as John C. Inscoe and Wilma A. Dunaway have done with issues of race in ante- and postbellum Appalachia (Dunaway 1996, 2003a, 2003b; Inscoe 2001). Those interested in literature from and about the mountains need to understand the seeming contradictions of the 1930s Agrarians Donald Davidson and Andrew Lytle in terms of Appalachia so we all can see what Appalachia has been rather than what many have wanted it to be. As demonstrated by MELUS (Society for the Study of the Multi-Ethnic Literature of the United States), more cross-cultural dialogue and learning is needed. Appalachian authors and literary scholars are very much cultural envoys, and purposeful conversations with other cultural studies organizations would push Appalachian studies forward in its own practices and in aligning with similar cultural groups for national action.

Finally, let everyone do unto literature as has been done with folklore—that is, make it the background to the study of rising forms of representation. Let those interested in Appalachian writing use the tools of literary study and criticism to think about Appalachians using video, smartphones, and the web.

Let us recover, transform, and advance our heritage. Let us proceed.

Notes

1. Condensed from a longer manuscript, the history provided in this chapter is a tentative overview based on the authors' limited experience and knowledge. We recognize that unseen influences, people, and movements inform this history, and we encourage readers to add to the ongoing work of its assemblage and renovation.

2. Tragically, Mike Mullins died in February 2012, but the legacy that he left at Hindman continues.

3. Monteagle, Tennessee, just six miles from Sewanee, was also home (until it moved to New Market) for the Highlander Center, which Don West cofounded, as well as later home for the Agrarian Andrew Nelson Lytle, who edited the *Sewanee Review* from 1961 to 1973. For an extensive analysis of the modernist canonical battle over the very definition of literature in Appalachia, see Green (2008).

4. In 1989 the *Proceedings of the Appalachian Studies Conference* would become the *Journal of Appalachian Studies*.

5. Perhaps due to her intercultural literacy, her active participation in Appalachian studies literary networks, and the nation's rising attention to women writers, Marilou Awiakta has been the most widely embraced Cherokee author in Appalachian studies and is also often the only Native American included in Appalachian literary collections, a situation that points to an absence in need of investigation.

6. Not as surprising is the absence of Glaydis Cardiff, Edwina Jones, Tony Mack McClure, and Mardi Oakley Medawar, all of whom identified on NativeWiki as being part of the Eastern Band but who have moved out of the region.

7. One welcome exception to this observation is the Fall 2012 *Appalachian Heritage* issue (40.4) that features Giovanni on pages 10–63.

8. Degrees (B.A., M.A., and Ph.D.) with theses awarded in Appalachian literature/ language by decade: 1920s, 4; 1930s, 7; 1940s, 5; 1950s, 1; 1960s, 4; 1970s, 12; 1980s, 33; 1990s, 70; 2000s, 118.

Works Cited

Ackerman, Kathy Cantley. 2004. *The Heart of Revolution: The Radical Life and Novels of Olive Dargan.* Knoxville: University of Tennessee Press.

Acoose, Janice, Lisa Brooks, Tol Foster, LeAnne Howe, Heath Justice, Phillip Carroll Morgan, Kimberly Roppolo, Cheryl Suzack, Christopher B. Teuton, Sean Teuton, Robert Warrior, and Craig S. Womack. 2008. *Reasoning Together: The Native Critics Collective.* Norman: University of Oklahoma Press.

Ballard, Sandra L., and Patricia L. Hudson, eds. 2013. *Listen Here: Women Writing in Appalachia.* Lexington: University Press of Kentucky.

Berry, Chad. 2008. "This Issue." *Appalachian Heritage* 36(3): 6.

Brosi, George. 2011. "Our History." *Appalachian Heritage.* Berea College. Site now discontinued.

Burriss, Theresa L. 2005. "Claiming a Literary Space: The Affrilachian Poets." In *An American Vein: Critical Readings in Appalachian Literature*, edited by Danny L. Miller, Sharon Hatfield, and Gurney Norman, 315–36. Athens: Ohio University Press.

Burton, Thomas G., Collection, 1967–1991. n.d. Biographical Note. 500/AppMs 160. Archives of Appalachia, East Tennessee State University. http://archives.etsu .edu/?p=collections/controlcard&id=245.

Byer, Kathryn Stripling. 2005. "Drawing from the Well." Interview by Beth English. *UNCG Magazine* (Summer): 29–30.

Chappell, Fred. 1986. "Fred Chappell." In *Contemporary Authors: Autobiography Series*, 4:113–26. Detroit: Gale Research.

Chung, Haeja K., ed. 1995. *Harriette Simpson Arnow: Critical Essays on Her Work.* East Lansing: Michigan State University Press.

Clabough, Casey. 2007. "The Imagined South." *Sewanee Review* 115(2): 301–7.

Clark, Amy D., and Nancy M. Howard, eds. 2013. *Talking Appalachian: Voice, Identity, and Community.* Lexington: University Press of Kentucky.

Cunningham, Rodger. 1996. "Writing on the Cusp: Double Alterity and Minority Discourse in Appalachia." In *The Future of Southern Letters*, edited by Jefferson Humphries and John Lowe, 41–53. New York: Oxford University Press.

Cuthbert, John A. 2006. "Louis Watson Chappell" and "John Harrington Cox." In *The West Virginia Encyclopedia*, edited by Ken Sullivan. Charleston: West Virginia Humanities Council.

Dunaway, Wilma A. 1996. *The First American Frontier: Transition to Capitalism in Southern Appalachia, 1700–1860.* Chapel Hill: University of North Carolina Press.

———. 2003a. *The African-American Family in Slavery and Emancipation.* Cambridge: Cambridge University Press.

———. 2003b. *Slavery in the American Mountain South.* Cambridge: Cambridge University Press.

Dyer, Joyce, ed. 1998. *Bloodroot: Reflections on Place by Appalachian Women Writers.* Lexington: University Press of Kentucky.

Dykeman, Wilma. 1962. *The Tall Woman.* New York: Holt, Rinehart and Winston.

———. 1966. *Prophet of Plenty: The First Ninety Years of W. D. Weatherford.* Knoxville: University of Tennessee Press.

Engelhardt, Elizabeth S. D. 2003. *The Tangled Roots of Feminism, Environmentalism, and Appalachian Literature.* Athens: Ohio University Press.

———, ed. 2005. *Beyond Hill and Hollow: Original Readings in Appalachian Women's Studies.* Athens: Ohio University Press.

Foster, Ruel E. 1970. "Notes toward the Coming Appalachian Literary Renaissance." *Pathway* 1(December): 14–17.

Fowler, Virginia C. 2008. "Nikki Giovanni's Appalachian Ties." *Appalachian Heritage* 36(3): 42–50.

Green, Chris. 2006. *Coal: A Poetry Anthology.* Ashland, Ky.: Blair Mountain Press.

———. 2008. *The Social Life of Poetry: Appalachia, Race, and Radical Modernism.* New York: Palgrave Macmillan.

Greene, Jonathan. 2005. "The Persistence of Folly: 40 Years of Gnomon Press, an Interview with Jonathan Greene." *Appalachian Journal* 32(4): 442–57.

Hague, Richard, Chris Holbrook, Jeff Mann, Frank X Walker, Marianne Worthington, Laura Sutton, and Robert Wallace [*sic*]. 2010. "Inaugural Event of Voices from the Hills: A Celebration of Appalachian Writers, in Honor of Danny Miller (1949–2008): Round-Table Discussion: The Future of Appalachian Literature." *Journal of Kentucky Studies* 27:141–59.

Hayden, Wilburn, Jr. 2004. "Appalachian Diversity: African-American, Hispanic/Latino, and Other Populations." *Journal of Appalachian Studies* 10(3): 293–306.

Higgs, Robert J., and Ambrose N. Manning. 1977. "More on Appalachian Literature." *Appalachian Journal* 4(2): 93–98.

Holman, C. Hugh. 1976. "Appalachian Literature? Two Views." Review of *Voices from the Hills,* edited by Robert J. Higgs and Ambrose N. Manning. *Appalachian Journal* 4(1): 73–79.

Inscoe, John C., ed. 2001. *Appalachians and Race: The Mountain South from Slavery to Segregation.* Lexington: University Press of Kentucky.

Kendrick, Leatha, and George Ella Lyon, eds. 2002. *Crossing Troublesome: 25 Years of the Appalachian Writers Workshop.* Nicholasville, Ky.: Wind Publications.

Krim, Arthur. 2006. "Appalachian Songcatcher: Olive Dame Campbell and the Scotch-Irish Ballad." *Journal of Cultural Geography* 24(1): 91–112.

LeRoy-Frazier, Jill. 2007. "Appalachian Literature and the Post-Colonial: A GPS for Appalachian Literary Studies." *Journal of Kentucky Studies* 24:125–32.

Lloyd, Teresa. 2010. "Early Anthologies of Appalachian Literature." Appalachian Studies Association Conference. Dahlonega, Ga.

Locklear, Erica Abrams. 2009. "Consenting to Create: The Affrilachian Movement." In *Crossroads: A Southern Culture Annual*, edited by Ted Olson, 169–85. Macon: Mercer University Press.

———. 2011. *Negotiating a Perilous Empowerment: Appalachian Women's Literacies.* Athens: Ohio University Press.

Lyon, George Ella, Jim Wayne Miller, and Gurney Norman, eds. 1993. *A Gathering at the Forks: Fifteen Years of the Hindman Settlement School Appalachian Writers Workshop.* Wise, Va.: Vision Books.

McCarthy, William Bernard. 1999. "Olive Dame Campbell and Appalachian Tradition." In *Ballads into Books: The Legacies of Francis James Child*, edited by Tom Cheesman and Sigrid Rieuwerts, 69–80. Bern, Switzerland: Peter Lang.

Miller, Danny L. 1996. *Wingless Flights: Appalachian Women in Fiction.* Madison, Wisc.: Popular Press.

Miller, Danny L., Sharon Hatfield, and Gurney Norman, eds. 2005. *An American Vein: Critical Readings in Appalachian Literature.* Athens: Ohio University Press.

Miller, James. 2003. "Coming Home to Affrilachia: The Poems of Doris Davenport." In *Her Words: Diverse Voices in Contemporary Appalachian Women's Poetry*, edited by Felicia Mitchell, 96–106. Knoxville: University of Tennessee Press.

Miller, Jim Wayne. 1980. *The Mountains Have Come Closer.* Boone, N.C.: Appalachian Consortium Press.

———. 1982. "Appalachian Studies Hard and Soft: The Action People and the Creative Folk." *Appalachian Journal* 9(2–3): 105–14.

———. 1990. "A People Waking Up." In *The Cratis Williams Symposium Proceedings: A Memorial and Examination of the State of Regional Studies in Appalachia*, 47–76. Boone, N.C.: Appalachian Consortium Press and Cratis D. Williams Graduate School, Appalachian State University.

Mission Statement. New Opportunity School for Women. http://www.nosw.org. Accessed September 9, 2011.

Mitchell, Felicia, ed. 2003. *Her Words: Diverse Voices in Contemporary Appalachian Women's Poetry.* Knoxville: University of Tennessee Press.

Morgan, Robert. 1994. "Autobiographical Essay." In *Contemporary Authors*, 201:258–86. Detroit: Gale Research.

Mullins, Mike. 2006. "'It's Not a Job to Me': Mike Mullins and the Hindman Settlement School." Interview by Dare Cook et al. *Appalachian Journal* 33(3–4): 310–34.

Newberry, Elizabeth. 2000. "Poets Turned Prophets: Affrilachian Poets Claim the Space between Two Worlds." *Sojourners* 29(50–51): 53.

Norman, Gurney. 1977. *Kinfolks: The Wilgus Stories.* Frankfort, Ky.: Gnomon Press.

Pancake, Ann. 2007. *Strange as This Weather Has Been.* Emeryville, Calif.: Shoemaker and Hoard.

Parrish, Nancy C. 1998. *Lee Smith, Annie Dillard, and the Hollins Group*. Baton Rouge: Louisiana State University Press.

Pérez-Torres, Rafael. 1995. *Movements in Chicano Poetry: Against Myths, against Margins*. Cambridge: Cambridge University Press.

Perry, Carolyn, and Mary Louise Weaks, eds. 2002. *The History of Southern Women's Literature*. Baton Rouge: Louisiana State University Press.

Sampson, Alice V., and Roberta T. Herrin. 2007. "The Appalachian Teaching Project: An Opportunity for Academic-Community Activism." *Appalachian Journal* 34(3–4): 352–83.

Schenkkan, Robert. 1993. *The Kentucky Cycle*. New York: Plume.

Shapiro, Henry D. 1978. *Appalachia on Our Mind: The Southern Mountains and Mountaineers in the American Consciousness, 1870–1920*. Chapel Hill: University of North Carolina Press.

Sickels, Carter. 2012. *The Evening Hour*. New York: Bloomsbury USA.

Smith, Nick, and Erik Tuttle, eds. 2005. *Wind: A Journal of Writing and Community, the Hindman Issue* 94 (with 2 CDs of oral history).

Stephenson, Jane. 1995. *Courageous Paths: Stories of Nine Appalachian Women*. Berea, Ky.: New Opportunity School for Women.

Stewart, Albert. 1973. "What It's All About." *Appalachian Heritage* 1(1): 4.

Turner, Bill. 2011. "*Affrilachia* as Brand." *Appalachian Heritage* 39(4): 27–30.

U.S. Department of the Interior, Bureau of Indian Affairs, Office of Indian Services. 2005. "American Indian Population and Labor Force Report." Accessed April 1, 2010, http://www.bia.gov/cs/groups/public/documents/text/idc-001719.pdf.

Weaver, Jace, Craig S. Womack, and Robert Allen Warrior. 2006. *American Indian Literary Nationalism*. Albuquerque: University of New Mexico Press.

Weiss, David W. 2006a. "Hunter, Kermit." In *Encyclopedia of Appalachia*, edited by Rudy Abramson and Jean Haskell, 1251. Knoxville: University of Tennessee Press.

———. 2006b. "Outdoor Drama." In *Encyclopedia of Appalachia*, edited by Rudy Abramson and Jean Haskell, 1258. Knoxville: University of Tennessee Press.

Wey, Herbert W. 1976. "Cratis Williams and Appalachian Studies at ASU." Box 15, folder 3, "Appalachian Consortium bulletins," series 5, 20003.046, Appalachian Consortium Historical Files. University Archives and Records Center, Special Collections, Appalachian State University, Boone, N.C.

Whisnant, David E. 1983. *All That Is Native & Fine: The Politics of Culture in an American Region*. Chapel Hill: University of North Carolina Press.

Wilgus, D. K. 1959. *Anglo-American Folksong Scholarship since 1898*. New Brunswick, N.J.: Rutgers University Press.

Williams, Cratis. [1979]. "Appalachian Consortium." Box 15, folder 3, "Appalachian Consortium bulletins," series 5, 20003.046, Appalachian Consortium Historical Files. University Archives and Records Center, Special Collections, Appalachian State University, Boone, N.C.

———. 1979. Letter to Pat Beaver, January 22. Box 15, folder 19, "Jim Wayne Miller Manuscript," series 5, 20003.046, Appalachian Consortium Historical Files. University Archives and Records Center, Special Collections, Appalachian State University, Boone, N.C.

Worthington, Marianne. [2009]. "Appalachian Music Fellowship Final Activity Report." Special Collections and Archives, Hutchins Library, Berea College. Web, accessed July 24, 2010.

4

Fixing Appalachia

A Century of Community Development in a "Depressed" Area

DONALD EDWARD DAVIS AND CHRIS BAKER

For more than a century, the people of Appalachia have been the recipients of numerous development and social uplift programs, all of which were designed to bring the region out of poverty or to improve the economic and cultural "backwardness" of its rural areas. From the settlement school movement of the early twentieth century to the Appalachian Regional Commission's distressed counties grants in the twenty-first century, private and public support has poured into the region in what ostensibly were attempts to make Appalachia more like the rest of America. Although few of these programs could be labeled outright successes, many had a lasting and important impact on the mountain region. And while some of the projects were conceived and implemented in good faith, others were misguided from their conception. In a few cases the jury is still out, especially for initiatives implemented in the first two decades of the twenty-first century.

What follows is a summary and analysis of the most well known attempts at solving the problems of inadequate education, poverty, and economic development in Appalachia. Also included in the discussion are community-based efforts, as well as initiatives involved in increasing the participation of mountain residents in local and state politics. For many, social problems exist in the mountains not as a result of underdevelopment but rather as a result of individuals unable to democratically control their own economic destinies. If communities had fair and open access to the region's vast natural resources, it is argued, they could become true stakeholders in the long-term development of the Appalachian region.

The Education Fix

Among the first to attempt to "fix" the problems of Appalachia were faith-based missionaries who began identifying the mountains as a place for educational and social reform a decade or so after the Civil War. Among the missionaries were educated elites, many of whom represented religious institutions such as the American Missionary Association or large Protestant denominations such as the Presbyterian Church. By 1915 nearly every major denomination in America had established educational facilities and relief programs in Appalachia. Other reformers followed in their footsteps, opening independent and nonsectarian schools and colleges, health centers, handicraft cooperatives, and governmental and nongovernmental social service agencies. By 1920 more than 150 such institutions could be found in the southern Appalachians alone (Alvic 2003, xi; Campbell 1921, 163; Tice 2006, 1150).

SETTLEMENT SCHOOLS

The most celebrated of the institutions seeking social reform in Appalachia during the early twentieth century were the so-called settlement schools. Although at least seven facilities had been established in the mountains before 1900, most were founded during the first two decades of the twentieth century. Directed largely by educated women from outside the mountain region, settlement schools were initially modeled after the settlement houses found in southern England and the northeastern United States and Jane Addams's Hull House in Chicago (Teets 2006, 123–24). While no two settlement schools offered identical educational programs, most of their founders shared a belief in "progressive education, organized collective action, recreation, modern hygiene, and preventive medicine—all cloaked in an activist, liberal Christianity" (Alvic 2003, 5; see also Whisnant 1983, 17–18, 24–33).

Although settlement schools had varying degrees of success as a result of individual leadership, geographic location, or institutional sponsorship, settlement school directors generally learned about conditions on the ground before responding to concerns they deemed important. Initially, their agendas focused on providing an adequate education for community residents—no small task, since large areas of Appalachia lagged behind the rest of the nation in both literacy and school-completion rates. Attendance was also extremely low, as children were often needed at home or in the fields as laborers. Those schools operating in the more "sparsely settled regions," noted Maryville College president Samuel Tyndale Wilson in 1914, did so for only "two or three months in the year."[1]

To increase the number of functioning schools in Appalachia, religious organizations funded the construction of establishments or supplied teachers, support staff, and educational materials to communities for a reduced fee or free of charge. Religious-sponsored community centers were also constructed in the region, as were boarding schools and trade academies. Perhaps the most visible religious denomination working in Appalachia during the first decades of the twentieth century was the Presbyterian Church, which served as the institutional headquarters for the Women's Board of Home Missions (McNeil 1995, 171; Wilson 1914, 72). In 1913 the Presbyterian Synod of East Tennessee and Western North Carolina supported no fewer than four colleges and universities, two academies, seven boarding schools, and fifteen day schools and community centers. Its twenty-eight properties were valued at more than $2.1 million at that early date, employed two hundred individuals, and were responsible for educating as many as four thousand students annually (Wilson 1914, 199).

The growth and development of mission-sponsored education centers across the region most certainly had an impact on the educational advancement of mountain residents. Although highly critical of their broader institutional goals, David E. Whisnant (1983, 29) admitted that missionary establishments provided good and basic educational training for many mountain children. Public schools in the mountain region also saw significant growth and improvements during this period, as they were the beneficiaries of improved roads and transportation networks, the passage of compulsory education laws, and the implementation, for much of the region, of a standard eight- and nine-month school year. As a result of these trends, by the mid-1920s many settlement schools were already shifting their focus away from the general education of young children, instead placing a stronger emphasis on adult learning and vocational training (Teets 2006, 125).

Perhaps the most well-known Appalachian institution focusing on adult education and vocational craft production during the period was the John C. Campbell Folk School. Olive Dame Campbell, the school's founder, named the institution after her late husband, who died in 1919. In 1908 John C. Campbell was approached by educator Philander P. Claxton and asked to investigate the "grown-up" schools of Denmark that would later become known as the Danish folk schools. Although John C. Campbell would draft several government reports about the applicability of the Danish folk school model to the Appalachians, his most comprehensive analysis of mountain education appeared after his death, in 1921, in *The Southern Highlander and His Homeland.*

After John Campbell's death, Olive Campbell continued to promote the ideals of the Danish folk school, which, she firmly believed, could be adapted "to meet the changing and varied needs" of mountain communities (Whisnant 1983, 130). At the Brasstown, North Carolina, facility, she and her staff developed a curriculum that included weaving and woodcarving, agricultural training, music instruction, and courses in world geography and Danish gymnastics. The school also operated several community-based agricultural cooperatives that produced small profits after several years of operation. One of the primary objectives of the folk school was to combine intellectual and vocational instruction so that students would be better prepared for life in the mountains. In the past, educational diplomas and certificates were viewed merely as postage stamps that aided in sending off young adults to areas where work was more plentiful, far away from mountain communities. By the mid-1930s, many in the region considered the folk school a success, especially its craft production enterprises, which had garnered national recognition. After World War II, however, for reasons discussed below, the school began to decline. By the end of the 1940s, further deteriorating conditions at the folk school would ultimately lead to a complete reevaluation of its formal mission (Alvic 2003, 17–20; Campbell 1921, 278–79; Teets 2006, 125–26; Whisnant 1983, 164–65).

Although the John C. Campbell Folk School was successful in many of its educational pursuits and remains in operation to this day, the institution's early curriculum and cultural programs did meet with some criticism (Shapiro 1978, 237–41; Whisnant 1983, 173–79). Ironically, during the first two decades of its operation, the school placed a strong emphasis on the celebration of Danish culture, which included learning Danish songs, folk dances, and gymnastic routines. Homegrown musical traditions, which might include the playing of banjo and guitar and shape-note singing, were less preferred than the recorder or dulcimer, the latter an Appalachian instrument that had long fallen out of popularity in many parts of the mountains. It was, after all, a more romantic instrument and one that could play to the heartstrings of wealthy benefactors who might sponsor individual students or a particular folk school initiative. Not surprisingly, labor ballads, coal-mining songs, and "hillbilly" music were not a part of the folk school's musical repertoire.

Of course, the John C. Campbell Folk School was not the only institution in the Appalachians that taught both vocational skills and book learning while embracing a strong cultural preservation mission. Numerous colleges and trade academies did so as well, including Berea College in Berea, Kentucky; Berry College in Mount Berry, Georgia; and Warren Wilson College in Swannanoa, North Carolina. Nor was the Campbell Folk School the only institution in the mountains influenced by the Danish education system. The Highlander Folk School, initially located near Monteagle in Grundy County, Tennessee, is another institution inspired by the Danish folk school movement. Founded in 1932 by Myles Horton and Don West, the Highlander Folk School would, by the 1960s, become closely associated with the civil rights movement and community organizing in Appalachia. Both Horton and West had visited Denmark on separate occasions, and each thought the Danish education system might prove helpful in solving the social problems of the mountains (Adams 1975, 1–6; Lorence 2007, 183–202).

Although Horton shared the basic idea that folk schools could provide answers to many of Appalachia's social problems, he found Olive Campbell's general approach too romantic, especially regarding her emphasis on preserving certain aspects of mountain culture. In Denmark, Horton had learned that folk schools also operated under a principle known as "dig where you stand," meaning that self-reliance and economic self-determination should be central goals in the education of rural folk (Myles Horton, pers. comm., March 23, 1988). Another important difference between the two was that Horton, a vocal supporter of the southern labor movement, would shape Highlander's education program to reflect his own views regarding social and economic democracy. Horton believed that education should come not from experts but from within the rural population. In that sense, the Highlander staff should only *assist* mountain folk in acquiring knowledge. In actual practice, there were some important similarities between Highlander and the Campbell folk schools, as each provided educational and recreational programs for students, initiated residential programs, organized community cooperatives, and incorporated music and theater into their curriculums.

The Great Depression had a severe impact on nearly all settlement schools and related institutions, forcing some to close their doors and others to look for more creative funding strategies. The Second World War further curtailed operations, especially in limiting the potential pool of pupils, as an entire generation of young adults was drawn into the global conflict. After the war, enrollment declined further as urban and suburban cultural hegemony made folk-school curricula less attractive to young adults. Less than a dozen such institutions survive into the twenty-first century, and only a few of those remain truly committed to preserving and celebrating Appalachian culture. In areas where settlement schools did prosper over long periods, communities were positively impacted in the economic sense, as they provided important jobs and incomes to local residents. Appalachian culture fared less well, as archaic ballads, traditional craft skills, and multigenerational subsistence practices were lost to memory and practice, even in those areas where settlement schools had been operating for decades.

The Federal Fix

Because settlement and mission schools were found in a minority of rural communities, it would have been impossible for them to shield the region from the economic downturn caused by the Great Depression—even if all had met with unqualified success. Additional measures would be needed. During the economic crisis, Appalachia had caught the attention of the federal government, whose own statistics painted a grim portrait of a region near collapse. In 1930 as much as 97 percent of Appalachia's rural residents lived without electricity (Black 2006, 1620). Infant and adult mortality rates also remained high, as did the presence of the so-called diseases of poverty, including pellagra, hookworm, and typhoid fever (Barney 2000; Campbell 1921, 209, table 9; Shannon 2006, 74). Annual income for mountain farmers was well below half the national average. In 1936 half of all families in the region were receiving some kind of government assistance (Straw 2006, 16–17; Thomas 2010, 126). Illiteracy rates also remained well above the national average, as did high school attrition and failure rates, as documented by the U.S. Department of the Interior's Office of Education in 1937. From the federal government's point of view, a fix was needed in Appalachia (Gaumitz and Cook 1938, 19–23).

THE TENNESSEE VALLEY AUTHORITY

In 1933, to combat these and other related problems in the mountains, including flooding and soil erosion, Franklin D. Roosevelt created the Tennessee Valley Authority (TVA), the first government agency to embrace the concept of *regional* development, an idea found in the writings of Lewis Mumford, Frederick Jackson Turner, and Howard W. Odum (Black 2000; U.S. National Resources Committee 1935). Public affairs analyst Ann R. Markusen labeled TVA's early development approach as "organic regionalism," which, she pointed out, culminated "in the advocacy of individually tailored regional plans based on the assumed dominance of natural factors in differentiating regions, reinforced by evolved cultures" (1987, 252). The government agency was also influenced by rhetoric found in New Deal programs, which called for increased citizen participation in federal policy making. Its mission: "the economic and social well-being of the people living in the [Tennessee Valley]," a geographic area encompassing the mountainous areas of six Appalachian states (Tennessee Valley Authority Act of 1933, 48 Stat. 69, 16 U.S.C., section 22; see also Owen 1973, 21; Selznick 1966, 43–45).

Under the leadership of Arthur E. Morgan, TVA followed closely the organic regionalist approach endorsed by Mumford, Turner, and Odum, as well as many other proponents of the development model. Morgan, a visionary who sought to make the agency operate more holistically, wanted TVA to work on projects ranging from labor relations and health care to the development of community cooperatives and the protection of forest preserves. The other important component of TVA's early mission was to democratize the decision-making process of the federal agency so that it would best serve the interests of local communities. TVA's two headquarters, for example, were located in the Tennessee Valley instead of Washington, D.C., and the administration itself was to be decentralized in order to ensure grassroots participation. In fact, codified in the agency's early mission was a "grassroots doctrine" that would, in theory, provide accountability and increase responsiveness to the needs of local communities (Hargrove 1994, 19–26; Morgan 1974, 197; Phillips 2007, 82–90; Selznick 1966, 12).

In reality, grassroots participation was considerably lacking, if not entirely absent, in most TVA programs during the first three decades of operation. By 1935 Arthur Morgan had been stripped of much of his authority and in 1938 was abruptly dismissed by President Roosevelt. Of course, throughout its entire history TVA has been plagued by an inability to include the grassroots in policy formation, as nearly every program surveyed by outside observers—including the agency's early reservoir resettlement, agriculture, and electrification programs—failed on this score (Black 2006, 1620; Hobday 1969; Selznick 1966, 12–14; Wengert 1952, 1–18; Williamson 1981). Historians Michael McDonald and John Muldowny, in their book *TVA and the Dispossessed*, documented a host of problems with TVA's reservoir resettlement program of the mid-1930s. After reviewing their study, it is clear that grassroots interests were not met during the land acquisition phase of the operation and that TVA did not deal openly with residents as the agency procured homes and property for the Norris Basin floodplain. McDonald and Muldowny conclude their work by calling the "social experiment" a failure, "brought about by the lack of a coherent and unified grassroots policy; by conflicting directorial roles and administrative structures; and by highly variant and persistent conceptual views held by people within TVA" (1982, 264).

Perhaps the most serious charge against TVA's so-called grassroots doctrine concerns the implementation of its agriculture and rural development programs. Norman Wengert, in his book *Valley of Tomorrow* (1952) criticized TVA for its excessive reliance on land-grant colleges and their extension departments for TVA's rural development activities during the 1930s and 1940s. In a slightly earlier study, sociologist Philip Selznick (1966, 211–13) proposed that because of its "co-optive" relationship with land-grant universities, TVA agriculture programs were conservative and class based, assisting only the most prosperous farmers in the valley. Agriculture economist Handy Williamson found that TVA omitted black agriculture schools from its rural development programs, thus ignoring an entire population of disadvantaged farmers. Without question, TVA's bias toward wealthier farmers and the agricultural establishment defies the notion that TVA's rural development programs were developed and controlled by the grassroots (Williamson 1981, 83–97).

In practice, TVA directors maintained an unwavering faith in solving economic and social ills with advanced engineering and technology, thus placing the burden of proof on agency experts who saw grassroots input as irrelevant at best and disruptive at worst. Moreover, the agency's technological proficiency in power production allowed it to continue a "growth-spiral" policy of increasing energy demand and consumer consumption across the region. In the 1950s, in order to keep up with these growing electricity demands, TVA built no fewer than ten coal-fired generating plants that further increased the mining and burning of surfaced-mined coal. By 1968 TVA coal purchases amounted to 5.5 percent of the total coal mined in the United States, making it—as it remains in the twenty-first century—one of the single largest purchasers of surfaced-mined coal in America. In the 1970s TVA could claim ownership of 365 million tons of coal reserves in southeastern Kentucky and eastern Tennessee alone and had, in essence, turned "the Tennessee Valley and adjacent coal-bearing areas of Appalachia into a national energy reservation in which every other consideration was subordinate to large-scale power production at the lowest possible dollar cost" (Whisnant 1988, 63).

The decade of the 1960s saw not only increased coal production in many parts of the Appalachian region but also increased hardship among local residents, particularly in areas that were most directly affected by TVA's coal-purchasing policies. In many communities, acid run-off from abandoned coal mines contaminated water supplies; in others, extensive flooding resulted from erosion caused by the strip-mining process itself. Unemployment rates also rose in coalfield counties as automation in underground mine operations further reduced the need for workers (Davis 2006, 105–6; Montrie 2003, 7–12,

85–90). As early as 1961, in Senate hearings designed to address the issue of unemployment in "certain economic depressed areas," it was reported that eastern Kentucky's Perry County had a 20 percent jobless rate, and the town of Pikeville had a 26 percent rate. U.S. senator Estes Kefauver testified that Grundy, Sequatchie, and Marion Counties in southeastern Tennessee were in nothing less than a "critical economic depression" (U.S. Senate 1961, 671; see also Whisnant 1988, 71).

THE OFFICE OF ECONOMIC OPPORTUNITY

Perhaps the most widely known federal initiative attempting to improve the impoverished state of Appalachian communities in the 1960s was the so-called War on Poverty. Although associated with the administration of President Lyndon Baines Johnson, who declared an "unconditional war on poverty" in his 1964 State of the Union address, the program actually had its roots in the administration of John F. Kennedy (Howley 2006, 1624). Kennedy was personally aware of the economic conditions in the coalfields and championed a variety of federal proposals that provided aid to the mountain region, most notably the Area Redevelopment Act of 1961. The act created the Area Redevelopment Administration (ARA), a federal agency responsible for channeling more than $500 million in grants or loans to economically depressed areas. In the end, the ARA became more effective at developing tourism than in reviving depressed economies in the mountains and was phased out after only nine months of operation (Gaventa and Lewis 1989, 58).

Appalachia remained in the media spotlight throughout the Kennedy administration, becoming part of a national dialogue that focused on the nation's escalating poverty and unemployment rates. In 1962 political scientist Michael Harrington published *The Other America*, a book that focused on Appalachia's "run-down" social conditions (40–44). Popular publications also got into the act, with *Look* magazine publishing a lengthy collection of black-and-white photographs in its December 4, 1962, issue. A year later, native-born Harry M. Caudill released his best-selling *Night Comes to the Cumberlands*, which placed the blame for Appalachian poverty squarely on the shoulders of large absentee corporations that had extracted millions of dollars in coal and timber resources but left little for local communities (1963, 334–51; Whisnant 1988). The *New York Times* followed with a two-part series about impoverished conditions in eastern Kentucky, depicting "a wasted landscape and a people so poor that children eat dirt out of chinks of chimneys to ease their hunger." Written by Pulitzer Prize–winning reporter Homer Bigart, the report was given the title "Kentucky Miners: A Grim

Winter; Poverty, Squalor and Idleness Prevail in Mountain Area, Poverty Grips Kentucky Miners with Winter's Ordeal Looming" and appeared on page 1 of the October 20, 1963, Sunday edition. By the time Johnson took office a month later, Appalachia was on the minds of many Americans.

Early in his administration, Johnson himself visited Appalachia, launching the official public campaign for the War on Poverty from the front porch of Martin County resident Tom Fletcher, an unemployed Kentucky coal miner. Months afterward, in August 1964, Johnson signed into law the Economic Opportunity Act, creating the Office of Economic Opportunity (OEO), a federal agency mandated to fight poverty in America's poorest communities such as those found in the Appalachian region (Howley 2006, 1624). Numerous other federal initiatives were created under OEO's auspices, including the preschool program known as Head Start, the Volunteers in Service to America (VISTA), Job Corps, Adult Basic Education, and the Community Action Program, the latter comprised of individually operated community action agencies (CAAs) to be located in America's poorest areas. While it would be impossible to assess all OEO initiatives, the Community Action Program is central to this discussion since it was one of the largest OEO programs and operated under the assumption that it would involve ordinary citizens in its efforts.

According to Ronald D Eller, the language of the Economic Opportunity Act called for the establishment of CAAs "run by local people, including the poor themselves" (2008, 85; Walls and Stephenson 1972, xiii-xv). The strategy was first embraced by community organizer and Ford Foundation staffer Richard Boone, who insisted that War on Poverty ground troops seek out the "maximum feasible participation of residents of the areas and members of the groups served." By mandating grassroots control over the CAAs, argued Boone, poor people not only could hold onto the balance of power but should use that power to challenge community elites or institutions that were seen as the ultimate source of their poverty (Eller 2008, 99; Moynihan 1969; Whisnant 1988). The Boone approach was basically a social conflict that stemmed from his earlier relationship with Saul Alinsky, Chicago's community organizer (Howley 2006, 1625). Boone, like Alinsky, believed that poverty was ultimately political and thus wanted to prevent community elites from co-opting CAAs and their antipoverty efforts.

In practice, however, this would not be the case. With a few important exceptions, the CAAs were unable to challenge the political status quo in most Appalachian communities. Although numerous agencies were able to create jobs, provide social services, and even turn several small businesses into profit-making enterprises, when CAAs introduced viable alternative strategies for long-term economic development (such as grocery store co-operatives) or challenged the political status quo (by endorsing grassroots candidates in county or state elections), political elites nearly always found ways of curtailing or stopping their efforts. One study, completed three years after the antipoverty program was first introduced into the mountain region, found that CAAs did little to change the institutional structure or decision-making processes of Appalachian communities, concluding that "the pattern of [political] alignments existing [when] the community action program began was not basically affected" (Street 1969, 7–8). In 1967 a Senate subcommittee report published similar findings in a study of thirty-five CAAs, three of which were located in Appalachian counties. At the end of the decade, after OEO lost a considerable amount of federal funding, the Community Action Program was irrelevant to most mountain residents (U.S. Congress 1967).

In retrospect, the War on Poverty did, in the long run, provide important social services to Appalachia, fund important community projects, and mobilize reform groups, public officials, and local citizens around the issue of poverty. However, as Senator Daniel Patrick Moynihan and others pointed out, OEO was unable to successfully incorporate grassroots participation in most of its antipoverty agendas. In Appalachia, the Community Action Program proved to be frustrating for those advocating real social and political change due to the "top-down" power structure long prevalent in mountain communities. According to one critic of CAAs, "maximum feasible participation was not even close to being pursued; conventional reforms produced no noticeable results; and county politics often stifled any meaningful change" (Gaventa and Lewis 1989, 58; see also Glen 1995, 67–73). Another shortcoming, argues Eller, is that OEO administrators—including activists from outside the region—envisioned themselves not as "poverty warriors" but as "culture commandos." They believed that their first priority should be to educate mountain people so that they might be better equipped to deal with the problems of the modern world—and thus pull themselves out of poverty. This "culture of poverty" bias, concludes Eller, was based on the erroneous notion that mountain residents were somehow outside "the cultural mainstream" and that poverty in Appalachia could be eliminated "without any significant restructuring of the political and economic system" (2008, 102; see also Billings and Blee 2000, 326).

THE APPALACHIAN REGIONAL COMMISSION

Another and no less important government agency created during the mid-1960s to improve living conditions in the mountains was the Appalachian

Regional Commission (ARC). Established during the Johnson administration as a result of the Appalachian Regional Development Act of 1965, the ARC was initially given $5 billion by Congress to provide infrastructure development, improve income levels and employment, and generally uplift the thirteen-state Appalachian region. Although the ARC has altered its development strategies over the last several decades, more than 80 percent of its total funding allocations have gone toward the construction of the 3,200-mile Appalachian Development Highway System (Eller and Taul 2006, 1570). Title I of the act also established the ARC as a "joint federal-state agency," which meant federal expenditures were to rely upon state plans and authority when identifying and budgeting projects. In theory, ARC's "new federalism" provided member states with a larger role in project implementation so that a more unified and effective rural development program would follow (Sundquist and Davis 1969, 3–9).

Also inherent in ARC's new federalism was the assumption that state and federal bodies could be responsive and accountable to mountain communities. However, ARC neither located its permanent office in the region nor appointed native residents to important staff positions. In fact, by 1970 almost no natives from Appalachia remained on the ARC staff at its Washington, D.C., headquarters. Moreover, the ARC governing board, consisting of a federal cochairman and the governors from thirteen states, simply approved or denied a list of projects submitted annually by each state (Eller 2008, 179–80; Eller and Taul 2006; Whisnant 1989, 143). This organizational structure, argued ARC critics, did not ensure grassroots representation or federal accountability when projects were flawed in concept or execution. What the "top-down" hierarchical structure did guarantee was that the interests of the ARC board would be given priority over the more immediate concerns of rural communities. As Thomas Gish, the editor of the *Mountain Eagle* and a resident of Whitesburg, Kentucky, stated in an editorial dated January 15, 1970, "The structure of the agency is such that . . . it can undertake only the most politically popular projects and is blocked from tackling any of the root causes of poverty in the mountains."

Initially, the ARC followed the development approach embraced by nearly all state-controlled, "high-modernist" planning agencies operating in the second half of the twentieth century. Like TVA, the ARC simply adopted a bricks-and-mortar strategy to solving basic social problems, ignoring existing institutional forces at work in the region's political economy. Social problems related to the environmental destruction caused by strip mining, the widespread absentee ownership of mountain lands, the inability of local governments to collect taxes on corporate-owned mineral resources, and the lack of essential human services in local communities were downplayed or even ignored by the agency. Instead of working on poverty or unemployment in the hardest-hit rural communities, the ARC chose instead to stimulate economic development by targeting regional "growth centers," that is, those places with the highest population densities. In doing so, the federal agency performed a kind of economic development triage by first approving projects that were in or near its major urban centers. Unemployment in the rural hinterlands would be solved later, *after* a network of highways had linked those areas to the region's growing metropolises (Eller 2008, 181–82; Shannon 2006, 77; Whisnant 1989, 139).

Although ARC continued to operate within the new federalism development paradigm for much of the 1980s, the commission did make some changes to its organizational structure in order to better accommodate the needs of rural communities. Nevertheless, poverty, hunger, high energy costs, high unemployment, and unfair labor practices continued to persist across much of the Appalachian region, as nearly two-thirds of the counties in the mountain region declined relative to the rest of the nation. In 1985, for example, four-fifths of the region's counties had an official unemployment rate higher than the national rate of 6.7 percent: eighty-five counties had double the national rate, and twenty-eight had triple the national rate, for an official unemployment rate of over 20 percent (Davis 1989). In the 1990s, after receiving considerable budget cuts, ARC appropriations stabilized, allowing the agency to expand its distressed counties program, which continues to provide funding for much-needed public services, including systems "to furnish clean drinking water and sanitary waste disposal, and human resource projects such as literacy training" (Appalachian Regional Commission n.d.a.). However, in 2012, after funneling more than $20 billion of federal aid into Appalachia, 96 of the commission's 420 counties—the majority of which were located in eastern Kentucky and east Tennessee—still qualified for distressed county funding.

While ARC, OEO, and TVA claimed to have operated in a decentralized and participatory fashion, these agencies were, in the final analysis, more accommodating to economic and political elites than to the direct needs of mountain residents. TVA, OEO, and ARC sometimes listened to the concerns of the grassroots but seldom acted or created federal policy on the behalf of the people. They did, nevertheless, improve the quality of life for those living in the mountains, contributing "significantly to the modernization of Appalachian life and culture" (Eller and Taul 2006, 1570; Shannon 2006, 77). At the same time, it is not clear that government policies emanating from "organic regionalism" or "new federalism" resulted in long-lasting community development by or for the people. In most cases, those agencies only used the rhetoric of participation to legitimize their "top-down" development agendas. Their organizational structures did, in fact, restrict grassroots participation in policy formation, often creating new and more complex social problems. As a result, Appalachian residents were periodically forced to respond to conditions on the ground with direct-action citizen protest. By the 1980s, grassroots community organizations in the region were politically challenging what was perceived as undemocratic federal policies and were embracing new, and perhaps more sustainable, forms of community development.

The Grassroots Fix

COMMUNITY ORGANIZING

During the 1970s and early 1980s, an increasing number of studies began to focus on community resistance in Appalachia as scholars and activists alike saw a need to document the ongoing struggles of mountain people. During that period, writers such as Si Kahn (1970), Helen Matthews Lewis (Matthews, Johnson, and Askins 1978), and John Gaventa (1980), among others, added critical and important insights into the understanding of Appalachian community protest and dissent. Although helpful in understanding the political and economic forces that were oppressing particular mountain communities, these studies did not anticipate the groundswell of grassroots activism that would occur in the mountains during the 1980s and 1990s. In fact, the growth and success of community activism in the region forced many to rethink important assumptions about the nature and extent of grassroots community organizing in Appalachia. Some commentators, such as Stephen Foster, uncritically accepted the notion that mountain residents universally oppose the forces of industry and modernization, ignoring differences of opinion among rural and urban dwellers, older and younger generations, or citizens of mountain, hill, and valley. Other scholars reinforced certain stereotypes about the Appalachian character, including the belief that residents maintain a fatalistic attitude toward political activism, making them unmobilizable as a social group (Foster 1988, 218–21; Gaventa 1980, 251–61).

Without question, the failure of the federal government to bring about substantive change during the 1960s and 1970s led to an increase in the number of nongovernmental organizations operating in the mountain region. Many War on Poverty activists remained in Appalachia during the 1970s, finding employment with community organizations, health clinics, or faith-based charities (Fisher et al. 2006, 87). Important regional coalitions were also created at this time, such as the Appalachian Alliance, as were national citizen organizations such as the Rural Coalition, which maintained organizational offices in the region. In the 1980s, partly in response to the Reagan administration's shifting of government funding to the states, community-based organizations (CBOs) began to devote more and more attention to the policies of local and state government (Couto 1999; Eller 2008, 253–54). Membership-based community organizations (MBOs) were also formed during this period, influenced by a larger grassroots movement that began to link environmental problems with issues of poverty and economic justice (Fisher 1993, 6–8).

SAVE OUR CUMBERLAND MOUNTAINS

Save Our Cumberland Mountains (SOCM) was one of several MBOs incorporated in the mountains of Appalachia during the early 1970s (Allen 1993). Although the group changed its name to Statewide Organizing for Community eMpowerment (SOCM) in 2008 and currently maintains chapters in west Tennessee, the majority of SOCM members have historically come from coalfield communities atop the Cumberland Plateau. MBOs such as SOCM employ professional full-time community organizers, distinguishing these organizations from other community groups in the Appalachian region. Throughout the 1980s and 1990s—and well into the twenty-first century—SOCM members worked on issues ranging from the control of strip mining and improving water quality to stopping hazardous incinerators and landfills from being located in mountain communities. In 2010 the group focused attention on the unregulated mining of large "fieldstone boulders sold in urban markets for landscaping and construction," a practice that causes irrevocable harm to mountain landscapes.

KENTUCKIANS FOR THE COMMONWEALTH

Another well-known MBO operating in the Appalachian region is Kentuckians for the Commonwealth (KFTC). KFTC currently has more than five thousand members, the majority of whom reside in the eastern portion of the commonwealth. Founded in 1980, KFTC has won numerous battles at both the local and state levels, including the elimination of the antiquated broad form deed, which for decades legally awarded mineral rights to coal companies rather than to local landowners. Under Kentucky law, companies holding broad form deeds "could legally strip-mine without permission to within 300 feet of the surface-property owner's house," as the surface rights of the property owner were viewed as "subservient to the mineral owner's" (Szakos 1990, 34). In 1984 KFTC members and state legislators passed a law forbidding the strip mining of private land without homeowner consent. However, the law had no immediate effect, as the state continued to issue strip-mine permits to coal companies holding broad form deeds. In 1987 the Kentucky Supreme Court overturned the 1984 law, again giving coal companies the legal right to destroy the property of surface owners (Kentuckians for the Commonwealth 1991, 66–75; Tetreault 1988, 2–3).

In response to the state's actions, KFTC members introduced and subsequently promoted a state constitutional amendment—Amendment #2—that would restrict the use of broad form deeds to deep mining only, the method of coal extraction in existence at the time the deeds were first signed. Although the new bill quickly passed in the General Assembly, it required a majority of the popular vote in a statewide election to become legally enforceable. Because of this fact, KFTC had to launch an aggressive grassroots campaign in order to convince not only coal interests that broad form deed practices should be abolished but also the general population living outside rural eastern Kentucky. After producing a series of television and radio advertisements, KFTC members set up information booths at county fairs and festivals and held bake sales at local supermarkets to raise additional funds and to increase broad form deed awareness. In the 1988 November election, Amendment #2 received 82 percent of the popular vote, winning in all of Kentucky's 120 counties, despite a five-hundred-thousand-dollar media campaign by the coal industry to defeat the amendment's passage. Only one of many such victories won by KFTC over the past several decades, in 2000 the group forced TVA to reconsider plans to auction forty thousand acres of land and mineral rights within the boundaries of the Daniel Boone National Forest. And in 2005 KFTC successfully lobbied state legislators to remove individuals "below the poverty line from state income tax rolls" and stopped the governor "from lowering tax rates on the wealthiest Kentuckians" (Kentuckians for the Commonwealth n.d.a.).

Exemplary grassroots organizations fighting for environmental and social justice in the Appalachian region, KFTC and SOCM are able to effectively involve members in state and local politics, winning battles once thought unwinnable by the region's most seasoned activists. Many communities in the mountain region remain unorganized, however, without the resources or the political power to influence state and local governments. In most Appalachian communities, political institutions are often viewed as obstacles to grassroots organizing, especially for those communities trying directly to influence the path of local economic development (Fisher 1989, 263–64). Across the region, development authorities are most often controlled by local elites, individuals who indiscriminately recruit big industry to communities in order to promote their own self-interests. This "chasing smokestacks" approach to economic development led a number of groups in the Appalachian region to call for "development from within," that is, the promotion of community development projects that foster more locally controlled economic growth.

THE IVANHOE CIVIC LEAGUE

One Appalachian community that embraced this economic development model is Ivanhoe, Virginia. The town of Ivanhoe is located on the border of Wythe and Carroll Counties, two of southwestern Virginia's poorest counties. For nearly a century, Ivanhoe was a prosperous mining center, possessing large iron, lead, zinc, and manganese deposits (Baker 1984, B7). Both National Carbide and the New Jersey Zinc Company were located in Ivanhoe during its boom days of the 1940s and 1950s. At that time, the town's population exceeded four thousand residents, and the community supported a railroad, school, hotel, movie theater, and restaurant. In 1966 National Carbide closed its facilities, leaving 450 local residents without jobs. New Jersey Zinc, which employed more than 350 people, shuttered its doors in 1981. Additional plant closings in the area left the town economically devastated. By the mid-1980s, the town no longer possessed a school, theater, or department store, and out-migration had reduced the population to less than 1,300 individuals. Employment opportunities were extremely limited for residents, and those who did find work commuted an average of sixty-three miles to low-paying jobs (Waller et al. 2000, 19–28).

In 1986 citizens formed the Ivanhoe Civic League, a CBO that initially focused its energies on stopping the county government from selling an abandoned industrial park. Most Ivanhoe residents believed that the sale announcement was "a signal that local economic development officials were giving up all hope of locating another industry to the community" (Gaventa and Lewis 1989, 58–59). In response, the Civic League started a grassroots initiative to stop the industrial park's sale and to recruit another outside industry. Their efforts made national news, including a "Hands across Ivanhoe" event in which "3,000 people paid $3 to hold hands in the cold rain in support of their community" (Hinsdale, Lewis, and Waller 1995, 7–13). That same year, local industrial development authorities agreed not to sell the park for at least two years, giving the community group time to recruit new industry to the park. As the Civic League began a vigorous campaign to bring new jobs to the community, county developers steered interested industries away from Ivanhoe to growth areas along the main interstate. After several failed attempts at securing industries, Ivanhoe residents began exploring other alternatives, focusing on smaller development projects. Civic League and other volunteers eventually cleaned up a large parcel of land along the New River, naming the space Jubilee Park. The completed park was comprised of camping facilities, bike and raft rentals, and a convenience store, all of which provided jobs and recreation for Ivanhoe residents (Davis 2006, 113–14; Waller et al. 2000, 20).

During hearings regarding the sale and development of the industrial park, government officials largely ignored Civic League members, giving experts and local development authorities priority in their deliberations. As a result of those encounters, the Civic League began focusing on other projects, including several based on their own community needs assessments (Lewis 1997). By 1989 the Civic League had successfully organized a senior citizen and youth recreation program and begun holding literacy education classes in the center of town. The Civic League later renovated the town's original company store and created a community-based education center where college extension classes could be permanently held. Participants in the school's extension classes researched the town's history and published a two-volume community history of Ivanhoe and the surrounding area (Lewis and O'Donnell 1990). In sum, the Ivanhoe Civic League worked toward creating a new model of community development, one that is place based, self-sufficient, and grassroots controlled.

SOUTHERN APPALACHIAN LABOR SCHOOL

Another CBO that has utilized this same development strategy is the Southern Appalachian Labor School (SALS), a nonprofit headquartered in Beards Fork, West Virginia (Baker 2007). One of SALS's most successful ventures is its housing program, which involves building new homes, rehabilitating substandard homes, and weatherizing existing ones. SALS's staff members determine eligibility for homeowners, write grants, and help local families apply for assistance. By 2006 these programs had been responsible for the expansion of entire neighborhoods, including Hilltop and the New Page housing complex. Community members and volunteers also work on the homes of black-lung widows and other low-income residents, creating new and safe environments for those vulnerable populations (Baker 2005). Many of the social problems associated with substandard housing fall disproportionately on the disabled, elderly widows, and young families with children, as low-income families often cannot afford repairs or have trouble finding reputable contractors who will work on small projects (Auvil 2001; U.S. Department of Housing and Urban Development 2005). SALS's housing projects receive monies and grants from a variety of state and federal sources, including the West Virginia Housing Development Fund, the U.S. Department of Agriculture, and the Federal Home Loan Bank (Baker 2005; Couto 1999).

Using local community capital, SALS draws on existing social networks to identify the needs of area residents, especially the elderly, infirm, and single mothers and children. Believing that both social capital and individual empowerment are central ingredients in rural development, SALS facilitates immediate self-help while ensuring longer-term fixes to the problems facing many mountain communities. For its ongoing work, SALS has been recognized by the United Mine Workers, the Department of Housing and Urban Development (HUD), the Appalachian Regional Commission, and the Appalachian Studies Association, the latter awarding it the Helen M. Lewis Community Service Award in 2004. Despite extensive federal and state funding cuts to nonprofits, SALS continues to build coalitions with other community groups and maintains a large volunteer staff. By 2012 the nonprofit had improved over fifteen hundred homes and annually works with two thousand volunteers in its programs, including GED candidates, college students, corporate executives, and numerous individuals from faith-based institutions (John David, pers. comm., January 28, 2010, July 14, 2012).

Grassroots initiatives like SALS, the Ivanhoe Civic League, KFTC, and SOCM clearly raise questions about conventional understanding of community organizing and economic development in the mountain region. These four groups, and many others like them, are effectively altering state policy and structure, creating the necessary preconditions for permanent social change in the Appalachian region. By challenging the formation and implementation of government policy and programs, grassroots organizations simultaneously alter the political process while holding the modern state to its democratic promise. While the state has had an important influence on the success or failure of most grassroots initiatives, it is seldom so hegemonic or monolithic that an organized and active citizenry cannot influence its planning or development authority. KFTC, in drafting and passing legislation, was able to change coal-mining policies that had existed in the state for more than a century. SOCM, by actively demonstrating against a proposed incinerator, convinced the local government to stop its construction while simultaneously challenging the state's entire permitting process. The Ivanhoe

Civic League was able to circumvent the plans of traditional industrial developers, providing residents with a community center, recreation park, and general store. SALS obtained hundreds of thousands of dollars in state and federal grants, ensuring both employment and adequate housing for hundreds of residents in Beards Fork and neighboring communities. Not merely isolated instances or random, self-interested actions, the activities of CBOs and MBOs make important and lasting contributions to the quality of life in Appalachia.

Nonetheless, in the twenty-first century, the limitations and challenges facing both MBOs and CBOs in Appalachia are numerous. The economic recession of 2008–13 severely limited the amount of private and public funds available to nonprofits, forcing many to cut staff and reduce budgets. In some areas, deindustrialization continues to impact communities historically dependent on manufacturing and industry. In other communities, especially those with a history of extreme inequality between the wealthiest and poorest inhabitants, grassroots groups still confront obstacles of violence, intimidation, and lack of resources when they do attempt to organize. Across the region, a deeper awareness of the international scope of "local" problems is also needed, as globalization has not only caused both industries and resources to leave Appalachia but also brought foreign workers into the mountain region. In the end, Appalachian communities must not only react to broader social forces but also, whenever possible, be *proactive*. In this sense, Appalachian communities must explore new and perhaps more creative solutions to the problems they currently face, especially if they are to maintain control over their economic futures (Marshall 1988).

The Final Fix?

The epicenter of bold (if sometimes ineffective) experiments by missionaries, the federal government, philanthropists, labor unions, and community organizers during the twentieth century, Appalachia is today still under repair. In the twenty-first century, a growing number of communities continue to explore development strategies that have important economic and environmental implications not only for the mountain region but for the United States as a whole. In the past decade, more and more individuals have been asking important questions about what constitutes long-term organizing success in Appalachia, focusing not only on traditional economic criteria but on an entire range of "quality-of-life" issues, including local food production, health and wellness, renewable energy, the manufacture of arts and crafts, green building construction, and unplanned growth and sprawl. These "place-based" approaches to community development add an important dimension lacking in earlier grassroots organizing efforts in Appalachia: the goal of sustainability (Fisher and Smith 2012; Fritsch and Gallimore 2007; Fritsch and Johannsen 2004; Nolt 2005; Reid and Taylor 2010).

APPALACHIAN SUSTAINABLE DEVELOPMENT

Perhaps the best example of a community organization adopting the new development approach is Appalachian Sustainable Development (ASD), a nonprofit based in Abingdon, Virginia. ASD focuses on developing "diverse and ecologically sound economic opportunities through education and training" and "creating cooperative networks and marketing systems" for distributing its products. Since 2000 ASD has focused on two issues in its southwestern Virginia/northeastern Tennessee coverage area: local organic food production and sustainable forestry. In a 2008 interview, Anthony Flaccavento, ASD's founder, discussed the nonprofit's economic development approach:

> We gathered environmental activists and some community activists together with more traditional economic development people, chambers of commerce, and a few entrepreneurs and friends, and we basically for about a year grappled with the question: can we create an economy that's good for people and good for the environment at the same time—in fact better for people and better for the environment—than we're getting on either end now? . . . What [ASD] has been trying to do . . . is to redefine what a healthy economy is and what economic development is. (Wheatley 2008; see also Flaccavento n.d.)

Flaccavento believes that "natural capital" is Appalachia's greatest asset, especially when communities are able to capture the value-added wealth of their natural resources. The principles of sustainable development, he says, ensure that the resources are developed both locally and wisely, thus providing long-term benefits for both mountain communities and ecosystems.

One of ASD's sustainable enterprises is the Appalachian Harvest Network (AHN), which in 2000 began helping small farmers make the transition from growing tobacco to organic food production (McDaniel 2001). Nearly all AHN growers sell their produce to local grocers, independent health food stores, area colleges, and large supermarket chains such as Whole Foods and Earth Fare. In 2008 the nonprofit cooperative was able to donate eighty-eight thousand pounds of organic produce to mountain families in need, and in 2011 AHN annual sales exceeded $1 million for the first time. According to Winrock International, AHN has "been invaluable" to the residents of

Southwest Virginia and upper East Tennessee, as it allows "tobacco growers who might otherwise have abandoned farming adopt a new strategy to continue farming." And by keeping more dollars circulating in the communities in which it operates, adds Winrock, AHN contributes "directly to the region's economic well-being" (Shuman, Barron, and Wasserman 2009, 44–45).

Although ASD maintains a staff of fourteen, has won numerous awards, and operates with an annual budget of nearly $2 million, it still faces daily challenges. In a 2009 report entitled *Community Food Enterprise: Local Success in a Global Marketplace*, the authors made note of AHN's limited financial viability, stating that "its operating expenses cannot be covered by sales alone" (Shuman, Barron, and Wasserman 2009). Not expecting to be operating in the black until sometime after 2014, Appalachian Harvest Network requires significant foundation grants and private donations to meet its annual budget. AHN has also struggled to manage the needs of both growers and buyers, as Appalachian farmers can be strongly independent when adopting new crop varieties, and grocery store chains can be uncompromising regarding quality control, as they tend to purchase produce that is uniform in both color and size. AHN suffered another setback in 2007, when its sorting and processing facility, a large wooden barn, was destroyed in a fire (Littrell 2007).

Another organization embracing the sustainable development model is HandMade in America (HIA), a nonprofit founded in the late 1990s by community leaders who believed that economic growth was not necessarily tied to luring modern industry to the region (Eller 2008, 257). Based in western North Carolina, HIA continues to receive national recognition for its collaborative and innovative community development strategies. Initially, HIA focused on marketing the rich craft traditions of the southern Appalachians and promoting the Blue Ridge Mountains as a heritage tourism destination. HIA does not subsidize craft production or even sell crafts directly but instead serves as a marketing support system for the western North Carolina industry, a two-hundred-million-dollar enterprise. Initially, the group simply involved itself in creating marketing networks for local communities, producing guidebooks, brochures, and other publicity tools for "mountain artists, galleries, inns, farmers' markets, and historical sites" (Eller 2008, 257). In the process of doing so, however, participating communities learned that by joining forces they were able to reach larger numbers of tourists, secure government grants, and collaborate on a myriad of projects, including the production of biofuels and other green-industry initiatives.

Organizations like HIA and other nonprofits dedicated to the principles of sustainable development are attempting to reverse the historical pattern of resource extraction in Appalachia and taking good advantage of the social and natural capital found in mountain communities. Many of them, however, still possess institutional weaknesses that make them vulnerable to larger social and economic trends. Nearly all rely heavily on external funding, including grants from large foundations or the federal government. While this is not an inherent shortcoming, it does create a dependency on unreliable funding sources, especially during economic recessions. While many of the groups intentionally operate as nonprofits, those that would prefer not to do so—such as Appalachian Harvest Network—cannot afford that luxury, since they continually operate above their annual budgets. Even HIA has had to engage in serious reflection regarding its marketing tactics, as the 2008–13 recession greatly reduced tourist traffic in the Blue Ridge Mountains. Some commentators even suggested that the craft items marketed by HIA were overpriced and targeted toward national or international buyers rather than local residents. To be truly sustainable, they argue, prices should reflect internal rather than external markets, so if extralocal or foreign tourists stay away, craft businesses do not suffer.

Appalachia's path to economic dependency has been a long and complicated one, involving the absentee ownership of both coal and timber resources, the decline of the region's agricultural economy, out-migration, and the destruction of entire ecosystems as the result of surface and mountaintop removal coal mining. For more than a century, Appalachia saw most of its natural resources leave the region, fueling the engines of development in urban centers far from its borders. This would change somewhat in the 1950s and 1960s, when many of those same resources would begin to be utilized internally, in Appalachia's own growing cities and towns. During the second half of the twentieth century, numerous counties, particularly in southern Appalachia, did experience economic growth and progress, becoming the target of second-home and retirement-community development. By the end of the millennium, large areas that had once been representative of rural Appalachia were beginning to look like the rest of the United States, complete with strip malls and suburban sprawl. In 2013, 223 (53 percent) of Appalachia's 420 counties were no longer classified as distressed or at risk, with as many as 15 counties (4 percent) classified as competitive or even surpassing national norms.

Despite obvious infrastructure improvements across much of the region, there are still many communities at risk in Appalachia. Residents living in the central Appalachian coalfields have been especially hard hit, facing high unemployment rates, lower-than-average wages, inadequate health care, and numerous problems associated with mountaintop removal (Zhang et al. 2008,

171–73, 180). While large-scale surface mining provides important jobs to local communities, a growing number of Appalachian residents are publicly opposing the practice, calling for a more sustainable and democratic use of their natural resources. Others have joined their efforts, including activists, authors, celebrities, filmmakers, and scientists.[2] Despite verbal and written protests and hundreds of arrests, mining has continued relatively unabated, even as President Barack Obama called for more green energy and the lowering of global greenhouse gas emissions during his first administration. Only a very small percentage of mountaintop-mining permits were altered or rejected by the Environmental Protection Agency after 2009, giving the impression that the federal government was more interested in protecting the interests of the coal industry than preserving healthy mountain ecosystems (U.S. Government Accountability Office 2009). While the coal industry did fund some intriguing sustainable development projects on abandoned mine lands, its efforts appeared to most observers as being too little, too late.[3]

The future of the coalfields may very well be linked to how mountaintop removal is ultimately regulated. If the forces of industry prevail, then more mountains will be lost, more streams will be polluted, and more communities will experience social and economic difficulties—or total abandonment. If sustainable development and environmental preservation win the day, then the people and places of central Appalachia will most certainly prevail. In an ideal world, communities should be able to chart their own economic futures, free from the narrow dictates of single industries and the absentee ownership of their land and natural resources. Indeed, all of Appalachia should be a place where individuals have enough economic control over their lives that they do not have to make a false choice between living in a healthy community or providing for their families (Fisher and Smith 2012, 1–15). In its purest form, sustainable development brings real economic choices to mountain communities, a path to self-determination and well-being that may require few, if any, fixes.

Notes

1. Using U.S. Census data, Campbell reported the 1910 illiteracy rate for Appalachia at 13.4 percent, which included all persons—black and white—age ten and over. For the nation as a whole the rate was 7.7 percent. For the Allegheny-Cumberland Plateau, which includes eastern Kentucky, the rate was 12.4 percent (Campbell 1921, 261).

2. Wendell Berry is the most well known author to have publicly denounced mountaintop removal. Notable celebrities who have criticized mountaintop removal include

country singer Kathy Mattea and actors Woody Harrelson, Ashley Judd, and Daryl Hannah. Mountaintop removal has also been the subject of numerous film documentaries, including *The Last Mountain* (2011), *Coal Country* (2009), *Mountaintop Removal* (2007), and *Black Diamonds* (2006).

3. By 2010 there was a growing consensus among scientists that the environmental impacts caused by mountaintop removal mining were "pervasive and long lasting and there is no evidence that any mitigation practices successfully reverse the damage it causes" (Palmer et al. 2010, 148–49).

Works Cited

Adams, Frank. 1975. *Unearthing Seeds of Fire: The Idea of Highlander.* Winston-Salem, N.C.: John F. Blair.

Allen, Bill. 1993. "Save Our Cumberland Mountains: Growth and Change within a Grassroots Organization." In *Fighting Back in Appalachia: Traditions of Resistance and Change*, edited by Stephen L. Fisher, 85–100. Philadelphia: Temple University Press.

Alvic, Philis. 2003. *Weavers of the Southern Highlands.* Lexington: University Press of Kentucky.

———. 2006. "Settlement, Mission, and Sponsored Schools." In *Encyclopedia of Appalachia*, edited by Rudy Abramson and Jean Haskell, 1151–52. Knoxville: University of Tennessee Press.

Appalachian Regional Commission. 1970. "The Urban-Rural Growth Strategy in Appalachia." Commission Staff Summary, Report 13. Washington, D.C.: ARC.

———. 2012. "Distressed Counties 2012." http://www.arc.gov/program_areas /MapofARCDesignatedDistressedCountiesFiscalYear.2012. Accessed July 13, 2012.

———. 2013. "County Economic Status in Appalachia, FY 2013." http://www.arc.gov /research/MapsofAppalachia.asp?MAP_ID=64. Accessed March 5, 2014.

———. n.d.a. "Distressed Counties Grants." http://www.arc.gov/index.do?nodeId=18. Accessed March 26, 2012.

———. n.d.b. "Maps of Appalachia." http://www.arc.gov/research/MapsofAppalachia .asp?MAP_ID=55. Accessed July 16, 2012.

Appalachian Sustainable Agriculture Project. n.d. Homepage. http://www .asapconnections.org/. Accessed January 29, 2012.

Appalachian Sustainable Development. n.d. Homepage. http://www.asdevelop.org/. Accessed January 30, 2012.

Asheville Citizen-Times. n.d. Online blog. http://www.citizen-times.com/article /20100121/LIVING/301210016. Accessed May 31, 2012.

Auvil, Ken. 2001. "Nation, State, Should Focus on Affordable Housing." *Charleston Gazette*, April 16, 1.

Baker, Chris. 2005. "Collaborations for Change: Who's Playing and Who's Winning in Community-Based Organization-Led Development in Rural Appalachia." *Humanity and Society* (August/November): 325–50.

———. 2007. "The Southern Appalachian Labor School: Communities of Difference and Development in Southern West Virginia." *Now and Then* 22 (Spring): 12–14.

Baker, Donald P. 1984. "Virginia Town Staves Off Disaster." *Washington Post*, February 12, B7.

Barney, Sandra L. 2000. *Authorized to Heal: Gender, Class, and the Transformation of Medicine in Appalachia, 1880–1930*. Chapel Hill: University of North Carolina Press.

Becker, Jane S. 1998. *Selling Tradition: Appalachia and the Construction of an American Folk*. Chapel Hill: University of North Carolina Press.

Bigart, Homer. 1963. "The Mine Patches." *New York Times*, October 21, 30.

Billings, Dwight B., and Kathleen M. Blee. 2000. *The Road to Poverty: The Making of Wealth and Hardship in Appalachia*. New York: Cambridge University Press.

Black, Brian. 2000. "Organic Planning: Ecology and Design in the Landscape of TVA." In *Environmentalism in Landscape Architecture*, edited by Michael Conan, 71–95. Washington, D.C.: Dumbarton Oaks Research Library and Collection.

———. 2006. "Tennessee Valley Authority." In *Encyclopedia of Appalachia*, edited by Rudy Abramson and Jean Haskell, 1620. Knoxville: University of Tennessee Press.

Campbell, John C. 1921. *The Southern Highlander and His Homeland*. New York: Russell Sage Foundation.

Caudill, Harry M. 1963. *Night Comes to the Cumberlands: A Biography of a Depressed Area*. Boston: Little, Brown.

Couto, Richard A. 1999. *Making Democracy Work Better: Mediating Structures, Social Capital, and the Democratic Prospect*. Chapel Hill: University of North Carolina Press.

Davis, Donald E. 1989. "Homegrown Activism Takes Root in Appalachia." *Utne Reader*, May/June, 26.

———. 2006. *Homeplace Geography: Essays for Appalachia*. Macon, Ga.: Mercer University Press.

Eller, Ronald D. 1982. *Miners, Millhands, and Mountaineers: Industrialization of the Appalachian South, 1880–1930*. Knoxville: University of Tennessee Press.

———. 2008. *Uneven Ground: Appalachia since 1945*. Lexington: University Press of Kentucky.

Eller, Ronald D, and Glen E. Taul. 2006. "Appalachian Regional Commission." In *Encyclopedia of Appalachia*, edited by Rudy Abramson and Jean Haskell, 1570. Knoxville: University of Tennessee Press.

Fisher, Stephen L. 1989. "National Economic Renewal Programs and Their Implications for Appalachia and the South." In *Communities in Economic Crisis: Appalachia and the South*, edited by John Gaventa, Barbara Ellen Smith, and Alex W. Willingham, 263–78. Philadelphia: Temple University Press.

———, ed. 1993. *Fighting Back in Appalachia: Traditions of Resistance and Change*. Philadelphia: Temple University Press.

Fisher, Stephen L., Patti Page Church, Christine Weiss Daugherty, Bennett M. Judkins, and Shaunna L. Scott. 2006. "The Politics of Change in Appalachia." In *A Handbook* to Appalachia: An Introduction to the Region, edited by Grace T. Edwards, JoAnn Asbury, and Ricky Cox, 85–100. Knoxville: University of Tennessee Press.

Fisher, Stephen L., and Barbara Ellen Smith, eds. 2012. *Transforming Places: Lessons from Appalachia*. Urbana: University of Illinois Press.

Flaccavento, Anthony. n.d. "Growing Local, Eating Local." Interview, PBS Enterprising Ideas website, http://www.pbs.org/now/enterprisingideas/asd.html. Accessed March 31, 2012.

Foster, Stephen. 1988. *The Past Is Another Country: Representation, Historical Consciousness, and Resistance in the Blue Ridge*. Berkeley: University of California Press.

Fritsch, Al, and Paul Gallimore. 2007. *Healing Appalachia: Sustainable Living through Appropriate Technology*. Lexington: University Press of Kentucky.

Fritsch, Al, and Kristin Johannsen. 2004. *Ecotourism in Appalachia: Marketing the Mountains*. Lexington: University Press of Kentucky.

Gaumitz, Walton H., and Katherine M. Cook. 1938. *Education in the Southern Mountains: Bulletin 1937*, No. 26. Washington, D.C.: U.S. Department of the Interior, Office of Education.

Gaventa, John. 1980. *Power and Powerlessness: Quiescence and Rebellion in an Appalachian Valley*. Chicago: University of Chicago Press.

Gaventa, John, and Helen Lewis. 1989. "Rural Area Development: Involvement by the People." *Forum for Applied Research and Public Policy* 4 (Fall): 58–62.

Glen, John M. 1995. "The War on Poverty in Appalachia: Oral History from the 'Top Down' and the 'Bottom Up.'" *Oral History Review* (Summer): 67–93.

Gray, Aelred J., and David A. Johnson. 2005. *The TVA Regional Planning and Development Program: The Transformation of an Institution and Its Mission*. Burlington: Ashgate Publishing.

HandMade in America. n.d. Homepage. http://www.handmadeinamerica.org/. Accessed January 30, 2012.

Hargrove, Erwin C. 1994. *Prisoners of Myth: The Leadership of the Tennessee Valley Authority, 1933–1990*. Princeton, N.J.: Princeton University Press.

Harrington, Michael. 1962. *The Other America: Poverty in the United States*. New York: Macmillan.

Hinsdale, Mary Ann, Helen Lewis, and S. Maxine Waller. 1995. *It Comes from the People: Community Development and Local Theology*. Philadelphia: Temple University Press.

Hobday, Victor C. 1969. *Sparks at the Grassroots: Municipal Distribution of TVA Electricity in Tennessee*. Knoxville: University of Tennessee Press.

Howley, Craig B. 2006. "War on Poverty." In *Encyclopedia of Appalachia*, edited by Rudy Abramson and Jean Haskell, 1624. Knoxville: University of Tennessee Press.

Kahn, Si. 1970. *How People Get Power: Organizing Oppressed Communities for Action*. New York: McGraw-Hill.

Kentuckians for the Commonwealth. 1988a. "Eighty-Two Percent of Kentucky Voters Say YES to Broad Form Deed Amendment." *Balancing the Scales*, November 17, 1, 5.

————. 1988b. "It's Time for a Change in Kentucky, Say KFTC Members Working for Passage of Broad Form Deed Amendment." *Balancing the Scales*, October 20, 1.

————. 1991. *Making History: The First Ten Years of KFTC*. Prestonsburg: Brown & Kroger.

————. n.d.a. "Our History." http://www.kftc.org/about-us/our-history. Accessed January 17, 2013.

————. n.d.b. "Press Room." http://www.kftc.org/press-room. Accessed November 19, 2012.

Lewis, Helen. 1997. "Community History." *OAH Magazine of History* 3 (Spring): 20–22.

Lewis, Helen Matthews, Linda Johnson, and Donald Askins. 1978. *Colonialism in Modern America: The Appalachian Case*. Boone, N.C.: Appalachian Consortium Press.

Lewis, Helen M., and Suzanna O'Donnell, eds. 1990. *Telling Our Stories, Sharing Our Lives: The Ivanhoe History Project*, vol. 2. Ivanhoe, Va.: Ivanhoe Civic League.

Littrell, Walter. 2007. "Stickleyville Produce Packing House Burns." *Kingsport Times*, May 15, A1.

Lorence, James J. 2007. *A Hard Journey: The Life of Don West*. Urbana: University of Illinois Press.

Los Angeles Times. 1942. "U.S. Civilian Payroll Hits 1,703,099." April 7, 1.

Markusen, Ann R. 1987. *Regions: The Economies and Politics of Territory*. Totowa, N.J.: Rowman and Littlefield, 1987.

Marshall, Gene. 1988. "Repair or Replacement: An Essay on Ecological Politics." *Realistic Living: A Journal of Ethics and Religion* 8 (June): 3–8.

McDaniel, Lynda. 2001. "Appalachian Harvest, Growing for the Future." *Appalachia Magazine* (September-December 2001), online version, http://www.arc.gov/magazine/. Accessed January 29, 2013.

McDonald, Michael J., and John Muldowny. 1982. *TVA and the Dispossessed: The Resettlement of Population in the Norris Dam Area*. Knoxville: University of Tennessee Press.

McNeil, W. K., ed. 1995. *Appalachian Images in Folk and Popular Culture*. Knoxville: University of Tennessee Press.

Montrie, Chad. 2003. *To Save the Land and People: A History of Opposition to Surface Coal Mining in Appalachia*. Chapel Hill: University of North Carolina Press.

Morgan, Arthur E. 1974. *The Making of TVA*. Buffalo, N.Y.: Prometheus Books.

Morgan, Thomas B. 1962. "Portrait of an Underdeveloped Country." *Look*, December 4, 25–33.

Moynihan, Daniel Patrick. 1969. *Maximum Feasible Misunderstanding: Community Action in the War on Poverty*. New York: Free Press.

Nolt, John. 2005. *A Land Imperiled: The Declining Health of the Southern Appalachian Bioregion*. Knoxville: University of Tennessee Press.

Owen, Marguerite. 1973. *The Tennessee Valley Authority*. New York: Praeger.

Palmer, M. A., E. S. Bernhardt, W. H. Schlesinger, K. N. Eshleman, E. Foufoula-Georgiou, M. S. Hendryx, A. D. Lemly, G. E. Likens, O. L. Loucks, M. E. Power, P. S. White, and P. R. Wilcocket. 2010. "Mountaintop Mining Consequences." *Science*, January 8, 148–49.

Phillips, Sarah T. 2007. *This Land, This Nation: Conversation, Rural America, and the New Deal.* Cambridge: Cambridge University Press.

Reid, Herbert, and Betsy Taylor. 2010. *Recovering the Commons: Democracy, Place, and Global Justice.* Urbana: University of Illinois Press.

Save Our Cumberland Mountains. n.d. "Annual Reports." http://www.socm.org/index .cfm/m/20/fuseAction/contentpage.main/detailID/31. Accessed May 18, 2012.

Scott, James. 1998. *Seeing like a State: How Certain Schemes to Improve the Human Condition Have Failed.* New Haven, Conn.: Yale University Press.

Selznick, Philip. 1966. *TVA and the Grassroots: A Study in the Sociology of Formal Organization.* New York: Harper and Row.

Shannon, Thomas. 2006. "The Economy of Appalachia." In *A Handbook to Appalachia: An Introduction to the Region*, edited by Grace T. Edwards, JoAnn Asbury, and Ricky Cox, 67–84. Knoxville: University of Tennessee Press.

Shapiro, Henry D. 1978. *Appalachia on Our Mind: The Southern Mountains and Mountaineers in the American Consciousness, 1870–1920.* Chapel Hill: University of North Carolina Press.

Shuman, Michael, Alissa Barron, and Wendy Wasserman. 2009. *Community Food Enterprise: Local Success in a Global Marketplace.* Arlington, Va.: Wallace Center at Winrock International Report.

Southern Appalachian Labor School. n.d. http://www.sals.info/programs/worker _ed.html. Accessed January 20, 2011.

Straw, Richard. 2006. "Appalachian History." In *A Handbook to Appalachia: An Introduction to the Region*, edited by Grace T. Edwards, JoAnn Asbury, and Ricky Cox, 1–26. Knoxville: University of Tennessee Press.

Street, Paul. 1969. "Case Study: OEO vs. Rural Poverty." *Mountain Life and Work* 45 (January): 7–8.

Sundquist, James L., and David W. Davis. 1969. *Making Federalism Work: A Study of Program Coordination at the Community Level.* Washington, D.C.: Brookings Institution.

Sutton, Willis A., Jr. 1969. "Differential Perceptions of Impact of a Rural Anti-poverty Campaign." *Social Science Quarterly* 50 (December): 657–67.

Szakos, Kristin. 1990. "People Power: Working for the Future in the East Kentucky Coalfields." In *Communities in Economic Crisis: Appalachia and the South*, edited by John Gaventa, Barbara Ellen Smith, and Alex W. Willingham, 29–37. Philadelphia: Temple University Press.

Teets, Sharon. 2006. "Education in Appalachia." In *A Handbook to Appalachia: An Introduction to the Region*, edited by Grace T. Edwards, JoAnn Asbury, and Ricky Cox, 119–42. Knoxville: University of Tennessee Press.

Tetreault, Maynard. 1988. "Broad Form Deeds in Kentucky: A Chronology." *Balancing the Scales*, October 20, 2–3.

Thomas, Jerry Bruce. 2010. *An Appalachian New Deal: West Virginia in the Great Depression*. Lexington: University Press of Kentucky.

Tice, Karen W. 2006. "Settlement House Movement." In *Encyclopedia of Appalachia*, edited by Rudy Abramson and Jean Haskell, 1150. Knoxville: University of Tennessee Press.

U.S. Congress. 1967. *Examining the War on Poverty: Staff and Consultant Reports Prepared for the Subcommittee on Employment . . . of the Committee on Labor and Public Welfare*. U.S. Senate, 90th Cong., 1st sess., vol. 4. Washington, D.C.: Government Printing Office.

U.S. Department of Commerce. Bureau of the Census. 1913. *Thirteenth Census of the United States, Abstract of the Census*. Washington, D.C.: Government Printing Office.

U.S. Department of Housing and Urban Development. 2005. *Affordable Housing Needs: A Report to Congress on the Significant Need for Housing, Annual Compilation of a Worst Case Housing Needs Survey*. Washington, D.C.: Government Printing Office.

U.S. Government Accountability Office. 2009. *Surface Coal Mining: Characteristics of Mining in Mountainous Areas of Kentucky and West Virginia*. GAO Report 10–21. Washington, D.C.: Government Printing Office.

U.S. National Resources Committee. 1935. *Regional Factors in National Planning and Development*. Washington, D.C.: Government Printing Office.

U.S. Senate. 1961. *Hearings before a Subcommittee of the Committee on Banking and Currency on Bills to Establish an Effective Program to Alleviate Conditions of Unemployment and Underemployment in Certain Economically Depressed Areas*. January 18-February 20. Washington, D.C.: Government Printing Office.

Waller, Maxine, Helen M. Lewis, Clare McBrien, and Carroll L. Wessinger. 2000. "'It Has to Come from the People': Responding to the Plant Closings in Ivanhoe, Virginia." In *Communities in Economic Crisis*, edited by John Gaventa, Barbara Ellen Smith, and Alex W. Willingham, 19–28. Philadelphia: Temple University Press.

Walls, David S., and John B. Stephenson, eds. 1972. *Appalachia in the Sixties*. Lexington: University Press of Kentucky.

Wengert, Norman. 1952. *Valley of Tomorrow: TVA and Agriculture*. Knoxville: University of Tennessee / Bureau of Public Administration.

Wheatley, Lois Carol. 2008. "Ag-Ventures: Appalachian Sustainable Development." *Appalachian Voices* (March), online archives, http://www.appvoices.org/. Accessed January 30, 2012.

Whisnant, David. 1983. *All That Is Native and Fine: The Politics of Culture in an American Region*. Chapel Hill: University of North Carolina Press.

———. 1988. *Modernizing the Mountaineer: People, Power, and Planning in Appalachia*. Boone, N.C.: Appalachian Consortium Press.

Williamson, Handy. 1981. "The Tennessee Valley Authority and Rural Development, 1979 Policy Study: The Role of TVA Programs in Regional Development." TVA Office of Planning and Budget, Knoxville, Tennessee.

Wilson, Samuel T. 1914. *The Southern Mountaineers*. New York: Presbyterian Home Missions.

Zhang, Zhiwei, Alycia Infante, Michael Meit, Ned English, Michael Dunn, and Kristine Harper Bowers. 2008. *An Analysis of Mental Health and Substance Abuse Disparities and Access to Treatment Services in the Appalachian Region*. Final Report. Washington, D.C.: Appalachian Regional Commission.

5

Developing Appalachia

The Impact of Limited Economic Imagination

AMANDA L. FICKEY AND MICHAEL SAMERS

> Appalachia is more striking in its homogeneity than in its
> diversity. Unlike though they may be, its subregions share
> an unhappy distinction: rural Appalachia lags behind rural
> America; urban Appalachia lags behind urban America; and
> metropolitan Appalachia lags behind metropolitan America.
>
> —PARC 1964

Appalachia has historically been represented as an enigma, a region that simply did not seem to fit within the rest of the United States. During the late nineteenth century, writers for national magazines often identified Appalachia as different by describing the region's inhabitants as "exotic" and "natural" (Williams 2002). Stories about feuding only fueled the perception that the region's inhabitants were somehow out of step with the rest of the country (Waller 1988). In the 1920s and 1930s, the region again made national headlines for miner strikes, predominantly in eastern Kentucky and southern West Virginia. Despite the fact that the 1950s were typically associated with national economic growth and prosperity, central Appalachia appeared in the news as a site of mine mechanization, unemployment, out-migration, and flood disasters, perpetuating the notion of "otherness."

By the 1960s Appalachia—which had thus far been understood as different, isolated, and rebellious—would also become associated with abject poverty, an image of the region that would become firmly ingrained in the imagination of most Americans (Eller 2008). It was the rural front in the War on Poverty. For example, in 1962 *Look* magazine published a series of photographs of Appalachia, including a caption that stated that Appalachian people lived in an underdeveloped country. "No less than Latin Americans or Africans," it read, "they can use more American aid. They are more entitled to it because they are our own people" (quoted in Eller 2008, 66). The use of the term "underdeveloped" can be understood as representative of the development discourse at the time. Such labeling was often used to substantiate poverty, implying that the underdeveloped region simply *lagged behind* others but would eventually *catch up*. This discourse supported claims for aid to "lagging" regions throughout the world (Ferguson 1999).

Similar discourse supported the 1964 creation of the Appalachian Regional Commission (ARC), an agency tasked with assisting economic development in the region. Rather than examine the creation of the ARC, which Ron Eller (2008), John Williams (2002), and others have already done, we take a different approach in this chapter. Looking back over almost five decades of ARC work, it is clear that its strategies have met with some success by providing federal funds for infrastructure projects such as highway construction, industrial park development for prospective businesses looking to locate in the region, vocational education enhancement to increase the availability of skilled labor, and increased access to health-care facilities (Gaventa and Lewis 1991; Keefe 2009).

Still, economic distress continues to differentiate counties in the central Appalachian coalfields of eastern Kentucky and West Virginia. Why is it that, despite large-scale federal efforts, mainstream development appears to have failed in this area?[1] We examine how "development" has been defined in the past and how Appalachian scholars might rethink that concept. Appalachian studies could contribute to a vision of an alternative future for the region, reimagining what is possible for Appalachian communities in both the field and the classroom. We begin by examining new possibilities for rethinking development in Appalachia by drawing upon the literature describing development studies from the Global South, then turn to studies of alternative economic practices. Each of these literatures offers new theories and methodologies that may prove fruitful in Appalachia. We then apply these theoretical and methodological ideas to the ways Appalachia was defined as an area in need of regional economic development, then examine how inhabitants of Appalachia have been represented in policy documents and what economic development strategies have been recommended. We close with a case study to better understand the history of development strategies—an examination of the final document produced by President John F. Kennedy's Appalachian Regional Commission, "Appalachia: A Report by the President's Appalachian Regional Commission, 1964" (hereafter the PARC report).[2] Our focus on this specific document, which helped to solidify and perpetuate a particular development discourse, is intended to reveal more about the development thinking applied to Appalachia. For the thirteen governors of Appalachian states, after all, the PARC report was the key to federal funding for state- and local-level development projects, providing the framework and foundation for the Appalachian Regional Development Act of 1965.

Our chapter emphasizes three themes that emerge in the language/ethos of the PARC report: (1) the problematic notion of isolation; (2) overemphasis on the role of state-organized economic development departments and private enterprise; and (3) the perception of the region's residents as human "resources" responsible for development policy outcomes. In the conclusion, we explore how today's local activists and researchers working in Appalachia, frustrated with the failure of conventional development practices, are searching for ideas beyond the borders of Appalachia and the ARC. Not only must new theories and methodologies be employed in the field, but Appalachian studies educators must convey critical theories to their students through engaged service-learning programs to provide opportunities to build ties between academic institutions and community-based organizations throughout the region.

Creating a New Regional Development Language

The future of the Appalachian region and Appalachian studies depends upon dialogue and collaboration with those working in poor, mountainous, rural regions around the world.[3] Critical literature on Global South ("Third World") development practices and policy documents provides a lens through which to conduct an analysis of the PARC report (e.g., see Crush 1995; Esteva 2010; Ferguson 1999; Li 2007, 2010; Wainwright 2008). This literature calls for an analysis of the narrative structures of Global North ("First World") economic development policy documents to determine "the ways that development is written, narrated and spoken; on the forms of knowledge that development produces and assumes; and on the power relations it underwrites and reproduces" (Williams 2002, 119; see also Crush 1995). Such language also reflects and creates the tensions, divisions, fractures, and struggles that occur as the result of particular development approaches (such as neoliberalization) and how groups and individuals experience the appropriation of resources (Jarosz 2011; Li 2007). "A close reading of documents can reveal an ethos, a way of defining problems and connecting them to solutions, that takes even the authors by surprise," adds Tania Murray Li. She further emphasizes that policy documents have *real effects*, often with unintended consequences. For example, "in the case of the [World] Bank program, the Indonesian nation took on $1 billion of debt on the basis of the document's narrative connecting problems to solutions. Hundreds of thousands of Indonesians participated in new ways of doing things prescribed by the Bank," Li observed (2010, 235).

It is important to conceive of development not as a thing but rather as a series of processes and performances, all of which, again, have real effects on groups and individuals. Researchers have found that development strategies employed by the ARC in the region tend to be short-term interventions. For example, economic geographer Michael Bradshaw, who has written about the ARC, observed: "The money available from government sources in countries with market economies will always be less than what is needed to make massive change possible; the involvement of politicians will always lead to a focus on short-term solutions to long-term problems. Public-policy regionalism is inevitably at most a catalyst: it may provide the structures and processes that assist change and improvement, but taking advantage of such provision must be done by individuals and groups at the local level" (2002, 330).[4] Unfortunately, short-term solutions, which render development strategies as "technical," often fail, especially when long-term problems such as a history of low wages, exploitation, out-migration, and resource extraction are not taken into account. Though many in the region have turned to alternative economic practices to make ends meet, development agencies around the world, including the ARC, have not generally deemed these methods as "development worthy" (for a detailed discussion, see Carnegie 2008).

Failing to acknowledge the importance of alternative economic practices in such a hostile economic context is a mistake (Carnegie 2008; Fickey 2011; Gibson-Graham 1996, 2006). For example, in central Appalachia the craft industry provides needed income to individuals who are no longer employed in mining and timber industries and to those who rely on state assistance (e.g., as a result of disability or black lung disease). Since the 1990s, employment in the coal industry has decreased as a result of mountaintop removal practices (MTR). Moreover, coal seams in eastern Kentucky are much thinner and far more difficult to access than those, for example, located in western states (such as Wyoming), leaving the region at a competitive disadvantage. Despite environmental devastation and loss of employment, proponents of MTR say it is needed to access smaller seams of coal. Although the use of MTR has increased over time, Appalachia has remained behind its western-based competitors in terms of overall U.S.-based coal production. In 2010, for example, the fourteen largest mines in the Appalachian region produced only

90,738,740 tons of bituminous coal, which was a little more than 8 percent of U.S. coal production for that year. In comparison, the top eleven U.S.-based mines in the same year produced about 444,565,767 tons of subbituminous coal, about 41 percent of total U.S. production. Nine of the top eleven mines are located in the Gillette coalfield of Wyoming. The remaining two are in Montana and North Dakota, respectively (Milici, Flores, and Stricker 2013).[5] Declining production, mechanization, MTR practices, and, most recently, cheap natural gas and worries about climate change have resulted in massive job losses in the Appalachian coalfields. The nonprofit agency Appalachian Voices (2012) reported that approximately 920 miners in Kentucky alone were laid off between December 2011 and April 2012.

The last decade has seen substantial growth in the study of alternative economic and political spaces (Fickey 2011; Fuller, Jonas, and Lee 2010; Jonas 2010; Leyshon, Lee, and Williams 2003), as well as the development of theories that challenge dominant discourses (Gibson-Graham 1996, 2005a, 2005b, 2006, 2008). Researchers studying economic diversity have encouraged scholars to "read for difference" and to demonstrate how noncapitalist *and* capitalist practices coexist in the economic landscape. Making visible activities that neoliberalism renders invisible expands the range of ideas for producing social livelihoods and economic development (Fickey 2011; Gibson-Graham 2008). In addition to craft production in central Appalachia, examples of such "alternative" economic practices include local currency systems such as local exchange trading systems, cooperatives, credit unions, barter networks, and social enterprises (Amin 2003; Fuller, Jonas, and Lee 2010; Jonas 2010; Lee 2006; Lee et al. 2004; Leyshon, Lee, and Williams 2003; North 2007; Williams, Aldridge, and Tooke 2003). Research pertaining to alternative economic practices is critical, because these practices can maintain livelihoods in rural regions with declining industries such as eastern Kentucky (Carnegie 2008; Fickey 2011; Oberhauser 2005; Pretes and Gibson 2008).

To consider them as development worthy, one must first recognize the prevalence of such alternative practices in the economic landscape and document the many ways in which people create sustainable livelihoods. In essence, the economic development community needs to broaden its language to incorporate more activities under the umbrella of "development." In a study of the village of Oelua in Indonesia, for example, Carnegie (2008) utilizes the heuristic framework created by Gibson-Graham (1996)—a typology of noncapitalist and capitalist practices—to catalog the ways in which noncapitalist practices sustain livelihoods, generate household income, and foster individual and community well-being. A primary goal is to create a language of economic diversity—recognizing the existence of noncapitalist economic transactions within the economy—that may then be utilized to widen the possibilities for local and regional economic development. Carnegie suggests that conversations with community members and researchers about how "surplus labor is (and could be) produced, appropriated, and distributed in ways that meet local needs, values and aspirations for building sustainable, ethical, place-based economies" should form the basis of economic development policy (2008, 367; quoted in Fickey 2011).

The President's Appalachian Regional Commission (PARC) Report of 1964

> At the request of the late President John F. Kennedy on April 9, 1963, the President's Appalachian Regional Commission was formed consisting of a representative designated by each of the Governors of the Appalachian States and a representative of the heads of major Federal departments and agencies. The President charged the Commission to prepare a comprehensive action program for the economic development of the Appalachian Region. Following the death of President Kennedy, our Commission received your direction to complete the preparation of this report.
>
> —Letter of transmittal, PARC 1964

The PARC report set a precedent for economic development strategies employed both inside and outside of Appalachia. The World Bank's "World Bank Report 2009: Reshaping Economic Geography" praised the 1965 Appalachian Regional Development Act (based on the 1964 report) as an excellent example of development policy that combined regionally coordinated social programs and physical infrastructure; in the report's language, such policies can "pay off" (World Bank 2009, 243). Despite the World Bank's attempt to provide a compelling narrative legitimating the 1965 Appalachian Regional Development Act, questions remain: If the 1965 act was so successful, why does poverty persist in Appalachia? Why is the World Bank blind to uneven economic development in the region? To address these questions, a close analysis of the language used in the 1964 report is required.

The PARC report depoliticizes economic problems, instead framing them as technical issues for development agencies to address. It disregards the region's legacy of absentee landownership, political corruption, low wages, and resource extraction and places the responsibility for development on Appalachian leaders and citizens. The report sees the role of the ARC as providing technical assistance and connective infrastructure to facilitate regional "modernization" so that Appalachia could eventually *catch up* with the rest of the United States. Three themes introduced earlier and repeated throughout the document call for closer examination.

THE "ISOLATION" OF APPALACHIA

> Appalachia is a region apart—geographically and statistically.
> —PARC 1964

Before a development agency can create and employ technical practices, a space for intervention must be defined. Identifying a space as distinct or different is an essential feature of development practices. As Li explains, "To render a set of processes technical and improvable an arena of intervention must be bounded, mapped, characterized, and documented; the relevant forces and relations must be identified; and a narrative must be devised connecting the proposed intervention to the problem it will solve" (2007, 126). The PARC report characterizes Appalachia as geographically and topologically isolated. The Appalachian region, the report states, is "upthrust between the prosperous Eastern seaboard and the industrial Middle West." The report further notes that "although the region includes a natural endowment of the nation's richest coal seams, abundant rainfall higher than the rest of the nation, and some of the most beautiful mountains in the Eastern United States, the Appalachian inhabitant (as a result of isolation) has failed to match his counterpart outside of the region as a participant in the nation's economic growth" (PARC 1964, xv). The report argues that to overcome this isolation, roads and air facilities must be built throughout the region "to serve a particular purpose, primarily to bring traffic into the region. This investment is seen as being crucial to stimulating economic growth" (28).

Appalachian studies has effectively challenged the assumption of regional isolation, documenting the many ways in which Appalachia has been socially, economically, and politically connected to other geographic areas (see, e.g., Billings and Blee 2000; Dunn 1988; Eller 1982, 2008; Gaventa and Lewis 1991; Schwarzweller et al. 1971). Because the PARC report preceded these studies, its authors did not have the benefit of this research. However, the authors of the PARC report failed to research the topic themselves and ignored any evidence of regional connection. Their assumption of isolation, without empirical investigation, justified the construction of transportation infrastructure as the central development strategy. The report states:

> The highland isolation must be overcome with modern roads and air facilities. The ribbon-towns must be provided with the amenities of urban life. A

substantial effort in education, health facilities, employment services, community apparatus—all the items of social overhead neglected for long decades—
must be made. The quality of such investment is essential. But its character is
even more important. It must be directed to the stimulation of growth, *and
not to the problems which result from growth as is the case with most of our
present public investment.* (PARC 1964, 28; emphasis added)

The ARC could not address all of the factors associated with economic
growth, such as lack of available housing or environmental degradation, nor
could the commission control the results of industrial growth that could take
place in the region once new roads were constructed. Thus, authors advocated investing capital in the region to stimulate growth through transportation infrastructure—this was the technical issue on which the ARC would
eventually focus. While tourism-related traffic is mentioned by the authors,
the report emphasizes the need to link the region to industrial centers to
increase exchanges among people, products, and ideas. The report's authors
argue that the region's "penetration by an adequate transportation network
is the first requisite of its full participation in industrial America," and they
go on to suggest that "the goal of the highway system would be to improve
travel to remote areas, to stimulate the flow of people and goods, and to open
areas where commerce has been inhibited" (PARC 1964, 32, 33).

Only a few pages later, the PARC report describes the relationship between
transportation infrastructure and the extraction of resources: the creation of
highways would provide access to previously unexploited areas. In regard to
timber production, the report recommends accelerating "the construction
of access roads in the national forests to enable the harvesting of the full al-
lowable cut of marketable timber" (PARC 1964, 41). As for coal, "all efforts
at increasing coal production—both for domestic and foreign uses—must
be vigorously pursued if the region is to obtain maximum economic benefit
from this resource" (42). When coal production is understood within the
context of the national economy—rather than in isolation—the results of
this federally subsidized highway construction effort become clear: it allows
energy corporations to export coal to fuel markets outside the region; feeds
and creates greater demand for coal (Weisenfluh et al. 1996); makes Appalachian coal more competitive with other fuel sources; and (eventually and
unintentionally) causes global climate change. Writing in 1996, Weisenfluh
and colleagues note that more coal in Kentucky was being mined than ever
before while using a smaller number of employees and providing a limited
amount of local surplus distribution, a trend that has continued until very
recently. In other words, the PARC report supports a deepening and extension

of the private capitalist resource extraction that had occurred in the region since the late 1800s, the same strategy that made the region economically depressed. Public investment in these transportation networks would only reinforce the class power of the elite, particularly of coal and timber company owners (Massey 2003).

State-Sponsored, Private Enterprise–Centered Development Schemes

> Private enterprise will be the ultimate employer.
> —PARC 1964

By the 1930s, many states had established development departments aimed at generating economic activity, a fact acknowledged in the PARC. Such agencies, it said, were "staffed by dedicated men and women who have created a climate of hope and enthusiasm throughout the region. Each of the development programs that had been established has the firm support of state political leaders and the cooperation of local officials in communities" (PARC 1964, 24). The role of regional entrepreneurs and development professionals was crucial to the success of this enterprise, as the PARC notes: "Serving in their individual capacities, as members of local committees formed under the area development or rural areas development programs, as members of state and local development organizations—they have provided a substance of effort *which no governmental effort could possibly attain*" (26; emphasis added). Note the care taken by PARC to diminish the efficacy of government development efforts in favor of the work done by private individuals and business leaders.

Tempered by the resistance to the Tennessee Valley Authority, the ARC was intended to provide federal funds to support state development agencies. The commission that was created, however, did little more than serve as a consultant to these states: "Advocates made much of this unique federal-state partnership, but the long-run implication suggested that the ARC was more a regional consulting than a coordinating body" (Williams 2002, 341). During a time of competition among states nationwide, the creation of the ARC met with opposition due to the competitive advantage it provided Appalachia. The act "would provide preferential treatment to one region of the U.S., thereby discriminating against other areas with equal or greater economic problems," noted ARC critics (quoted in Farrigan and Glasmeier 2005, 11), although it passed in spite of opposition. Smaller regional plans had been developed in the United States, including the Four Corners, Ozarks, Coastal Plains, New

England, and Upper Great Lakes regions. The multistate plan for Appalachia was different, however, as Estall explains: "An unusual feature of the Appalachian Regional Development Act was its provisions for local planning organizations and its requirement that the public investments made in the region under this Act shall be concentrated in areas where there is a significant potential for future growth and where the expected return on the public dollars invested will be the greatest" (1982, 47). This policy led to the practice of investing in growth centers, which often widened the gap between urban and rural locations. The commission argued that funding would provide the *thrust* for growth in the region (particularly in the growth centers), and it would be individual private entrepreneurs who would be responsible for the success of development. As the report states, "The final purpose of the actions recommended in this report is to assist growth and development at the local level—*to enable people to help themselves*" (PARC 1964, 53; emphasis added), a stance that anticipates the neoliberal policies of the 1980s and 1990s.

Once the commission injected monies, it was argued, responsibility for the further improvement of the region would be shifted to the rational and maximizing entrepreneur who would have the skill set and capital to stimulate growth (Amin 2003, 48). As the report stressed, most local businessmen would indeed have "access to traditional channels for private equity capital, and private sources of short- and long-term credit required for the regional development activities included in the report" (PARC 1964, 53). Thus, the report once again reaffirmed the class power of the local elites—those who have access to capital to invest in the proposed projects. How do the nonelite regional residents fit into this economic development scheme? They are the main *resources* in the region.

> Humans: the most important resource in the region

> On behalf of the people of the Appalachian Region, for whom this program can bring sorely needed new opportunity and upon whose shoulders will rest the final responsibility for success, we express our appreciation to the late President John F. Kennedy for his action in establishing this commission. (letter of support on behalf of the Conference of Appalachian Governors, Washington, D.C., in PARC 1964, iv)

Under the heading "Human Resources," the PARC report states, "The programs of access and physical resource development in the foregoing are validated only by the enlargement of hope and genuine opportunity they offer to this region's most valuable resource—its people. But programs must also be initiated which are focused more directly on the people themselves" (PARC

1964, 48). These programs would focus on meeting the basic needs of the region's inhabitants, including food, clothing, medical care, housing, education, skills, and jobs. Again, these issues are framed as technical. Rather than addressing *why* these problems existed, the report simply offers technical ways of addressing such issues. For example, vocational schools were to be built in more remote areas, job training offered, financial support made available for children and the elderly, regional health centers constructed, the school lunch program expanded, and inadequate housing improved (PARC 1964).

The Office of Economic Opportunity (OEO), part of President Lyndon Baines Johnson's "War on Poverty," would assume responsibility for most of these human-resource initiatives, while the ARC would handle infrastructure-related concerns. Unfortunately, most of the federal dollars sent to the region were diverted and absorbed by local elites. Hence, the federal government consistently failed to address class relations when generating development policies. A situation was created in which the improvements sought by the ARC could not be realized because federal funds reinforced the status quo and did not encourage social change. The failure to examine social history critically, common among First World development agencies, resulted in a failure of economic development policy. Or, as Li explains it, "an important reason promised improvements are not delivered is that the diagnosis is incomplete. . . . [I]t cannot be complete if key political-economic processes are excluded from the bounded, knowable, technical domain" (2007, 18).

The dismantling of the OEO by the Reagan administration in 1981 caused conflict among local elites. As Ronald D Eller writes, "Elites fought over control of poverty dollars. Authority over public housing and economic development programs became as important as control of county roads and schools, and local political machines clashed with state and even federal authorities to maintain their influence" (2008, 156). A crack developed in the foundation of elite power in Appalachia, and the region's citizens began to articulate a more critical awareness of regional poverty. ARC and OEO failures can be usefully compared and contrasted to those of development agencies in the Global South (Ferguson 1999; Li 2007; Wainwright 2008). For example, Li (2007) finds that the people of Sulawesi came to share the same desires as the development professionals. Rather than become depoliticized through failed technical development projects, the people there applied a critical sensibility to these development schemes (Li 2007). In an analysis of development efforts in the Zambian Copperbelt, Ferguson (1999) demonstrates how inhabitants had the same aspirations for development as the developers. However, as mining in the Copperbelt began to decline, leading to an overall economic decline, socioeconomic opportunities were taken away from Zambians, prompting a critical awareness of their forcible exclusion from a global market. Wainwright's (2008) work echoes these sentiments, documenting how Mayans who suffered from multiple development failures experienced their own critical awakening and became involved in countermapping practices in collaboration with Wainwright and several geographers from the University of California–Berkeley.

This analysis of recent critical Global South development scholarship allows us to highlight the significance of Eller's (2008) work within the context of Appalachian studies. Following a similar line of thinking as these researchers, Eller notes the unintended effects of the failed development initiatives implemented by the ARC and the War on Poverty on Appalachia's inhabitants. Paradoxically, while the War on Poverty failed, it unintentionally succeeded in mobilizing residents of the region to express their understanding of the political, rather than the technical, aspects of regional poverty, as Eller explains:

> The War on Poverty generated a degree of independence and assertiveness that undermined the old tradition of deference to authority and laid the groundwork for collective action on a variety of labor, health, and environmental issues. Low-income community leaders found common ground with their counterparts in neighboring counties on problems of welfare and social services; coal mining families from eastern Kentucky joined with others in West Virginia and Ohio to press for mine safety and union reform; young volunteer organizers from across the region established networks to oppose strip mining, outlaw the broad form deed, document absentee land ownership, and lobby for fair taxation. Out of the crucible of community action came a variety of regional movements and a new space of regional organizations. (2008, 157)

Although the ARC and OEO may not have anticipated these outcomes, their development efforts played a crucial role in fomenting resistance in Appalachia; the field of Appalachian studies became an added voice in that resistance.

Rethinking "Development" and Imagining Alternatives

> These mountains have stood throughout history as nearly impenetrable barriers to socioeconomic interaction, commerce, and prosperity. Appalachia is a place apart, a place where people have long-suffered the chronic economic consequences of physical isolation.
> —Appalachian Regional Commission 2009

In setting the standard for federal- and state-led economic development, the PARC report raises questions: were the recommendations in this report the only possible options for this region? If we think outside the dominant discourse of economic development practices, what might we imagine? Apparently, the ARC is unable to think outside its own discursive box, because in November 2009 it released a new study: "Networking Appalachia: Access to Global Opportunity." Once again, the report focuses on the "commercial importance of intermodal transportation networks." Building its argument on the same misconception of regional isolation that Appalachian scholars have worked diligently to deconstruct, the 2009 report replicates the 1964 PARC report discourse. Even though Appalachian studies has demonstrated that Appalachia's poverty is a result of the terms of its integration with the global capitalist economy—not isolation (Billings 2002; Billings and Blee 2000; Eller 1982; Gaventa 1980)—the introduction to the 2009 report (sections 1.0 and 1.1) begins *literally* with the same framework as the 1964 PARC report:

> Recognizing both obstacles and the potential facing the Region, the President's Appalachian Regional Commission (PARC) opened its 1964 report to President Lyndon Johnson, thus the following: "Appalachia is a region apart—geographically and statistically. It is a mountain land boldly upthrust between the prosperous Eastern seaboard and the industrial Mid-West—a highland region which sweeps diagonally from New York to Mississippi . . ." Recognizing the linkage between the isolation and economic distress, the PARC report emphasized, "Developmental activity in Appalachia cannot proceed until the regional isolation has been overcome." (Appalachian Regional Commission 2009, 2)

The 2009 report once again advocates for the construction of transportation networks to attract new business and employment to the region while pointing out the disjointedness and disorganization of regional transportation networks, many of which were developed through the ARC's own Appalachian Regional Highway Development program.

Based on the inadequacy of conventional development practices, the search for new ideas has moved well beyond the borders of Appalachia and beyond the reach of the ARC's Washington, D.C., beltway. Promising models for the region can be found in worker cooperatives in Spain's Mondragon region, networked niche-based firms in Italy, and the World Social Forum in Brazil (Billings 2002). Rural regions, especially those dominated by one extractive industry, must begin advocating for economic diversity and fighting for control of surplus distribution. Such an aim is in direct contrast to the ARC, whose highway projects have historically provided access to previously "untouched" resources, thus facilitating not only the extraction of such resources but also the extraction of wealth from the region, not to mention out-migration.

These problems are not unique to Appalachia; they can be found in rural, poor communities throughout the world. Struggles to foster economic diversity and to fight for redistribution of resources, however, must be grounded in local contexts to succeed. Activists, scholars, and development practitioners must understand the social solidarities and fissures of different communities and be attuned to the wants and desires of community members. They must push for policy change rather than promote decontextualized technical strategies. Given intraregional diversity, policy makers must allow economic development strategies for Appalachia to emerge from the bottom up rather than force them on communities from the top down. More space must be given to "alternative" or noncapitalist approaches, such as cooperatives, local currencies, credit unions, and social enterprise, even as they will necessarily become entangled with neoliberal practices and conventional development models operating in the region and the world.

In spite of the ascendancy of neoliberal policies globally since the 1980s, noncapitalist practices continue to thrive in Appalachia and elsewhere (for examples of diversity, see Gibson-Graham 1996; for Appalachian-related examples, see Graham, Healy, and Byrne 2002; Oberhauser 2005). Take, for example, the diversity that exists within eastern Kentucky's craft industry. The Kentucky Craft Marketing Program, as a state-based initiative, offers workshops that teach entrepreneurialism and self-sufficiency. Artists are encouraged to participate in microfinancing opportunities, such as Small Business Administration loans, to obtain the capital needed to support opening their own business and supporting production. Craft producers do not always embrace a state-promoted campaign of self-sufficiency, however. In recent years, independent craft cooperatives have reemerged in eastern Kentucky's handicraft industry, and, in some cases, artists collectively pool time and capital.[6] One such example is the Sheltowee Co-op Art Shop, located in Somerset, Kentucky. Income generated through the sale of craft items is given back to the artists. In this scenario, artists become the first distributors of the surplus (profit) generated. Furthermore, artists allocate a collectively agreed-upon percentage of surplus to a community reserve that all artists may access, directly challenging the "you're on your own" premise of neoliberalism. The Sheltowee Co-op members control the surplus they generate, thus avoiding a central trauma of capitalist exploitation: the inability of workers to access surplus in order to pursue projects, or "social possibilities" (Community Economies Collective 2001). A cooperative approach provides an expansion of social possibilities, allowing crafters to create and revise their own notions of "the good life" and decide for themselves how surplus should be distributed.

Other examples, both new and old, include David Appalachian Crafts, a nonprofit crafts cooperative organization located in David, Kentucky. Founded in 1971 and in existence until its closing in 2013, David Appalachian Crafts provided opportunities for over sixty-five craft producers to supplement their income (http://davidappalachiancrafts.com). The organization received funding from St. Vincent Mission, a Catholic mission serving the Appalachian region. Many religious organizations, such as David Appalachian Crafts and Red Bird Mission Crafts (a Methodist organization that remains open), have managed to keep themselves afloat through national and international support received from church members. Regrettably, St. Vincent Mission is no longer able to provide financial support for David Appalachian Crafts, and the organization was closed in August 2013. With regard to such faith-based organizations, however, questions of poverty and social justice remain crucial. These organizations market their products based on tradition and authenticity but also poverty amelioration.[7] According to one person interviewed,

> With David Appalachian Crafts and Red Bird Mission, they can incorporate into their marketing social justice issues as well as quality work. So they can market a finely made basket not only as a finely made basket, but as a finely-made basket that supports a low-income family in Appalachia. And that, to the consumer, means that they can do twice as much with their dollar because they can buy something they like for themselves personally or to give as a gift, and, they can also feel like, *and actually be making a contribution to a family and a region that is a little bit out of the economic mainstream.*[8]

Note that this interviewee, an industry leader who had worked with arts-related programs throughout the region for over thirty years, sees the region as "a little bit out of the economic mainstream." Again, the idea that the region's poverty is caused by a disconnection from the "national" and the "global economy" is common. It also attests to the hegemonic assumption about the region's being in but not of America. Such (mis)understanding of the "regional economy" limits the possibilities that might be imagined for Appalachia's future.

Inspiring a New Generation of Critical Thinking about Development in Appalachia

The search for alternative development practices must involve rethinking surplus distribution in communities and acknowledging the impact of globalization throughout the region. Appalachian studies must work in and with communities in the region to collectively reimagine what is possible for Appalachia. The process of reimagining must also inspire a new generation of Appalachian studies students, researchers, activists, and practitioners to work within and for the region, exploring new theories and methodologies in both research and pedagogy. It must encourage students to examine alternative economic practices, teach them to recognize these practices in the economic landscape, and engage such practices directly with community members and activists.

To this end, service-learning projects should be designed to apply classroom learning, to teach critical thinking, to inspire hope, to nurture a commitment to social change, and to create a useful product (for both the students and the community). Indeed, Appalachian studies instructors must ensure students get out of the classroom and into the region to deepen learning. For example, in the fall of 2010, the first author took students in a University of Kentucky Appalachian geography class to a postmining community in southeastern Kentucky, providing them with insights how postmining communities create livelihood strategies (Fickey and Rieske-Kinney 2011; Grabbatin and Fickey 2012; Oberhauser 2005). Before traveling to the community, students learned about the history and geography of Appalachia over the past two hundred years in a course ("Land, People, and Development in Appalachia") and completed readings about critical development, diverse economies, and alternative economic and political spaces.

The University of Kentucky Appalachian Center, Appalachian Studies Program and an AmeriCorps VISTA worker located in the southeastern Kentucky community helped to build relationships between local community members and the students. During the field trip, students spoke with local entrepreneurs and government officials to gain a deeper understanding of the difficulties faced by rural people with limited capital. This place-based approach challenged the students from Appalachia and those who grew up outside the region to examine place through the lens of critical development and alternative economic practices by exploring new and diverse understandings of "the good life" (Fickey 2011; Fickey and Hanrahan 2014; McKinnon 2010). After completing the field trip, students conducted interviews with regional leaders and wrote reports about southeastern Kentucky organizations engaged in alternative economic development strategies. Each student examined the development practices of organizations of their own choosing. They also participated in those organizations and assessed the benefits they offered to the region.

Final reports were submitted for review to the Mountain Association for Community Economic Development (MACED), located in Berea, Kentucky. Several of the reports were published as part of the Alternative Transitions Initiative, which featured the stories under the heading "Student Stories" (see http://appalachiantransition.net/stories).[9] For example, a student explored the value in small-scale sustainable agricultural practices and conducted an interview with Dr. Bill Best at the Sustainable Mountain Agriculture Center in Madison County, Kentucky (Coleman 2011). Even though the project was limited to a semester-long time frame, students learned that they could critically analyze development discourse in Appalachia. Through this project, students made visible the alternative economic practices that a capitalist discourse renders invisible (Gibson-Graham 1996, 2006; Lee 2010).[10]

Conclusion

The preceding analysis of the top-down development recommendations of the 1964 PARC report demonstrates how Appalachia was defined as an area in need of regional economic development, how Appalachians were represented by the ARC, and how economic development discourse limited the strategies deployed by the ARC. This report provided a limited development discourse that continues to be invoked today.

For those who are committed to social change, new paths were suggested for rethinking development strategies in Appalachian studies in terms of both literatures to engage and methodologies to use in classrooms and communities. It is not fruitful to perpetuate the idea that regions move through a preset series of stages, as modernization theory strives to do. Instead, a new discourse is needed that encourages Appalachians to define "the good life" in their own terms and in places of their own choosing. Appalachian studies has taken the first step in deconstructing the predominant discourse concerning the Appalachian region as isolated, deficient, and a social problem. Now it is time to think even more critically about the economic development policies deployed in the region and to commit the field to expanding economic development language, imagination, and practices.

ACKNOWLEDGMENTS

We would like to thank our editors, Shaunna Scott, Phil Obermiller, and Chad Berry, for providing us with the opportunity to contribute to this collection and offering thoughtful comments throughout the writing process. We are also grateful to Sue Roberts and Martin Hess for their comments on an earlier draft of this chapter.

Notes

1. In her work on participatory development in Appalachia, Susan Keefe (2009) notes that "well over three-quarters of all ARC money goes to build highways and more than 2,600 miles have been constructed at a cost almost $10 billion" (6).

2. The analysis of this report is based on Fickey (2011), and portions of the original analysis have been edited/expanded throughout this chapter. The Appalachian Regional Commission has made the full PARC report available online for researchers and instructors: http://www.arc.gov/about/ARCAppalachiaAReportbythePresidents AppalachianRegionalCommission1964.asp.

3. For an engaging and thoughtful roundtable discussion on the future of Appalachian studies, see the Spring/Fall 2010 issue of the *Journal of Appalachian Studies*.

4. See also Bradshaw (1992), which provides a very detailed and engaging analysis of this federal agency.

5. It is important to note that Milici, Flores, and Stricker (2013) do make the point that reduced transportation costs may actually result in maintaining competitiveness of Appalachian coal in certain regional markets: "The costs of transporting these western coals to markets in the eastern and southern parts of the United States, however, allow coals mined in the Interior and Appalachian Regions to remain competitive in nearby markets. Also, their significantly higher heat content allows these coals to be competitive" (3).

6. We are deeply cognizant of the contradiction that is engendered by our implicit and sometimes explicit critique of "capitalist social relations" and capitalism, on the one hand, and by our affinity for the Co-op's use of "capital," which can only be generated from capitalist social relations in themselves, on the other. This is then clearly an acknowledgement of the "reformist" tendencies of the diverse/alternative economies literature, tendencies that not only underscore the variety of noncapitalist and quasi-capitalist organizations illuminated by this body of work but also strike at the heart of some of the criticisms of the diverse/alternative economies literature.

7. This section draws upon Fickey (2011) and Fickey and Samers (2014). Please see these works for a full discussion pertaining to the role of state-based craft-marketing programs, geographical lores, and alternative economic practices within eastern Kentucky's craft industry.

8. Interviewee 2, interviewed by Amanda Fickey, 2008, emphasis added, Eastern Kentucky Handcraft Industry, University of Kentucky Louie B. Nunn Oral History Center.

9. The Alternative Transition Initiative, led by MACED and Kentuckians for the Commonwealth, seeks to advocate for economic development strategies other than the extraction of natural resources.

10. For a detailed discussion pertaining to service learning within the field of geography and academia in general, see Grabbatin and Fickey (2012).

Works Cited

Amin, Ash. 2003. "An Institutionalist Perspective on Regional Economic Development." In *Reading Economic Geography*, edited by Trevor J. Barnes, Jamie Peck, Eric Sheppard, and Adam Tickell, 48–58. Malden: Blackwell Publishing.

Appalachian Regional Commission. 2009. "Networking Appalachia: Access to Global Opportunity." http://www.arc.gov. Accessed November 1, 2012.

Appalachian Voices. 2012. "Appalachian Coal Jobs Update—June 2012." http://www.appvoices.org. Accessed December 27, 2012.

Ball, C. E. 2000. "Historical Overview of Beef Production and Beef Organizations in the United States." *Journal of Animal Science* 79:1–8.

Billings, Dwight B. 2002. "Economic Representations in an American Region: What's at Stake in Appalachia?" Economic Representations Essay, part of the Economic Representations Conference held at the Rockefeller Foundation's Bellagio Study and Conference Center, Bellagio, Italy. http://www.nd.edu/~econrep/bellagio.html. Accessed November 14, 2012.

Billings, Dwight B., and Kathleen Blee. 2000. *The Road to Poverty: The Making of Wealth and Hardship in Appalachia*. New York: Cambridge University Press.

Bradshaw, Michael. 1992. *The Appalachian Regional Commission: Twenty-Five Years of Government Policy*. Lexington: University Press of Kentucky.

———. 2002. "A Political Approach to Regional Development." In *Appalachia: Social Context Past and Present*, 4th ed., edited by Phillip J. Obermiller and Michael Maloney, 318–69. Dubuque, Iowa: Kendall/Hunt Publishing Company.

Carnegie, Michelle. 2008. "Development Prospects in Eastern Indonesia: Learning from Oelua's Diverse Economy." *Asia Pacific Viewpoint* 49(3): 354–69.

Caudill, Harry M. 1963. *Night Comes to the Cumberlands: A Biography of a Depressed Area*. Boston: Little, Brown.

Coleman, Caroline. 2011. "Sustainable Agriculture." Student Series: Saving Seeds and Sustainable Agriculture. http://appalachiantransition.net/content/student-series-saving-seeds-and-sustainable-agriculture. Accessed November 29, 2012.

Community Economies Collective. 2001. "Imagining and Enacting Noncapitalist Futures." *Socialist Review* 28: 3–4.

Crush, Jonathan, ed. 1995. *Power of Development*. London: Routledge.

David Appalachian Crafts. "About Us." http://davidappalachiancrafts.com/AboutUs.asp. Accessed November 20, 2012.

Dunn, Durwood. 1988. *Cades Cove: The Life and Death of a Southern Appalachian Community*. Knoxville: University of Tennessee Press.

Eblen, Tom. 2009. "East Kentucky's Future Hinges on Altering Relationship with Coal." *Lexington Herald-Leader*, April 25.

Eller, Ronald D. 1982. *Miners, Millhands, and Mountaineers: Industrialization of the Appalachian South, 1880–1930*. Knoxville: University of Tennessee Press.

———. 2008. *Uneven Ground: Appalachia since 1945*. Lexington: University Press of Kentucky.

Estall, Robert. 1982. "Planning in Appalachia: An Examination of the Appalachian Regional Development Programme and Its Implications for the Future of the American Regional Planning Commissions." *Transactions of the Institute of British Geographers* 7(1): 35–58.

Esteva, G. 2010. "What Is Development?" In *The International Studies Compendium Project*, edited by Robert A. Denemark and Renée Marlin-Bennett. Oxford: Wiley-Blackwell.

Farrigan, T. L., and A. K. Glasmeier. 2005. "Economic Development Administration: Legislative History." In *Poverty in America: One Nation, Pulling Apart*, edited by A. K. Glasmeier. http://povertyinamerica.mit.edu/products/publications/.

Ferguson, James. 1999. *Expectations of Modernity: Myths and Meanings of Urban Life on the Zambian Copperbelt*. Berkeley: University of California Press.

Fickey, Amanda. 2011. "'The Focus Has to Be on Helping People Make a Living': Exploring Diverse Economies and Alternative Economic Spaces." *Geography Compass* 5(5): 237–48.

Fickey, Amanda, and Kelsey Hanrahan. 2014. "Thinking beyond *Neverland*: Reflecting upon the State of the Diverse Economies Research Program and the Study of Alternative Economic Spaces." *ACME: An International E-Journal for Critical Geographies* 13:394–403.

Fickey, Amanda, and Lynne K. Rieske-Kinney. 2011. "Cultural Industries and Invasive Species: Ecological Threats to Handicraft Production in Central Appalachia." *anthropologies* (open source, online journal) 8, http://www.anthropologiesproject.org/2011/11/issue-8.html.

Gaventa, John. 1980. *Power and Powerlessness: Quiescence and Rebellion in an Appalachian Valley*. Oxford: Clarendon Press.

Gaventa, John, and Helen Lewis. 1991. "Participatory Education and Grassroots Development: The Case of Rural Appalachia." Gatekeeper Series No. 25, Sustainable Agriculture Programme of the International Institute for Environment and Development, London.

Gibson-Graham, J. K. 1996. *The End of Capitalism (as We Knew It): A Feminist Critique of Political Economy*. Minneapolis: University of Minnesota Press.

———. 2005a. "Surplus Possibilities: Postdevelopment and Community Economies." *Singapore Journal of Tropical Geography* 26(1): 4–26.

———. 2005b. "Traversing the Fantasy of Sufficiency: A Response to Aguilar, Kelly and Lawson." *Singapore Journal of Tropical Geography* 26(2): 119–26.

———. 2006. *A Postcapitalist Politics*. Minneapolis: University of Minnesota Press.

———. 2008. "Diverse Economies: Performative Practices for 'Other Worlds'" (includes online bibliography). *Progress in Human Geography* 32(5): 613–32.

Grabbatin, Brian, and Amanda Fickey. 2012. "Service-Learning: Critical Traditions and Geographic Pedagogy." *Journal of Geography* 11(6): 254–60.

Graham, Julie, Stephen Healy, and Kevin Byrne. 2002. "Constructing the Community Economy: Civic Professionalism and the Politics of Sustainable Regions." *Journal of Appalachian Studies* 8(1): 49–60.

Hunts, G. L., and H. Daniels. 2008. "Coal: Inconvenient Truths." *Public Utilities Fortnightly* 146(2): 1–66.

Jarosz, Lucy. 2011. "Gender and the Dialectics of Development." *Annals of the Association of American Geographers* 100(1): 225–26.

Jonas, Andrew E. G. 2010. "'Alternative' This, 'Alternative' That . . . : Interrogating Alterity and Diversity." In *Interrogating Alterity: Alternative Economic and Political Spaces*, edited by Duncan Fuller, Andrew E. G. Jonas, and Roger Lee, 3–30. Farnham: Ashgate Publishing.

Keefe, Susan. 2009. *Participatory Development in Appalachia: Cultural Identity, Community, and Sustainability*. Knoxville: University of Tennessee Press.

Lee, Roger. 2006. "The Ordinary Economy: Tangled Up in Values and Geography." *Transactions of the Institute of British Geographers* 31:412–32.

Lee, Roger. 2010. "Spiders, Bees, or Architects? Imagination and the Radical Immanence of Alternatives/Diversity for Political Economic Geographies." In *Interrogating Alterity: Alternative Economic and Political Spaces*, edited by Duncan Fuller, Andrew E. G. Jonas, and Roger Lee, 273–87. Farnham: Ashgate Publishing.

Lee, Roger, Andrew Leyshon, J. Tooke Aldridge, Collin Williams, and Nigel Thrift. 2004. "Making Geographies and Histories? Constructing Local Circuits of Value." *Environment and Planning D, Society and Space* 22: 595–617.

Leyshon, Andrew, Roger Lee, and Colin C. Williams, eds. 2003. *Alternative Economic Spaces*. London: Sage Publications.

Li, Tania Murray. 2007. *The Will to Improve: Governmentality, Development, and the Practice of Politics*. Durham, N.C.: Duke University Press.

———. 2010. "Revisiting 'The Will to Improve.'" *Annals of the Association of American Geographers* 100(1): 233–35.

Massey, Doreen. 2003. "Uneven Development: Social Change and Spatial Divisions of Labor." In *Reading Economic Geography*, edited by Trevor J. Barnes, Jamie Peck, Eric Sheppard, and Adam Tickell, 111–24. Malden: Blackwell Publishing.

McKinnon, K. 2010. "Diverse Present(s), Alternative Futures." In *Interrogating Alterity: Alternative Economic and Political Spaces*, edited by Duncan Fuller, Andrew E. G. Jonas, and Roger Lee, 259–72. Farnham: Ashgate Publishing.

Milici, Robert C., Romeo M. Flores, and Gary D. Stricker. 2013. "Coal Resources, Reserves, and Peak Coal Production in the United States." *International Journal of Coal Geology* 113:109–15.

North, Peter. 2007. *Money and Liberation: The Micropolitics of Alternative Currency Movements.* Minneapolis: University of Minnesota Press.

Oberhauser, Ann M. 2005. "Scaling Gender and Diverse Economies: Perspectives from Appalachia and South Africa." *Antipode* 37(4): 863–74.

Oxford English Dictionary (online). http://www.oed.com. Accessed November 1, 2010.

PARC (President's Appalachian Regional Commission). 1964. "Appalachia: A Report by the President's Appalachian Regional Commission, 1964." http://www.arc.gov. Accessed October 25, 2012.

Pretes, Michael, and Katherine Gibson. 2008. "Openings in the Body 'Capitalism': Capital Flows and Diverse Economic Possibilities in Kiribati." *Asia Pacific Viewpoint* 49(3): 381–91.

Raitz, Karl B., and Richard Ulack. 1984. *Appalachia, a Regional Geography: Land, People, and Development.* Boulder, Colo.: Westview Press.

Salstrom, Paul. 1994. *Appalachia's Path to Dependency: Rethinking a Region's Economic History.* Lexington: University Press of Kentucky.

Samers, Michael. 2005. "The Myopia of 'Diverse Economies,' or a Critique of the 'Informal Economy.'" *Antipode* 37(4): 875–86.

Schwarzweller, Harry K., James S. Brown, and J. J. Managalam. 1971. *Mountain Families in Transition: A Case Study of Appalachian Migration.* University Park: Pennsylvania State University Press.

Wainwright, Joel. 2008. *Decolonizing Development: Colonial Power and the Maya.* Malden: Blackwell Publishing.

Waller, Altina L. 1988. *Feud: Hatfields, McCoys, and Social Change in Appalachia, 1860–1900.* Chapel Hill: University of North Carolina Press.

Waselkov, Gregory A., Peter H. Wood, and Michael T. Hatley, eds. 1989 (revised 2006). *Powhatan's Mantle: Indians in the Colonial Southeast.* Lincoln: University of Nebraska Press.

Weisenfluh, G., J. Cobb, J. Ferm, and C. Ruthven. 1996. "Kentucky's Coal Industry: Historical Trends and Future Opportunities." In *Exploring the Frontier of the Future,* edited by Kentucky Long-Term Policy Research Center, 145–55. Frankfort: Kentucky Long-Term Policy Center.

Williams, Colin C., Theresa Aldridge, and Jane Tooke. 2003. "Alternative Exchange Spaces." In *Alternative Economic Spaces,* edited by Andrew Leyshon, Roger Lee, and Colin C. Williams, 151–67. Sage: London.

Williams, John Alexander. 2002. *Appalachia: A History.* Chapel Hill: University of North Carolina Press.

World Bank. 2009. "World Bank Report 2009: Reshaping Economic Geography." http://web.worldbank.org. Accessed November 13, 2012.

6

Studying Appalachia
Critical Reflections

PHILLIP J. OBERMILLER AND SHAUNNA L. SCOTT

This chapter seeks to identify both strengths and weaknesses in the field of Appalachian studies, its insights and contributions, as well as its blind spots and omissions. The chapter functions as a signpost for people who are interested in Appalachian studies, guiding them toward areas, projects, and questions in need of attention. As a signpost, however, the chapter contains many arrows pointing toward a variety of locations and issues, because Appalachian studies, like the region, is not monolithic; it encompasses a variety of participants with their own points of view.

In an effort to capture the diversity, contradictions, and tensions inherent in the field, our essay is based on interviews with thirty-two people involved with the region as scholars, artists, practitioners, and activists, as well as previously published collections and essays about the field of Appalachian studies. The latter includes special issues of the *Appalachian Journal,* "A Guide to Appalachian Studies" and "Assessing Appalachian Studies"; the "Rethinking Appalachian Studies Series" published in the *Journal of Appalachian Studies*; and various other collections, speeches, and essays.

This chapter, however, is not a simple compilation of these opinions. It is, rather, our version of a conversation that has unfolded in recent decades. Appalachian studies is an interdisciplinary educational, research, artistic, and practical enterprise that extends well beyond its professional association and journals. The field can trace its roots to missionary, literary, and activist projects more than a century old, and many influential works were published or under way before the study of the region coalesced into a formal academic field in the late 1970s (Caudill 1963; Ford 1962; Shapiro 1978;

Weller 1965). This essay does not retread that ground; instead, it provides critical reflection about Appalachian studies based on more recent readings and conversations in the field.

Reflecting on Appalachian Studies

Around the time that the Appalachian Studies Conference was formed in 1977, the *Appalachian Journal* published a special issue assessing the field.[1] In it, Steve Fisher's (1977) introductory essay presaged some of the matters with which the field still grapples. Fisher noted a tendency to organize "safe" or noncontroversial courses that would not raise administrative or collegial eyebrows by making tradition, culture, and heritage focal topics, relegating social, political, and economic analyses to the margins. He found a need for more and more rigorous scholarly research on the region and its people. Fisher noted that the field had strengths in some areas, such as literature, folklore, ethnomusicology, history, sociology, political science, and anthropology, but was missing specific disciplinary perspectives from psychology, economics, education, and the natural sciences.[2]

Five years later, the *Appalachian Journal* published a second collection of essays assessing Appalachian studies.[3] In his introduction, sociologist John Stephenson was frank about the tension within the field: "The 'pure academics' never feel quite safe from the threat of attack by the realpolitickers, they still hold back from the muck of social activism. The battle-scarred, slightly graying knights of social action wonder if they aren't becoming outnumbered by the arrogant and irrelevant literaturists, historians, folklorists, geographers and others who, their critics believe, reinforce inequalities in the region by not attacking them" (1982, 99). The other essays in this issue include a strong emphasis on and commitment to working alongside people in communities and identifying the practical implications of Appalachian studies. At that time, issues of social class were not a focus: only two of the sixteen contributors were women, and race was barely mentioned. While this collection was a milestone in the evolution of Appalachian studies, concerns about globalization, postmodernism, rigorous scholarship, and sexual identities had yet to emerge.

A decade later, in their study "Where Have We Been? Where Are We Going? A History of the Appalachian Studies Association," Logan Brown and colleagues (2003) noted that Appalachian studies journal articles and conference proceedings were dominated by historians, literary critics, folklorists, ethnomusicologists, and social scientists. In addition, they noted that both panelists and publications omitted African American, minority, and sexuality issues in Appalachia (Brown et al. 2003, 71). They recommended that more attention be paid to racial/ethnic and sexual/gender minorities and other underrepresented topics, such as family issues, work, technology, crime, tourism, museums, and the Civil War.

While accurate at the time, the findings in the three summarized endeavors represent trends and conditions in the field that are now decades old. Their observations are included here so that readers may gauge for themselves the degree of progress achieved in the intervening years. For instance, Appalachian studies began to address the lacunae surrounding race/ethnicity and gender through several initiatives. Marshall University held a conference on the topic in 2000, which led to the establishment of its Center for the Study of Ethnicity and Gender in Appalachia in 2003. About this time, Ohio University Press initiated a book series, Race, Ethnicity, and Gender, which has to date published a dozen books, including studies of the relationship between feminism and environmentalism, women activists, gay life in the mountains, migration, women's literacy, and memoirs focusing on family life and the relationship between class and race. In 2007 the Appalachian Studies Association (ASA) began to support and collaborate with the emergent Black Belt Studies Association by offering meeting opportunities at the ASA conference, by including black belt studies organizers in ASA committee work and leadership, and by setting up a committee to liaise between the two organizations. In 2008 the ASA established a postdoctoral fellowship named to honor prominent Appalachian author Wilma Dykeman in order to support research on gender, sexuality, race, and ethnicity in Appalachia, although the fellowship has been awarded only twice. Clearly, more work could be done in these and other areas of long-standing weaknesses.

Theoretically, the field of Appalachian studies seems to embrace some aspects of postmodernism, albeit hesitantly, by simultaneously seeking a better understanding of the region's heterogeneity and recognizing the contested, socially constructed, and politically charged terrain of regional identity and cultural heritage movements. The ontological questioning and uncertainty inherent in postmodernism, however, often pits academics against activists who seek firmer grounding from which to leverage social change. Without resolving this tension, Alan Banks, Dwight Billings, and Karen Tice (1993) advocate for a moderate postmodernist approach that avoids both universalism (identifying a characteristic or characteristics that apply to all of the region or its residents) and essentialism (a belief that there is a core set of characteristics that make something or someone quintessentially Appalachian).

Still, some believe that the granularity and heterogeneity of postmodernist thought carries the seeds of its own destruction, as seen in some of the profound contradictions found in parts of women's studies and African American studies (Bawer 2012). For this reason, Rodger Cunningham, along with many Appalachian scholars (Berry 2002), is leery of some tendencies in postmodernism: "Universal fragmentation did not mean universal liberation; on the contrary, it meant the strongest would now have a free hand to sweep up the fragments into their own universal system of exploitation. And what could oppositional voices say? If everything was particular and nothing was universal, how could one appeal to universal ideas of justice and freedom?" (2003, 380). Cunningham points out, however, that there is heterogeneity among postmodernist approaches, and this variety makes postmodernism useful to Appalachian studies. He distinguishes between a constructed discourse about the region and an authentic dialogue carried out among Appalachians and between Appalachians and the world, thereby "navigating between the Scylla of all-swallowing constructivism and the Charybdis of rock-hard essentialism" (382).

In a similar vein, Herbert Reid and Betsy Taylor note that the postmodern/poststructuralist concern with the problem of essentialism has "increasingly and unnecessarily become a debate about representation in general" (2010, 173), a tendency that distracts from the political struggles and social interactions that really matter in Appalachia. "The key problem of our age is not so much that things are slippery and cannot be safely lassoed by words," they write. "The key problem of our age is the political economy in which markets, technocracy, and bureaucratic governance displace democratic public space with hegemonic regimes of interlocking and ever expanding grids that pre-label things and beings," making them "infinitely exchangeable" (174). It is this tendency that Appalachian studies (and other area studies) combats through its insistence on particularity and its refusal to erase place-based (and other) differences. With the exception of some literary studies, Appalachian studies has not fully embraced postmodern/poststructural theory and the strict social/linguistic constructivism this theoretical move entails.

Reid cautions against being too celebratory about the field's accomplishments, however. He writes, "Those of us who have grown old with Appalachian Studies since 1978 are not likely to provide models of intellectual responsibility by slipping into a celebratory mood and heralding our achievements with no attention to our slag piles" (2005, 172). One such pile is the persistence of insider/outsider distinctions that emerged from the colonial development models of the 1970s. Participating in this insider/outsider discourse, according to Reid, weds Appalachian studies to an outmoded region/nation framework that is not useful to the challenges that we now face. Such a framework encourages the mystification and reification of "Otherness," resulting in an unproductive identity politics and a "dehistoricizing trap" that prevents us from recognizing that the civic and environmental "commons" is being destroyed by neoliberal globalization elsewhere, not just in Appalachia (164).[4]

Related to this reified insider/outsider dichotomy is the tendency of some Appalachian studies scholars, artists, and activists to represent Appalachian communities in an ahistorical, idealized fashion that neglects political oppression and economic exploitation within the region's localities. Such a tendency results in a "reactionary nostalgia" that, at best, does little to address economic inequality and, at worst, is complicit in the perpetuation of such inequality. Another slag pile littering the field is its frequently uncritical adoption of the federal definition of the region as articulated by the federal Appalachian Regional Commission, an indication that Appalachian studies has not escaped the hegemonic forces of the corporate state (Reid 2005, 166). An overreliance on ARC "tools" and "maps," coupled with a lack of systematic critical interrogation of the relationship between local, regional, national, and global scales, poses an obstacle to the transformation of Appalachian studies into global regional studies. Lastly, according to Reid, some in Appalachian studies have confused the reality of American cultural pluralism with pluralist models of power, the latter positing that the state provides a neutral terrain through which political "interest groups" compete equally in a political contest to formulate U.S. policy (171). According to Reid, such intellectual sloppiness is another conceptual error in the field that obscures key features of the current global political economy.

While critical of its failings, Reid (2005) and Reid and Taylor (2002) have hope for the future of Appalachian studies, especially if the field attends to the social movements and citizens' organizations that are resisting economic globalization and seeking to create democratic civic spaces through which a healthier, more sustainable, future can be realized. Reid writes, "[As] one of several global regions where there is significant community-based action, Appalachia provides an ideal setting for academics, artists, educators, and citizens to join forces with those from *elsewhere* to resist the destruction of places by globalizing capital and the corporate state" (2005, 169). Those who are willing to partner with communities to resist technocratic domination will play an important role in moving the field forward from "Appalachian studies" to "global regional studies" to become "part of the mix of a new democratic politics that dares to raise questions of global justice" (173).

When Stephen Fisher's 1993 classic *Fighting Back in Appalachia* appeared, there was no mention of globalization. Some twenty years later, *Transforming Places: Lessons from Appalachia,* edited by Fisher and Barbara Ellen Smith, featured a metanarrative about the placelessness of global capitalism: "The global is continuously produced through the activities of human beings in specific locales" (2012, 269). Today we take as a matter of fact that place matters, even in a transnational political economy that argues otherwise.

Dwight Billings (2007), in contrast to Fisher, Cunningham, and Reid, approaches Appalachian studies from the perspective of the discipline of sociology, tracing the historical arc of the "sociology of Appalachia" from structural functionalism to postmodernism/poststructuralism. In so doing, he demonstrates that Appalachian studies has evolved over the decades as a counterpoint to structural-functionalist "culture of poverty" analyses that cast the region as an isolated frontier from which developed a regional folk culture characterized by familism, traditionalism, and fatalism. Appalachian studies scholars have demonstrated compellingly that nineteenth-century Appalachian communities were not so different from their contemporary counterparts elsewhere (see especially Pudup, Billings, and Waller 1995).

Rather than accept static notions of traditionalism as characteristic of the region, others have demonstrated time and again how Appalachian residents make, remake, negotiate, and reinterpret the meaning of the past in an ongoing effort to cope with the present and plan a future. Challenging conceptions of culture as a fixed store of traits and traditions or an authoritatively sanctioned worldview, Mary Anglin, for instance, writes that "regional culture encompasses material resources, systems of kin / community ties, and pragmatic information about how to live in specific settings, in addition to perspectives on what is a life well-lived. It reflects a particular history and set of socio-economic conditions, and is the means by which individuals come to terms with, or contest, these particularities" (1993, 263). The placement of meaning in an historical, geographical, and material (class) context continues to be a central aim of "mainstream" Appalachian studies scholarship, a characteristic some attribute to the circumstances of the field's birth and ongoing engagement with neo-Marxian and world-systems theories.

Some value this tendency in Appalachian studies scholarship, arguing that nonmaterialist postmodern/poststructural frameworks are best applied to representations of Appalachia (see Shapiro 1978) rather than to explanations of people's practices. According to Banks, Billings, and Tice, the Appalachian

Studies Association's conferences provide "a social space where oppositional discourse has flourished . . . [and] the research carried out by many Appalachian scholars has not come primarily from the intellectual agenda of academic disciplines, but rather from a regional conversation among activists and scholars" (1993, 283–84). This regional activist-scholar conversation may also help to account for the relative lack of traction that postmodern and poststructuralist theory has had in Appalachian studies.

All of these commentators on the field place a high value upon "dialogue" in the region, especially as practiced through campus and community partnerships, community engagement, and participatory action research. Appalachian studies scholar and activist Helen Matthews Lewis also acknowledges the importance of participatory action research in the history and future of Appalachian studies, but she provides a trenchant critique of the field's lack of success in that regard:

> Rather than bringing the university or college into Appalachian experiences and changing the university [by] integrating education and action—we [have] academized Appalachian studies. . . . We take life and objectify it, neutralize it and make it apolitical. When we make something into a course, structure it into periods with term papers, tests, exams—we neutralize and objectify it. The attitude stance of the classroom is: tolerance of ideas, dispassionate evaluation of alternatives, disinterested scrutiny, and objectivity. If one is tolerant and objective, one does not resist; one adjusts to all situations, [but] does not challenge the situation. (2007, 10)

This is far from the origins of a field based in a social movement and directed toward social change (Wagner, Obermiller, and Wagner 2013). It is also far from the trajectories advocated by members of the field (Billings 2007; Reid 2005; Reid and Taylor 2010) and exemplified by studies of Appalachian landownership (Appalachian Land Ownership Task Force 1983), alternative regional policies and strategies (Fisher 1993; Fisher and Smith 2012), community development (Hinsdale, Lewis, and Waller 1995), and environmental issues (McSpirit, Faltraco, and Bailey 2012). Although some Appalachian studies courses include a service-learning component, this does not necessarily make those courses transformative for students, communities, or institutions of higher learning, as Lewis points out: "Much activism through service learning emphasizes service to the victims and amelioration of damages rather than changing the destructive system. Studies of globalization and corporate control of the region seem missing from many programs" (2011, 3). Lewis's point here resonates with Reid's (2005) argument that Appalachian studies should be engaged in a struggle to reclaim a democratic commons through which to deliberate and seek global social and environmental justice and sustainability (see also Reid and Taylor 2010).

To accomplish this goal, there is clearly a need to change the relationship between institutions of higher learning and communities in the region to include both *outreach* (engagement) to transform communities in Appalachia (Fisher and Smith 2012) and *inreach* to change the culture and structure of higher education (Scott 1995; Taylor, Faltraco, and Isla 2012). Though this has been recognized by many in Appalachian studies (and other area studies as well), it has proven difficult to achieve. In some institutional contexts, it is a challenge for scholars to gain recognition and reward for doing community-based work, because such research takes longer to complete and may not lend itself to the production of the refereed academic journal articles that have long provided the "ticket" to academic tenure and promotion (Kezar and Rhoads 2001). Indeed, the entire enterprise of community-based, participatory-action research raises unsettling questions concerning the basis of knowledge and the locus of expertise, questions that challenge the position and role of universities and colleges in society, or, as Reid calls it, "technocratic, top-down research" (2005, 170). But then, such pedagogies and inquiries have always been designed to do just that.

Furthermore, some institutions of higher learning continue to reorganize along corporate/business administrative models, encouraging specialization, hierarchy, and attention to a market-driven "bottom line" rather than educational, democratic, and other prosocial values (Reid 2001; Scott 1995; Slaughter and Rhoades 2000). With the declining commitment of tax money to higher education, colleges and universities are increasingly vulnerable to pressures from wealthy donors, boards of trustees (often dominated by members of the business community), corporate research funding, and tuition dollars (and the parents who provide them), pushing some institutions in a conservative, procorporate direction (Washburn 2008). More pragmatically, school terms do not always coincide with the schedules and cycles of activity within nonacademic communities, making it difficult to coordinate community-based research and build social relationships of trust over time (McSpirit, Faltraco, and Bailey 2012). In spite of these obstacles, Appalachian studies has a clear tradition of community engagement and participatory research, from the region to the neighborhood level. Important community-based research initiatives are documented, for instance, in Fisher and Smith (2012), Ludke and Obermiller (2012), and McSpirit, Faltraco, and Bailey (2012).

In sum, these reflective articles and speeches agree that Appalachian studies is a work in progress, often falling short of its goals and aspirations. Though the field is somewhat interdisciplinary, there remains a clear predominance of history, literature, folklore, sociology, and anthropology and less representation in psychology, economics, and the natural/environmental sciences, just as there was in 1977 (Fisher 1977). The field also experiences a tension between those who see postmodernism/poststructuralism as a valuable orientation that should play a more central role in the field and those who are wary of the limitations of these orientations, and between activists and academics whose different agendas, schedules, practices, and institutional constraints make collaboration difficult. There is a consensus, however, that community engagement and participatory research should be centerpieces of Appalachian studies as it moves forward, even though the writers cited here disagree as to the quality of the field's performance in these areas.

Discussing Appalachian Studies

Between July and September 2012, the first author conducted telephone and email interviews with thirty-two people, asking for their perspectives on Appalachian studies, its strengths and contributions, weaknesses and omissions, and the prospects and directions for its future. While the sample was not randomly selected, it incorporated a variety of ages, gender and sexual identities, races, and occupations both in communities and on campuses. The interviewees also came from a variety of occupational and disciplinary backgrounds, including literature and writing; history and American studies; folklore and communication; social sciences, including anthropology, political science, and sociology; education and social work; planning and economic development; and health and library sciences. In addition, the sample is geographically diverse, with participants located in northern, central, and southern Appalachia; nine Appalachian states, as well as Texas and California; and Canada. Interviewees were involved in Appalachian studies in a variety of capacities, including students, teachers, activists, researchers, members or officers of the Appalachian Studies Association, or some combination thereof. On average, participants had been involved in Appalachian studies for twenty-eight years (median: thirty years), indicating a predominance of advanced scholars and practitioners over early career participants in the group.[5]

Participants were provided in advance with a short list of topics for discussion (e.g., perceived strengths of Appalachian studies; criticisms of

Appalachian studies) and were also encouraged to explore other topics they thought relevant to the general theme. Although each discussion covered a wide range of relevant topics, seven key themes emerged: community, diversity, globalization, quality of scholarship, social change, omissions, and the future of Appalachian studies. Throughout the balance of this chapter, direct quotes will not be attributed to the person who voiced them—all of the interviewees agreed to remain anonymous in order to emphasize ideas over personalities.

COMMUNITY

The interviewees generally agreed that the most important aspect of Appalachian studies was the strong sense of community that participants experience. Most said that they enjoy working and interacting with one another: "These are people you can eat lunch with." This camaraderie, they said, is rooted in a shared enthusiasm and dedication to the region. Appalachian studies participants, one said, "are passionate about topics, personally touched, involved in scholarship, and share ideas that have meaning." For that reason, "I am tremendously grateful for being involved in Appalachian studies," said another. This passion, which was brought up more than once, is not a self-centered one. The words "kindness," "compassion," and "collegiality" resonate throughout the interviews, while regional pride, diversity, and open-mindedness are seen as identifying values. Because of this passion and collegiality, Appalachian studies is seen as a field that offers purpose and inspiration to young people. The field is also seen as bringing recognition and acceptance to the region, as well as developing a stronger regional identity: "The passion of people teaching, writing, thinking, and speaking about places where they live is obvious." People in the field view their colleagues as ready to lend support, seek common ground, and offer challenges to one another: "Appalachian studies is a diverse group involved in inspiring and complementing each other's work, enjoying and learning from each other's work. It's a field that's stronger than other area studies, some of which are dying out."

A celebratory attitude is tempered and, in some cases, contradicted by deeply held concerns. Some participants say that the field can be *too* accepting: "Healthy families have fights," it was said, implying that Appalachian studies participants tend to eschew open disagreement. It is not always clear where the line should be drawn between being polite and cooperative, on the one hand, and unhealthy conflict avoidance, on the other. "I am sometimes disappointed that we take the easy road," said one participant. "We like to jump on stereotypes like dogs on a bone, but sometimes we shy away from the tougher and potentially more divisive issues of power or race and class or corporatization of our institutions. Perhaps the flip side of our generosity and inclusiveness is that we avoid conflict and controversy." The value of cooperation is so instilled, however, that one participant complained, "Conferences are a lopsided love-fest that don't tolerate dissonance." That individual encouraged the Appalachian Studies Association to seek diversity by including more Appalachian businesspeople in its conference sessions.

There was some disagreement on how well the older generation communicates with and mentors young Appalachianists. Older participants in the field are generally seen as welcoming, generous, and noncompetitive but not always open to new ideas or ready to hand the reins over to the younger generation. One noted that "there should be more collaboration across disciplines and experience," while another says the field is inclusive and especially strong in mentorship of new scholars. Senior scholars speak positively of graduate students and young scholars, saying, "They're sharper and know a lot more than we did." While generally laudatory about the field, the interviewees, like the commentators reviewed above, see room for improvement. Said one, "It is impossible to care this much about a field of studies without wanting more for it." Some of the areas for improvement mentioned include incorporating more racial/ethnic and gender/sexual diversity into our scholarship, art, and discourse; creating more connections between Appalachia and other regions; increasing the rigor of the scholarship; maintaining the field's grassroots, activist, and community focus; and attending to topics to which we have not paid sufficient attention in the past.

DIVERSITY

Just as the field's sense of "community" can have the negative consequence of discouraging dissent and debate, it can also have a homogenizing influence on Appalachian studies. Other chapters in this volume document the white, androcentric, heteronormative focus of much of Appalachian studies scholarship and popular discourse about the region. It comes as no surprise, then, that the interviewees were concerned about the field's lack of African American representation. "Although the field is aware of the work of William Gates, Jr., Alessandro Portelli, John Inscoe, Joe Trotter, Ron Lewis, Bill Turner, Ed Cabell, and Carter G. Woodson, it has missed the mark on promoting an Appalachian identity among regional blacks themselves," said one participant. Likewise, while the Affrilachian poets have gained much attention in the past ten years, not enough has been done to celebrate other black artists in Appalachia, noted another.

In spite of the initiatives that the Appalachian Studies Association and other regional institutions have taken to encourage the involvement of a more diverse group of people in Appalachian studies, ASA membership remains predominantly white. "Without inclusion, blacks may not feel connected, even if their work fits within a regional perspective," an interviewee observed. The same can be said of the Cherokees, other ethnic groups, and LGBT Appalachians. Notably, however, in spite of a history of androcentrism, women are well represented in Appalachian studies art, film, scholarship, and organizational leadership.

GLOBAL CONNECTIONS

Many in Appalachian studies note that the region, with its large population and abundant natural resources, has a major impact on the rest of the world. However, they are concerned that the field itself is ignored outside the region. Appalachian studies has failed, in other words, to convince others not only of Appalachia's significance but of its own. As one interviewee put it, "We haven't put enough stress on comparative analysis. It [comparative analysis] was always an undercurrent; and now the stress on transnational and global issues is helping matters. But to the extent our work is not done in comparison to other U.S. and global regions, we unintentionally reinforce our own insularity."

While it may be true that too few conference papers and journal articles take an explicitly comparative approach, there are nevertheless several long-standing connections between Appalachia and other global regions. In 1974, for example, John Gaventa, who was soon joined by Helen Lewis, initiated a videotape exchange between miners in Appalachia and Wales. The exchange has continued for forty years and resulted in visits between Welsh and Appalachian miners, a study-abroad program in Wales established at Appalachian State University in 2001, and, most recently, the production of a documentary film by Tom Hansell and Patricia Beaver entitled *After Coal: Welsh and Appalachian Mining Communities*. For about thirty years, there has been an exchange of faculty and graduate students between the University of Kentucky Appalachian Center and the University of Roma La Sapienza. Alessandro Portelli (2010), an oral historian who studied Harlan County, Kentucky, helped spearhead this program. In addition, Appalshop, a grassroots, multimedia cooperative producing documentary film, radio, recording, and performances, has initiated several exchanges, tours, and performances with artists from around the world. The Highlander Center has organized visits of Appalachian workers to Mexico to document the places to which their jobs had been exported (Gaventa 1988). In 1994 Phillip Obermiller and William Philliber edited the first scholarly book putting the region in a global perspective, *Appalachia in an International Context: Cross-National Comparisons of Developing Regions*. The University of Kentucky Appalachian Center, a proponent of a more globalized Appalachian studies, launched the Rockefeller Fellowship Program (2001–5) to bring activists from Appalachia and around the world to the university to work on research projects of interest to them and their communities (Taylor, Faltraco, and Isla 2012). Donald Davis and the Loyal Jones Appalachian Center at Berea College have worked to bring scholars from Western Ukraine's Carpathian Mountains in closer connection with the Appalachian studies community. In October 2012 the University of Kentucky Appalachian Center held a Global Mountain Regions conference that brought together academics, activists, artists, and practitioners from around the world to discuss their work in mountainous areas. These are just a few examples of the kind of global outreach that has occurred in Appalachian studies, leading one interviewee to note: "Appalachian studies is strongest when rooted in an understanding of place in a global context and builds links to that context." After all, "you can't transform someone else's community."

QUALITY OF SCHOLARSHIP

In spite of this outreach, some believe that Appalachian studies and the region often go unnoticed. Appalachia "drowns in the large pool of Southern history after early frontier settlement," one participant noted. Another observed, somewhat contradictorily, "No major Southern historian can function without recognizing the mountains [i.e., Appalachian scholarship]." The field's disengagement from other area studies encourages people to find validation exclusively within Appalachian studies, a form of tunnel vision that often affects area studies and the standard disciplines. Meanwhile, many keep a careful eye on American studies and southern studies without necessarily reaching out to them (see Creadick 2013). This watchful but passive stance invited the question from one participant, "Would publishing in venues outside the usual Appalachian serials solve the problem, or prove self-defeating?" There have been some significant exceptions, such as in the work of Larry Griffin and Ashley Thompson (2002), southern studies scholars who made a foray into Appalachian studies to find common ground and generate new questions (see also Billings, Berry, and Inscoe 2002). Some questions have also periodically been asked by Ozark scholars as they investigate that region's similarities with Appalachia.

Many participants were impressed by what the field has achieved with little university, government, or foundation support. However, this knowledge is not being communicated well enough to cause the greatest impact on local communities or the wider world. "People laugh in my face, make crude comments when they hear I teach Appalachian studies," one participant commented. Many involved scholars want to know why? Why would studying and teaching about a vital part of the American experience be considered a joke?

Opinions on this question are mixed. The type of research is one possible explanation for why some view the field as a "joke." Appalachian studies tends to produce more qualitative research than quantitative; and it is focused around the humanities and social sciences, rather than the more funding-rich natural, medical, and engineering sciences. This could result in the field's devaluation, especially among Research-I institutions. Second, Appalachian studies values local, grassroots knowledge, seeks to resist academic elitism, and therefore is easily dismissed as inferior by intellectual elites who believe that only credentialed scholars can produce legitimate knowledge. Yet, one interviewee countered, "the skills, knowledge, and research in Appalachian studies are equal to any other field." Some also report that Appalachian scholarship is increasing in quality but is not yet top-tier due to a lack of theoretical development and sophistication. Finally, one interviewee went so far as to say that a lack of theoretical sophistication in Appalachian studies is the result of a lower level of intellectualism, a contention that should inspire further reflection and debate.

It is not surprising to find opinions so varied in a field that embraces disciplinary and occupational diversity and seeks to provide a common investigative and expressive space for scholars, educators, practitioners, writers, artists, musicians, filmmakers, and poets. Yet this kind of diversity sometimes results in fragmentation, incoherence, and communication barriers. "Appalachian studies is stronger for being multidisciplinary, but it's harder to communicate the substance of the field precisely because it is multidisciplinary," one participant notes. It is difficult for traditional academics to grasp what the nonprofit sector and artists are doing, and vice versa. Yet these groups seem to share a sense of community and a genuine desire to deepen their understanding of the region. While the field labors to include a variety of types of knowledge (local, expert, practitioner, scientific, humanities) and to represent many disciplines, Appalachian studies walks a fine line between being broadly inclusive and lacking depth and rigor. "In a field built on passion and dedication for the people of a region," said one interviewee, "choosing between ensuring everyone is covered and narrowing focus to produce specific measurable results is a decision that nobody seems to feel fully ready to make. It's a tug-of-war between breadth and depth; and we're pulling on both ends." "I think sometimes we are not rigorous enough," another states. "I want to be careful, however, not to hold up the mainstream disciplines as a model of rigor, because what too often passes for rigor in the academy is a limited scope of highly specialized, technical, and narrow questions as well as the fetishization of methods. That said, we could be more penetrating, more critical, more exacting."

On the positive side, Appalachian studies has built a large research base and an extensive collection of archival material about the region and its people. "A valuable scholarly record is being established in Appalachian studies," said one participant. "It is a marriage between scholarship and making a difference, research for a purpose, not just [for] other scholars." Looking back, another noted, "There is amazing scholarship by the early people in the field, the methodological bases soundly laid, important questions were asked and answered. The early scholars set the stage for the next generation, but maybe [they did it] too well [because] old models are still maintained beyond their usefulness."

SOCIAL CHANGE

Along with this urge to strengthen Appalachian studies' rigor as an academic field, there is fear that moving in this direction will take the field away from its activist roots. Some fear that it already has done so, as indicated by a participant who says, "Something has been lost here—success is killing us. Appalachian studies began in an activist era, but we no longer gather in nonacademic settings."[6] Some also note a growing classroom versus community mentality that reduces the field's effectiveness and collegiality, while others complained that Appalachian studies has become elitist and cliquish. The growing gap between scholars and the community and the ongoing tension between cultural heritage interests and political and economic interests causes anxiety about the future of the field.

The quest for social change and justice, however, often attracts people into the field. In addition, scholars see the benefits within their own academic lives of being involved in communities of place in addition to the academic, abstracted "communities" with which they might identify. "Even if we all do not do participatory action research directly, that model has made all of us scholars more attuned to our relationship and responsibilities to the grassroots," one interviewee noted. "The [Appalachian Studies Association] conferences are a strange mix," observed one interviewee. "You can walk into a conference and find 30 banjo players picking away . . . and yet hear some of the most effective community activists making great sense in the panels."

While that may seem "strange" to some, others value the mix between cultural, activist, and scholarly influences in Appalachian studies. The commitment to place and community is seen as the motivating factor that brings scholars, activists, practitioners, and artists together. Some observe that Appalachian scholars, authors, and artists do not frequently or obviously engage in a naked, egotistical competition for prestige but, rather, emphasize their pursuit of change and justice in the region. Perhaps this type of purposeful scholarship is the reason people notice a richness and passion not common in traditional academic disciplines. The annual Appalachian Studies Association conference, one observed, is "a banquet where you just can't eat enough." While other fields of "disciplinary activism" may have a shortage of scholar-activists, Appalachian studies seems to have an abundance of them. One participant reported that a colleague was "amazed and delighted about the real-world engagement that is still such a strong component that we sometimes take for granted. This is not the case in very many other academic or professional organizations." Many conversations expressed the hope for a wider range of participation in Appalachian studies and more interaction with local communities. "When community-involved people are on Appalachian studies panels, they are visceral, real, and compelling in a way that standard scholarly panels are not," it was said. However, one person's "visceral, real, and compelling" may be another person's lack of "rigor" and "intellectualism."

OMISSIONS

As noted, the field of Appalachian studies has focused on some topics to the exclusion of others. In this section the interviewees present a variety of sometimes contradictory opinions about what we have overlooked thus far.

First, there is general consensus that Appalachian studies has a rural bias. "Except for studies of the Appalachian out-migrant populations and communities, our stress on the rural has caused us to neglect urban and small-town life, and along with that the middle class in the region, especially civic life," noted one interviewee. In addition, there has been a working-class bias to our studies, with many focusing on coal miners. This has led one interviewee to note that "middle-class life in Appalachia is there, but ignored." By too selectively focusing on the rural working class, this interviewee contends, the field overlooks other potential sources of social transformation.

In addition, the field has not systematically investigated intimate family life, especially recently. "We had a significant number of early studies of kinship and family . . . James Brown, John Stephenson, etc. . . . and while we are much better about gender now than then, what do we know about intimate life, sexuality, childhood, or aging? We don't seem to be updating that sort of work," one participant said. Geographically, there is some consensus that Appalachian studies has historically focused upon the central Appalachian coalfields, where a history of violent class conflict, extreme poverty, and environmental disaster has captured much scholarly, artistic, journalistic, and popular attention. As a result, the southern and especially the northern subregions have been relatively ignored. Likewise, industries such as tourism, steel, chemicals, gas, manufacturing, farming, prisons, and timber are largely overlooked. Our attention to transnational energy companies and coal miners means that small businesses, professionals, and a wide variety of occupations are excluded from economic analyses. A shift of focus to the economies in northern and southern Appalachia would alleviate some of the imbalance, as would a shift from energy to other types of corporations and businesses. Subregional differences affect not only economic patterns but also academic perspectives: "I grew up in southern Appalachia, so I was unaware of coalfield politics until I moved to West Virginia." How researchers, artists, and activists are affected by the localities in which they were raised, especially in terms of their representations of the region writ large, is itself worthy of more attention.

The region's economies relate to its coal, timber, gas, waterways, and scenic mountain views. As one contributor put it:

> This will sound odd, given the rightful attention to mountaintop removal and our early, but now declining, attention to labor issues in coal mining . . . strikes and the United Mine Workers of America, union democracy, black lung, etc. . . . but I don't think we know enough about coal beyond mountaintop removal: the mineral and how much is left of it—so geology is another field we should have been better in touch with—and the coal industry itself. And speaking of labor, we write as if Don Blankenship and big machines and explosives alone do the work of mountaintop removal, but the [Appalachian] workforce is ignored.

The field needs to take a closer look at how coal, timber, gas, and steel relate to wealth and poverty today. Forty years ago, activists and miners worked together to improve coal mining safety and make it a beneficial livelihood. Now many in the field of Appalachian studies, which prides itself on its relationship with the people of the region, are at odds with many regional residents on a range of topics, especially related to jobs, the economy, and the environment.

Another interviewee claimed that many studies of the region's economies are outdated; more "critical approaches to economics" are needed rather than "mainstream neoclassical" approaches. Instead, Appalachian studies should focus more on the scholarship needed to assist communities with economic development and planning. "There has been no real progress in understanding regional economic development in twenty years," this individual claimed. With a few exceptions (Eller 2008; Keefe 2009), much of the research on economic development has been organized through the Appalachian Regional Commission rather than Appalachian studies. Such a feeling may be because much of the research on Appalachian economic development has been organized not through Appalachian studies but through the Appalachian Regional Commission. It may explain not only Appalachian studies' critical view of existing economic analyses of the region but also the lack of economic, demographic, and planning analyses from within Appalachian studies proper. This omission is, however, not surprising for a field heavily tilted toward literary, historical, folkloric, anthropological, and artistic perspectives.

Still, it is important not to cede the territory of economic development entirely to the Appalachian Regional Commission. Appalachian studies scholars and activists are not absolved from doing their own analyses of the important issues involved: How should the definitions of Appalachia be determined? How should planning policies be set and economic conditions interpreted? How should issues of power and governance be addressed? Who should evaluate the outcomes of past and present federal interventions in the region and recommend new strategies? Most of these efforts are pursued at a state and subregional level through community organizations such as the Mountain Association for Community Economic Development (MACED) in Kentucky rather than at the regional level.

History remains an important element of Appalachian studies, yet there are various aspects in the region's historical record that need attention. One participant stated, "Appalachian studies needs to recapture our own intellectual history: . . . How and why did we get to this place?" Another omission is military history: everything from the Revolutionary War through World War II up to the Middle East needs further assessment in terms of its impact on the region and its people. The civil rights movement, desegregation, and the overturning of Jim Crow laws have yet to be fully investigated from a regional perspective. Many of these subjects should not only be considered from regional and subregional aspects but also be placed in a larger context.

As one interviewee noted, "Appalachia is part of a larger story. Progress was made in the 1990s to place Appalachian history in the larger perspective of American history, but the momentum has stalled."

The interviewees generally agreed that Appalachian studies is weak in specific areas, for instance, political science. As one said, "We've had some fine political scientists contributing to the conversation, but they could use some coworkers." Even more acute, as noted earlier, has been a lack of disciplinary representation from the natural, environmental, and medical sciences and psychology. The interviewees, however, were far more interested in addressing the gaps in political decision making and policy analysis in Appalachian studies. "In a region with such a strong labor history, it's amazing how apolitical Appalachian studies can be," one interviewee noted.

Our discussions also revealed a need for more attention to food, nutrition, and health. *Journal of Appalachian Studies* editors have noted that much of the research done on health in the region comes from the fields of public health and nursing, fields that are poorly integrated into Appalachian studies. As a result, many health studies are done without familiarity of recent research on the region. Health researchers, many of whom utilize outmoded conceptions of culture and accept as true flawed understandings of the region promulgated in the 1960s "culture of poverty" discourse, sometimes reproduce stereotypes about the region's residents and contribute to a discourse that blames the individual for negative health outcomes. This, of course, is a tendency in many applied, practical fields such as health care, where the focus is on the individual patient and her or his behavior rather than the larger structural and sociohistorical context that may cause ill health (Rush 1997), though this may now be slowly changing (Hendryx and Ahern 2008). Notable for its avoidance of these pitfalls is Ludke and Obermiller's *Appalachian Health and Well-Being* (2012).

The inclusion of artists enhances the regional conversation by combining scholarship with music and the arts: "Years ago there would be one candidate for the Weatherford Awards [an honor given to fiction, nonfiction, and poetry authors whose work brings Appalachia to the page]. In recent years, the awards have grown to have multiple candidates in each category." There are many artists and a wide variety of musicians, filmmakers, poets, and writers involved in the field, and the resulting conversation has become more sophisticated and of higher quality. At the same time, literature syllabi seem to some outdated. "There's an emphasis on 'classic Appalachia' versus the good contemporary writing that is constantly being produced. A canon seems to have developed that doesn't necessarily speak to contemporary issues in the region," expressed one concerned interviewee.

So, what are the major challenges to Appalachian studies as we move forward? Is there a future for the field? Is it sustainable, still relevant? What should we do to maintain and enhance its utility for the region?

THE FUTURE

Interviewees identified serious challenges threatening the future of Appalachian studies. First, they noted that the field has a vulnerable position in campus hierarchies and therefore needs to develop alliances with disciplines and other area studies programs on their own campuses and beyond in order to advance its work. "We need to knit things together with our academic allies," as one person put it. The field has not been sufficiently engaged in discourse and action related to new trends such as MOOCs (Massively Open Online Courses), the rising costs of tuition and student debt, the emphasis on STEM (Science, Technology, Engineering, and Mathematics) curricula, the increasing use of contingent labor for higher education teaching (adjunct and lecturer positions, challenges to tenure), and the new austerity budgets being promulgated on campuses nationwide. All area studies programs will be affected by these developments, and Appalachian studies will be no exception.

Many university and college administrators lack an understanding of Appalachian studies. "With every new academic administration you have to revalidate, re-educate, re-convince administrators," a participant said. The mental energy, resources, and time it takes to repeatedly prove to administrators that Appalachian studies is a valuable asset to their curricula distracts from other goals in the field. Systems need to be in place to alleviate some of the stress of selling the field to administrators over and over again. Adding to the problem, administrators who deem the field unimportant damage it by assigning inexperienced or untrained instructors to teach the subject. Separate course catalog designations similar to those for African American studies or women's studies are needed to validate an Appalachian-focused curriculum in the minds of students picking their concentrations.

In this context, it is not surprising that many interviewees are concerned about developing and educating the next generation of Appalachian leaders, artists, scholars, educators, and practitioners. While the field is still attracting students, the question remains whether there are enough new people to do the work that lies ahead. An equally compelling question is, Will this work provide a living wage and career to those who choose it? Changes in higher education have resulted in fewer tenure-track academic positions and the use of more contingent and temporary labor. Appalachian studies programs and centers exist only at some of the colleges and universities in the region, and some of these have already been closed, such as at Radford University,

Eastern Kentucky University, and Western North Carolina University. Appalachian studies, unlike women's and African American studies, is not national (or global) in scope. Government funding for research, art, and other activities has decreased in the past decade. These developments are nothing new in many parts of Appalachia that have undergone repeated economic and ecological crises and have always had a small middle class between the wealthy and poor. Clearly, Appalachian studies needs to expand its thinking about learning and pedagogy in the region at all levels and also broaden its purview beyond students enrolled in Appalachian studies courses to students in other areas and even Appalachian residents and migrants who are not enrolled in school. The field also needs to broaden its thinking and teaching to prepare students for nonacademic careers in community organizations, social entrepreneurship, community planning and economic development, environmental remediation, sustainable forestry and agriculture, appropriate technology, the arts, public service, health care, and other fields.

Appalachian studies has been slow to adopt new technologies and adapt to trends in digital texts, online courses, and virtual classrooms, but then so has most of academia. Despite the publication of many edited readers about the region, one participant noted, "In a way, we're still just teaching from Kinko's." Digitization of research and curricula is relevant to globalization, area insularity, and our communication difficulties with new generations, as well as those outside the field of Appalachian studies. A hopeful note here is Appalachian State University's new online Appalachian studies certificate program. Nonetheless, if a global conversation is being held online, the field of Appalachian studies cannot fully participate in that dialogue without digitalization of its courses, scholarship, and databases.

The academic publications focused on Appalachia are slowly adapting to new digital distribution systems. The *Encyclopedia of Appalachia* is in a multiyear process of being digitized, for example. Many Appalachian journals, including *Appalachian Heritage*, *Appalachian Journal*, and *Journal of Appalachian Studies*, are available online through such aggregators as EBSCO, JSTOR, and Project Muse. These publications are taking steps in the right direction but may not come up to speed before the rate of technological change passes them by. The field has a wealth of graphically appealing and pedagogically important information in regional archives and at Appalshop, but only few seem to understand their importance in the digital age. A possible model for the future is the website constructed for the University of Kentucky's Appalachian Center by Kate Black and Sheli Walker (2012). Using interviews, commentary, music, and scholarly research along with archival photos, newspapers, and other documents, Black and Walker's "Background to the 1931–32 Strike" may make Appalachian studies more accessible to younger generations and a global audience. In addition, Berea College's Special Collections and Archives has embarked on a robust digitization effort.

As higher education becomes increasingly digitized and virtual, Appalachian studies may well experience a second "digital divide" that the field has yet to acknowledge. The first is a widely acknowledged lack of access to computers and high-speed Internet connections in some parts of the region. The second may be based on the growth of online courses (including MOOCs) that are not well suited to the intimate, person-based classroom experience that "communicates the passion, electricity, camaraderie, and real commitment" many students currently experience in Appalachian studies courses. Those who can afford only a low- or no-cost MOOC may not find an Appalachian studies course available; by contrast, those who can afford the cost of a traditional university or private college education have access to a potentially life-changing experience not available to many others.

Funding for Appalachian studies research is seen as minimal. The Appalachian Regional Commission, for instance, has historically been more concerned with infrastructure than people. Participants acknowledge that an emphasis on government funding is no longer working, that resources will have to come from outside the government. Competition for scarce private foundation dollars is intense, and the marginality of the field, which mimics the region it studies, contributes to a lack of institutional and financial support for scholarship. The critical issue facing Appalachian studies is

> the insularity or marginalization of the field. I certainly won't say we should shoulder all or even much of the blame for it; but I'm disappointed that we rarely seem to escape the regional studies ghetto such that the important experiences, insights, exemplary actions, and scholarship rarely seem to travel beyond our confines. The term Appalachia itself serves as a container. After all, if our region is a national sacrifice zone and our peoples and cultures are marked as "others," how can we be of value elsewhere? [Our work] is, of course, of value but not if the rest of the country has 150 years' worth of reasons not to listen.

Conclusion

Although this volume is the first book about Appalachian studies, it is clearly not the first look at the field. Appalachian studies has consistently been a self-conscious and reflective endeavor, as evidenced by the number of special issues of journals, book chapters, journal articles, and speeches devoted to the subject. These considerations of the past, present, and possible futures of the field provide a sense of how it has evolved.

While the study of the region and its people has become less scattered, more coherent, and more cooperative and coordinated, it is far from mature. Its full scholarly potential awaits. "Everything is still in play, which is a good thing," one participant points out. Almost everything about the field is a double-edged sword. To the extent it is multidisciplinary and inclusive of grassroots people, Appalachian studies has avoided the "gated community" characteristics of academic disciplines and higher education in general. Yet that very strength can contribute to the lack of respect that Appalachian studies receives from academic administrators and funding agencies. From the perspective of many involved in it, the field stands head and shoulders above many disciplines and other area studies in terms of its attention and responsiveness to regional issues, its legacy of participatory research, and the prominent roles that residents play in regional scholarship. From the perspective of communities in the region, however, the field still has a long way to go inasmuch as it is sometimes cliquish, apolitical, and at odds with some of the region's residents concerning jobs, economic development, and the environment.

Social media and technology will play a role in the future of Appalachian studies. People all over the world should know more about the region via social media and the Internet from such resources as Appalshop, the Appalachian Studies Association, regional institutions of higher learning, and community organizations. Appalachian studies must use these resources to establish itself firmly as a digital resource in the United States and internationally; add other resources such as digital texts, online courses, and virtual classrooms; and make more creative use of social media. Appalachian studies needs a new way of thinking and teaching, new theories, and new methods: "It's not just an academic process, but a whole new pedagogy."

Though the field has sometimes been slow to adopt new technologies, the developments of the past few decades give Appalachian studies hope for the future. One participant commented, "Although many times it has been on the doorstep of doom organizationally, it has a resilience, a presence that continues to exist. That Appalachian studies is still going strong after nearly forty years is extraordinary." There is much work yet to be done in Appalachian studies, but the progress made to date is encouraging.

Notes

1. The Appalachian Studies Conference became the Appalachian Studies Association (ASA) in the 1990s and simultaneously began publishing the peer-reviewed

Journal of Appalachian Studies in lieu of conference proceedings. At the time of this writing, the ASA's annual conference attendance and journal circulation are above 900, while its mailing list exceeds 2,200. The ASA's 841 members are currently located in 29 states and the District of Columbia, as well as Canada, Italy, France, Japan, New Zealand, and Ukraine. The association has a full-time executive director based at Marshall University and has developed a five-year strategic plan that is primarily administrative rather than academic.

2. Fisher's essay was informed by responses to an Appalachian studies questionnaire "mailed rather haphazardly to over 1,000 people" that, in addition to other information, asked respondents "to offer their own thoughts about Appalachian Studies" (Fisher 1977, 5). Participants in the 2012 interviews were still raising similar issues.

3. These essays and the commentaries that follow them were based on presentations made at the University of Kentucky Appalachian Studies Conference, May 21–22, 1981 (McGowan 1982).

4. In what is perhaps the best insight on the insider/outsider dichotomy in Appalachian studies, Wendell Berry distinguishes between natives of Appalachia and citizens of Appalachia. The former are those who are simply born in the region, while the latter are those who consciously assume responsibility for it or, as Berry puts it, become "consciously native" (Minick 2004, 307). Clearly, many natives of Appalachia are also citizens of the region.

5. It is likely that the age of the sample reflects the age (and social networks) of the editors of this volume, all of whom are fifty years of age or older; this reinforces some of the concerns about the field that emerged from the conversations.

6. In its early years the Appalachian Studies Conference was held in off-campus settings, such as state parks, in alternating years to make gatherings more accessible to community participants. As the conferences grew in size, they could no longer be accommodated by these alternative venues and are now hosted solely by hotels or educational institutions.

Works Cited

Anglin, Mary. 1993. "Engendering the Struggle: Women's Labor and Traditions of Resistance in Rural Southern Appalachia." In *Fighting Back in Appalachia: Traditions of Resistance and Change*, edited by Stephen L. Fisher, 263–81.

Appalachian Land Ownership Task Force. 1983. *Who Owns Appalachia? Land Ownership and Its Impact*. Lexington: University Press of Kentucky.

Appalachian Studies Association. 2012. "Mission Statement." http://www.appalachian studies.org/content/about/. Accessed December 12, 2012.

Applebome, Peter. 2009. "Scholar and Witness: John Hope Franklin Reshaped the Study of Black History in America." *New York Times*, March 29, 1, 5.

Banks, Alan, Dwight B. Billings, and Karen Tice. 1993. "Appalachian Studies, Resistance, and Postmodernism." In *Fighting Back in Appalachia: Traditions of Resistance and Change*, edited by Stephen L. Fisher, 283–301. Philadelphia: Temple University Press.

Bawer, Bruce. 2012. *The Victims' Revolution: The Rise of Identity Studies and the Closing of the Liberal Mind.* New York: HarperCollins Publishers.

Bell, Shannon E., and Richard York. 2010. "Community Economic Identity: The Coal Industry and Ideology Construction in West Virginia." *Rural Sociology* 75(1): 111–43.

Berry, Chad. 2000. "Upon What Will I Hang My Hat in the Future? Appalachia and Awaiting Post-postmodernity." *Journal of Appalachian Studies* 6(Fall): 121–30.

Billings, Dwight B. 2007. "Appalachian Studies and the Sociology of Appalachia." In *21st-Century Sociology: A Reference Handbook*, vol. 2, edited by Clifton D. Bryant and Dennis L. Peck, 390–96. Thousand Oaks, Calif.: Sage Publications.

Billings, Dwight B., Chad Berry, and John C. Inscoe. 2002. "Three Responses to Larry Griffin and Ashley Thompson, 'Insularity, Advocacy, and Postmodernism in Appalachian Studies'; 'Looking for Common Ground'; and 'Encouraging Cross-Pollination.'" *Appalachian Journal* 29:328–40.

Black, Kate, and Sheli Walker. 2012. "Background to the 1931–32 Strike." https://appalachiancenter.as.uky.edu/coal-strike/background-coal-strike. Accessed May 13, 2013.

Bradshaw, Michael. 1992. *The Appalachian Regional Commission: Twenty-Five Years of Government Policy.* Lexington: University Press of Kentucky.

Brown, Logan, Theresa Burchette-Anderson, Donovan Cain, and Jinny Turman Deal with Howard Dorgan. 2003. "Where Have We Been? Where Are We Going? A History of the Appalachian Studies Association." *Appalachian Journal* 31(1): 30–85.

Caudill, Harry M. 1963. *Night Comes to the Cumberlands: A Biography of a Depressed Area.* Boston: Little, Brown.

Creadick, Anna. 2013. "The *AppalJ* of My Eye: From Appalachian Studies to American Studies, and Back." *Appalachian Journal* 40(3–4): 166–72.

Cunningham, Rodger. 2003. "Appalachian Studies among the Posts." *Journal of Appalachian Studies* 9(2): 363–86.

De Sousa-Brown, Semoa C. B., and Tesfa G. Gebremedhin. 2004. "An Empirical Analysis of Poverty and Income Inequality in West Virginia." http://ageconsearch.umn.edu/bitstream/20223/1/sp04de06.pdf. Accessed May 9, 2012.

Eller, Ronald D. 2008. *Uneven Ground: Appalachia since 1945.* Lexington: University Press of Kentucky.

Fisher, Stephen L. 1977. Introduction to the special issue, "A Guide to Appalachian Studies," edited by Stephen L. Fisher, Jerry W. Williamson, and Juanita Lewis. *Appalachian Journal* 5(1): 4–12.

———, ed. 1993. *Fighting Back in Appalachia: Traditions of Resistance and Change.* Philadelphia: Temple University Press.

Fisher, Stephen L., and Barbara Ellen Smith, eds. 2012. *Transforming Places: Lessons from Appalachia.* Urbana: University of Illinois Press.

Ford, Thomas, ed. 1962. *The Southern Appalachian Region: A Survey.* Lexington: University Press of Kentucky.

Gaventa, John. 1988. *From the Mountains to Maquiladoras: A Case Study of Capital Flight and Its Impact on Workers.* Issue 10, Working Papers Series. Knoxville, Tenn.: Highlander Research and Education Center.

Griffin, Larry, and Ashley Thompson. 2002. "Collective Memory, Identity, and Representation in Appalachia and the South." *Appalachian Journal* 29(3): 296–327.

Hendryx, Michael, and Melissa M. Ahern. 2008. "Relations between Health Indicators and Residential Proximity to Coal Mining in West Virginia." *American Journal of Public Health* 98(4): 669–71.

Hinsdale, Mary Ann, Helen M. Lewis, and Maxine Waller. 1995. *It Comes from the People: Community Development and Local Theology.* Philadelphia: Temple University Press.

Keefe, Susan E., ed. 2009. *Participatory Development in Appalachia: Cultural Identity, Community, and Sustainability.* Knoxville: University of Tennessee Press.

Kezar, Adrianna, and Robert A. Rhoads. 2001. "The Dynamic Tensions of Service Learning in Higher Education: A Philosophical Perspective." *Journal of Higher Education* 72(2): 172–204.

Lewis, Helen M. 2007. "Appalachian Studies as a Model of Education for Social Change and Regional Stewardship." Unpublished manuscript of a speech given at Ohio University.

———. 2011. "The Future of Appalachian Studies." Unpublished manuscript of a speech given at Morehead University.

Ludke, Robert L., and Phillip J. Obermiller, eds. 2012. *Appalachian Health and Well-Being.* Lexington: University Press of Kentucky.

McGowan, Thomas A., ed. 1982. "Assessing Appalachian Studies." Special issue, *Appalachian Journal* 9 (Winter-Spring): 2–3.

McSpirit, Stephanie, Lynne Faltraco, and Conner Bailey, eds. 2012. *Confronting Ecological Crisis in Appalachia and the South.* Lexington: University Press of Kentucky.

Messinger, Penny. 1998. "Leading the Field of Mountain Work: The Council of Southern Mountain Workers, 1913–1950." Ph.D. diss., Ohio State University.

Minick, Jim. 2004. "A Citizen and a Native: An Interview with Wendell Berry." *Appalachian Journal* 31(3–4): 300–313.

Obermiller, Phillip J., and William W. Philliber, eds. 1994. *Appalachia in an International Context: Cross-National Comparisons of Developing Regions.* Westport, Conn.: Praeger.

Paletta, Anthony. 2009. "The Bucks Stop, but Will Colleges Notice?" *Wall Street Journal,* July 10, W-13.

Portelli, Alessandro. 2010. *They Say in Harlan County: An Oral History.* London: Oxford University Press.

Pudup, Mary Beth, Dwight B. Billings, and Altina L. Waller, eds. 1995. *Appalachia in the Making: The Mountain South in the Nineteenth Century.* Chapel Hill: University of North Carolina Press.

Reid, Herbert G. 2001. "The Resurgence of the Market Machine-God and the Obsolescence of Liberal Democracy: On Academic Capitalism as Unsustainable Professionalism." *Rethinking Marxism* 13(1): 27–44.

———. 2005. "Appalachia and the 'Sacrament of Coexistence': Beyond Post-colonial Trauma and Regional Identity Traps." *Journal of Appalachian Studies* 11(1/2): 164–81.

Reid, Herbert G., and Betsy Taylor. 2002. "Appalachia as a Global Region: Toward Critical Regionalism and Civic Professionalism." *Journal of Appalachian Studies* 8(2): 6–28.

———. 2010. *Recovering the Commons: Democracy, Place, and Global Justice.* Urbana: University of Illinois Press.

Rush, Kathy L. 1997. "Health Promotion, Ideology, and Nursing Education." *Journal of Advanced Nursing* 25(6): 1292–98.

Scott, Shaunna L. 1995. "Teaching for Democracy: Reflections on Teaching Appalachian Studies." *Journal of Appalachian Studies* 7:131–39.

———. 2009. "Discovering What the People Knew: The 1979 Appalachian Land Ownership Study." *Action Research* 7(2): 185–205.

Shapiro, Henry D. 1978. *Appalachia on Our Mind: The Southern Mountains and Mountaineers in the American Consciousness, 1870–1920.* Chapel Hill: University of North Carolina Press.

Slaughter, Sheila, and Gary Rhoades. 2000. "The Neo-liberal University." *New Labor Forum* 6:73–79.

Stephenson, John. 1982. "Politics and Scholarship: Appalachian Studies Enters the 1980s." *Appalachian Journal* 9(2–3): 97–104.

Taylor, Betsy, Lynne Faltraco, and Ana Isla. 2012. "Social Theory, Appalachian Studies, and the Challenge of Global Regions: The UK Rockefeller Humanities Fellowship Program, 2001–2005." In *Confronting Ecological Crisis in Appalachia and the South*, edited by Stephanie McSpirit, Lynne Faltraco, and Conner Bailey, 217–32. Lexington: University Press of Kentucky.

Wagner, Thomas E., Phillip J. Obermiller, and Melinda B. Wagner. 2013. "Fifty Years of Appalachian Advocacy: An Interview with Mike Maloney." *Appalachian Journal* 40(3–4): 174–218.

Warren, Kenneth. 2011. "Does African-American Literature Exist?" *Chronicle of Higher Education.* http://chronicle.com/article/Does-African-American/126483/. Accessed March 2, 2011.

Washburn, Jennifer. 2008. *University, Inc.: The Corporate Corruption of Higher Education.* New York: Basic Books.

Weller, Jack E. 1965. *Yesterday's People: Life in Contemporary Appalachia.* Lexington: University Press of Kentucky.

Whisnant, David E. 1988. *Modernizing the Mountaineer: People, Power, and Planning in Appalachia.* Boone, N.C.: Appalachian Consortium Press.

7

Imagining Appalachia

Three Landscapes

DOUGLAS REICHERT POWELL

One of the signal achievements of Appalachian studies, I believe, is to establish that the southern mountains have been not a backwater but a vanguard, a kind of laboratory of society and culture, with a distinctive role to play in many of the watershed periods and themes of American and global history: from migration to inhabitation, settlement, colonization, and development. Fault lines of race, class, gender, sexuality; the conflicts of social and, perhaps above all, environmental change—all have left their curious marks on the Appalachian landscape in ways that shed new or different light on larger historical dynamics. The traces of all of this incredible cultural dynamism can be seen taking fascinating shape in the panoply of cultural work the mountains' inhabitants produce.

Too often, however, those marks have been at best troubling and at worst immensely destructive. Mountaintop removal is the apotheosis of an entire series of experiments in social order that have not perhaps gone off as smoothly as one would hope. One could write a veritable *United States of Appalachia II: The Empire Strikes Back* based on the region's more unfortunate innovations, starting with ethnic cleansing and going up through mountaintop removal by way of predatory capitalism, the atomic bomb, and the meth lab.[1] Even the experiments in state socialism have produced mixed results at best; the Tennessee Valley Authority's best intentions in its early days paved the road to Pigeon Forge—a neon-lit spectacle powered today by surface mining.

A lot of the critical work on Appalachian studies has focused on these undesired and undesirable interventions in Appalachia. Much cultural scholarship maintains a defensive posture, identifying errors in depictions of the region or caricatures of the people who live there, and issuing corrections or refutations. This is important work: the cultural wing of Appalachian studies has produced an impressive body of work arguing that cultural works have material consequences for the people depicted in them.

But do we need to be so focused on arguing the negative? If Appalachia as a sociohistorical laboratory has been the site of many experiments that blew up in everybody's faces, could it not also be a laboratory for testing new kinds of solutions to social and economic crisis? I hope that the future of Appalachian studies is enmeshed with arguments about the future of Appalachia, learning to teach people to make use of the historical and cultural narratives we have documented, to learn from both the triumphs and the mistakes of life in our region, and to make new contributions that extend, expand, and evolve our regional relationships.

How can we make Appalachian studies resources—institutional, informational, and analytical—more accessible to local communities to use in developing tactical responses to their particular economic, political, and cultural situations? What forms of culture might at least ameliorate some of the crises the region faces today? What if, instead of declaring "Not this," we ask, "If not this, then what?" (Ross 1998, 161).

In what follows, I offer three scenarios, three instances in which crisis opportunities for Appalachian studies present themselves. What do all of these sites have in common? They are all alignments of time and space in which knowledge has the opportunity literally and figuratively to shape the place in which what we think "Appalachia" is, what it actually is, and what we wish it to be are in a complex, dynamic relationship. To some extent, in theory, every place in the region is like this. In every speck of dirt of the southern mountains you might truly see a world, and indeed many of us do see Heaven in each wildflower.

But there are some sites, some spaces, in which for some period of time the terms of the deal, the bases on which the seeming "nature" of the place operate, come into a particularly distinct relief. In each of the cases I contemplate here, politics, economics, culture, and history join forces literally to rework the shape of the land itself to tell a particular kind of story about the relationship of a specific place to progressively broader patterns of the circulation and distribution of knowledge, power, material.

I offer these stories as examples of the kind of moment we should be alert for, events in particular places that offer us the opportunity to see the cultural meet the material, where images or versions of the region that are built into broader Appalachian landscapes are created in ways that have real material consequences—as well as farther-reaching and more abstract political ones—for residents of the region.

In all these spaces the opportunity appears to put forward a version of region in a public way. They are the kind of situations to which Appalachian studies could bring useful expertise not just in the interest of making sure that the account of regional life is accurate but that it engages the public in the difficult challenge of rethinking its inaccurate versions of regional life. And in so doing, our scholarly community could help create the conditions for Appalachia to become a new kind of experiment, in creating a version of the region that promotes the possibility of confronting the failed experiments of the past in such a way as to learn from them how to do it right the next time.

As the examples that follow demonstrate, these opportunities may turn up in all kinds of places: beside interstate highways, in secondhand stores, in public parks, in caves. The examples tend to run toward the landscape, built environment, and in particular public space, partly because I believe these are especially important points of intervention, as sites where ideas take material form, where landscapes proffer narratives, where the movements of people and goods and ideas and money through the region are literally reshaped. But they are also the kinds of situations that my academic training has equipped me and conditioned me to recognize.

All of us in Appalachian studies should be looking for the analogous situations within our own areas of expertise, where our resources can help build arguments and plans for a better version of the region out of the misfires of the past. We need to borrow thoughtfully from each other's projects to help create a truly useful version of what the region is. Maybe this also might involve crossing some professional lines and looking for those opportunities to take our work public in ways that traditional academic value systems might not fully recognize, as parents, volunteers, activists, consultants, commentators.

Bad information about the land and people of the Appalachian Mountains has helped sponsor some of its more heinous chapters. In Appalachia, as everywhere, bad assumptions based on spurious narratives about people, places, and histories create the preconditions for both material and symbolic injury. Perched on the edge of the Ivory Tower, looking intently at the way folks actually live in the Appalachian Mountains, maybe we can help find out what happens when those assumptions are rooted in good information, the kind our intellectual community exists to discover and circulate.

These are moments where that complicated, braided cordillera that is the very idea of region is visible in its workings. And when those workings become visible, they also become susceptible to change.

Dateline: Scottsboro

Scottsboro, Alabama, is a town with an image problem. It can't be easy having your town's name known, when it is known at all, for a watershed moment in the sordid history of racism in America.

This railroad town of about fifteen thousand is the site of the infamous "Scottsboro Boys" trial, in which a group of black teenagers, nine in all, were convicted by all-white juries, despite strong evidence for acquittal and blatantly incompetent defense counsel, of raping two white women on a freight train en route from Chattanooga to Memphis, Tennessee, on March 25, 1931. An armed group described in the local press of the day as a "posse" intercepted the train in the middle of the night at the whistle stop of Paint Rock and delivered the young black men they captured there to the county seat. The convictions were swift, greeted with thunderous applause from the crowd gathered on the square (who in the period prior to the decision had posed a serious threat to the prisoners). The verdict was followed almost immediately by death sentences for all but the youngest (age twelve) of the "Boys."

The next seven years saw a legal struggle in which appeals led by the International Labor Defense, the legal wing of the American Communist Party, twice reached the Supreme Court. And twice the Court handed down landmark decisions, one (Patterson v. Alabama, 1932) that asserted that the right to counsel required that said counsel actually be effective, and the other (Norris v. Alabama, 1935) declaring that potential jurors could not be stricken from the pool based only on their race. Undoing the verdicts, however, proved a much slower task than the original convictions, and full absolution for the Scottsboro Boys would not come until posthumous pardons for the last three defendants were issued by the Alabama Board of Pardons and Paroles in November 2013.

This is momentous stuff.[2] Many historians believe the Scottsboro Boys' case marks the origins of the contemporary civil rights movement. It took over seventy years for a standard-issue bronze marker to be erected on the courthouse square (in 2004). Only very recently (February 2010) has the Scottsboro Boys Museum and Cultural Center opened, and then only after an anonymous buyer tried to purchase their building, an old AME church, out from under organizers—and even then, it's open only two Saturdays a month and by appointment (Patterson 2010). The town's own promotional video makes no mention whatever of the Scottsboro Boys' trial, though it does plug the town's historic brick factory.[3]

The problem is, of course, if they came to make a Scottsboro Boys movie on location, most of the folks in this 91 percent white, 6 percent African American community would be cast as extras in the "angry racist crowd" scenes on the town square. Small-town white folks—the kind of people who make up almost all of the town's population today—don't come off too well in this story, and it's understandable that a lot of townspeople don't necessarily want to help maintain that bloodthirsty-racist image.

And they kind of have a point. Corruption of blood is forbidden in the Constitution just as much as the stacked-deck trials the Scottsboro Boys faced were. There's almost no one left in town with a direct, firsthand connection to those increasingly distant events.

What's more, the whole incident is tied to this particular county seat to some degree by chance. The scene of the supposed crime was a moving train. None of the accusers or accused had any ties to the town—all were transients looking for work, set in motion by the Great Depression. Had the train moved a little faster, or the lynch mob a little slower, and the whole spectacle crossed the Madison County line, we might well be talking about the Huntsville Boys today.

But while those exigencies might let area residents somewhat off the hook, that argument itself has a gloomier implication: this could have happened anywhere, especially anywhere in the South. Scottsboro's crooked trials and angry mobs were not anomalous but symptomatic. Trying to explain away culpability just leads to bigger, more disturbing, questions, questions turned not just on the white townspeople but on their white, small-town neighbors and visitors. The town's very name on the map is an uncomfortable reminder.

Here's what they're staking their reputation on instead. Scottsboro's big draw for the out-of-town guest is now the Unclaimed Baggage Center, "a one-of-a-kind store snuggled in the foothills of the Appalachian Mountains," unclaimedbaggage.com proclaims. It's a sprawling building complex—"more than a city block!" the website enthuses—filled with the stuff travelers from all across the globe checked in but never met at the carousel: seven thousand new items every day, the website promises. You can get good deals on suitcases, for sure, but also everything else under the sun: lots of secondhand clothing, jewelry, paperback books, outdated personal electronics, and a vast miscellany of every other kind of personal possession. The in-house "museum" includes such finds as Egyptian artifacts, a two-hundred-year-old violin, and a huge Muppet from the Jim Henson movie Labyrinth, which means Scottsboro has for years had more museum space dedicated to a gigantic, misplaced Muppet than it has for all nine Scottsboro Boys.

Even in a town with an image problem, this seems like a bit of an overcorrection: a warehouse full of placeless, wandering stuff, a global lost-and-found, the anti-place where things come to rest that people who had somewhere to be cast aside. It's a unique site, but one that could happen literally anywhere.

And it's the best example of a syndrome plaguing many of Appalachia's and America's small towns. Though they have a reputation for their unchangingness, most of the American small towns I know have changed pretty dramatically over the last few decades at the very basic level of how the landscape looks and works in daily life. Urbanites often fear the parochialism, the eccentricity, of small towns, but lots of these towns aren't eccentric at all. They offer the exact same landscape, architecture, goods, and services in the areas that are most active and significant in daily life—a least-common-denominator design centered on short hops from parking lot to parking lot.

Scottsboro is no exception, with a recently sprouted patch of sprawl growing up around the town's only exit off of US-72. The late economic unpleasantness has perhaps slowed its metastasis, but the big box stores are welling up all around: a new Home Depot and a Sears anchor a rash of strip malls, the Jameson Hotel and the Hampton Inn square off for primacy in the realm of the better class of mass-produced lodging, and casual dining restaurants complete the smattering. If there's a way for the town to beat the Scottsboro Boys' rap without addressing it directly, this is probably it: just blend in with the crowd.

The irony? Scottsboro's anonymizing project is brought to you in part by the Appalachian Regional Commission (ARC), which has designated this stretch of US-72 "Development Corridor V" of the Appalachian Development Highway System (ADHS) (http://www.arc.gov/adhs). ADHS is an infrastructure project of the old school: 3,090 miles of highway, still basically working from a plan in place since 1965 designed to provide linkage with the interstate.

Like the TVA's efforts toward rural electrification in the 1930s and 1940s and the ARC's own expanding work on connecting Appalachian communities to the Information Superhighway, the ADHS has helped to plug the region into a larger grid, changing not just the physical infrastructure but also the cultural structure of the region as a whole, leveling it up or down (depending on your point of view) in the direction of the American mainstream.

But the ARC has also, in recent times, demonstrated a commitment to "asset-based" development (http://www.arc.gov/abd). In sponsoring projects such as The Crooked Road, a music heritage trail that runs across southwestern Virginia, the ARC is making an effort to highlight and cultivate the things that are special about Appalachia's heritage and terrain in a way that might encourage an influx of consumer dollars to economically stressed communities throughout the mountain South. Development, in other words, that invigorates local cultures rather than obliterating them.

Maybe there's a clue toward a third way for this town to deal with its past that neither perpetuates nor obliterates the tragic public memory. There's a situation here that calls for the involvement of people who have the patience and the training and the knowledge to offer a critical understanding of events. Maybe there's a way to present this story in a way that resists sanitizing it yet doesn't necessarily disgrace Scottsboro's current residents in the process?

To achieve that goal by somehow denying (or, more passive-aggressively, deliberately forgetting) the involvement of the local residents in the larger incident would be deeply at odds with the truth of the story. It would be an insult to the price paid by the various players in the story, most especially the Scottsboro Boys themselves, who all eventually found freedom, only to find that, for most, their lives had been destroyed anyway.

Having an albatross like the Scottsboro trials hung on you might be hard to see as an asset. To even attempt it demands that people understand the incident in a different light: one that's not about blaming or celebrating racial and ethnic groups but about the fact that broader historical, cultural, political, economic, and geographical factors somehow managed to collide in this particular way, with global-historical reverberations.

To recognize the significance of Scottsboro as a locus of public memory is not to decide whether or not the people here are good or bad, guilty or innocent. Focusing exclusively on the culpability of the locals omits an important part of the story, too: the parts about regional networks of transportation, employment, politics, justice, and culture.

It's about the fact that this place is interesting, worth taking a closer look at, because this happened here—but it's bigger than that. There are things we can and ought to learn here about relationships among places and the problem of place itself. How do we tell the truth about places when the truth can be unflattering, even hurtful, and to fail to tell all would constitute a lie of omission? Can people understand the significance of history of the region, even when that significance is born of the need to remember, through the landscape of the places where they happened, the trauma of history? Can people embrace a regional heritage that might seem antithetical to their near-term interests?

We'd all better hope the struggle for cultural justice is not a zero-sum game. That means that whatever was gained for Americans in Scottsboro, despite the shame and horror of the way that it was realized, was gained for all Americans, including the people of Scottsboro present and future. In this view, Scottsboro is not just healthy but, more profoundly, vital.

These are pages from the notebook of a cultural critic on the move. I have long argued that the word "region" denotes not a thing but a complicated set of relationships, that region is itself a relational term. In recent years my ties to Appalachia have gotten more complicated and a lot more relational. Over the past few years I've had fewer and fewer personal ties to the region but more and more professional ones. Though I still go home to East Tennessee a couple of times a year, I have spent a lot more time driving up and down the Appalachian Valley gathering information for my writing and research, looking at Appalachia through a windshield for a couple of weeks at a time before heading back to life and work in Chicagoland. It is the Hillbilly Highway in reverse, my family ties centered on the Rust Belt, migrating to the mountains to pick up some work.

This is a point of view with some serious limitations, for sure, in terms of its organic relationship to the people and events that shape Appalachia. But it also has certain virtues, especially if one's work, like mine, involves sussing out bigger patterns in the shape of the operations of culture across a broad swath of the landscape. The contrast between my life-world and the Appalachian places I have visited, driving two-lane highways from Fort Payne, Alabama, to Berkeley Springs, West Virginia, between 2005 and 2012, poking around in archives, conducting interviews, has sharpened my perception of how regional difference is perceived from a distance, how the idea of Appalachia figures in the ways other people imagine their own places.

Appalachian studies might be well served to devote more deliberate attention to the issue of how the region figures in the geographical imaginary of the mobile majority. The point of view of those just passing through has real consequences for the economic, cultural, political, and environmental life of the region. In some situations the tail wags the dog: the cultural landscape of the region realigns itself in response to the way it is perceived. When this happens, the landscape itself becomes a site of public argument about what these regional relationships are and what they ought to be. At stake is the question not only of what the region is but of what the region does. It is not just about "us" but about the way our lives intersect with others, how the borders of "we" and "they" are constantly shifting.

Rootedness is important, but it is also necessary to understand how the meanings of places are constantly on the move. For Appalachian studies, the chance to shape Appalachia's future is premised on changing the kinds of ideas in circulation. To do that, we might look less for the quintessentially Appalachian features and more to those spaces and places where the idea of the region taps into the mainstream.

Dateline: Tamarack

I admit, I love Tamarack. Where else can you get braised kale with buttery slices of garlic just as easily as you can get a five-dollar footlong at Subway? But I'm supposed to love Tamarack: middle-class, out-of-state traveler, with strong sentimental ties to the mountain landscape. The place is literally made for me.

Anyone who has crossed West Virginia by interstate in the last fifteen years has had occasion to wonder, "What the hell is Tamarack?" prompted by official signs noting your distance from the place scattered all over the state. Despite its crisp, official Highway Gothic ethos, Tamarack's signage borrows a page from the more garish marketing campaigns of South of the Border or Wall Drug or SEE ROCK CITY, as by sheer repetition it makes you start to feel like you have got to stop there just to see what could be worth all these signs.

So when you get to the outskirts of Beckley on I-77 and they've made it so easy for you to pull off at the dedicated Tamarack exit ramp and it's been awhile since you've had a handy turnoff and you kinda have to go . . . there you are, walking in the front door of Tamarack, a craft store / conference center / food court / regional rebranding project for the interstate age.

The building itself is worth pulling over to take a look at; it's one of the most high-profile examples of a stab at critical regionalist architecture in (and about) the Appalachians. Designed by Charleston, West Virginia, architect Clint Bryan and completed in 1996, it's a big spiky circle, done up in autumnal reds, highlighted with highbrow triangular dormers of metal and glass (Casto 2010). The composition could seem too aggressive, too stark for the sinuous hills, but instead it (deliberately) calls to mind a starburst quilt pattern and all its attendant domestic tranquility. And the building's low eaves and dense plantings at the base visually attach it to its hilltop like a hobbit hole or a flying saucer that landed there long enough ago to be absorbed by the hill and the ivy and the bushes.

Rustic but classy. Polished but folkie. The mood carries over into the interior, where the sloped ceilings and earthy tile floors and natural light create a sales floor that feels like a very sophisticated barn. (I mean this in a good way.) All the merchandise (and there's a lot of it everywhere you turn) has a kind of folkloric air—even the kitsch has an artisanal quality. This is a place where you can buy poetry about coal. Like the architecture, Tamarack's retail sales area comes off simultaneously nostalgic but contemporary.

And the institution itself focuses not just on West Virginia's past but on its future. Tamarack's mission: to develop the economy of West Virginia by providing a marketing network and a retail outlet for upmarket folk arts and crafts throughout the state for the good of the artists, the state, and culture more generally. The nonprofit Tamarack Foundation, operators of the complex on behalf of its owners, the West Virginia Parkways Authority, go so far as to term it their "vision": "We envision a vibrant cottage industry in West Virginia where jobs, market opportunities, training, and educational resources abound for West Virginia's artists, artisans, craftspersons, and food producers, and our rich cultural heritage and artisan skills and traditions are preserved and strengthened for future generations of West Virginians" (Tamarack Foundation 2009). The mission statement makes clear, however, that the means to this end is putting a better foot forward. "The Foundation celebrates West Virginia's cultural heritage in the context of Tamarack's brand of excellence," it asserts, by "exploring new markets" and "communicating success stories."

But lofty as this vision is, and as sophisticated as the building's design is, and as carefully calibrated as its brand identity is, Tamarack still seems to have learned a few things about the good old-fashioned rules of roadside attraction that governed the Mystery Hole and Cudjo's Caverns.

Tamarack's foods—rustic fare like my kale or their fried green tomatoes courtesy of the folks at the Greenbrier, the old-world-elegant mineral springs resort—are toward the back of the circle, guaranteeing a little bit of ambling time for every hungry visitor.

And there's a lot to look at: books, jam, clocks, lamps, mugs, and staves. Through the neatly arranged merchandise you can regularly catch glimpses of the big windows overlooking the artisan studios: glassed-in workspaces where you might see glassblowing or basketry or carpentry going on before your very eyes.

When you come to a place like this equipped with Appalachian studies radar, of course, your antennae naturally bristle to pick up vibes of commodification, of exploitation, of any trace of condescending "uplift." And it's hard not to feel a little ambivalent about the craftsman-under-glass, the way it positions the buyer of products as an anthropological observer peering into the hillbilly habitat, or worse, as a kid at the zoo.

But that isn't quite fair this time. If there's a problem with Tamarack, it's that maybe it's a bit too classy for anybody's good. Tamarack dramatizes a middle-class-friendly version of regional culture, one in which the skills that sustained the yeoman farmers have been not only sustained but refined almost to the point of high art by contemporary craftspeople whom you can see, working in a clean modern settings, right over there, prosperous and provided for. It all bespeaks the kind of robust local scene that might appeal to, say, someone planning a family vacation or considering a second home. Exploitation is the last thing you'd think of here.

And indeed the project has not been without its benefits. A 2009 report from the Tamarack Foundation documents the victories of the charm offensive via a study by Marshall University's Center for Business and Economic Research. The report found that Tamarack's retail arm grossed over $89 million in sales, collected $4.5 million in sales tax, gave shelf space to over three thousand West Virginia artisans, and brought in more than 5.6 million visitors. Plus, the report noted, "as the money earned at Tamarack is spent and re-spent within the state, additional output, income and jobs grow by a multiple of the original spending" (Tamarack Foundation 2009).

Ultimately, though, it's all about that branding x-factor, the message that Tamarack turns loose about Appalachia on America's interstate-driving public, but for that, the researchers have decidedly less hard data. "'It is important not to overlook the positive image that Tamarack creates for those visiting the state,' said Jennifer Price, one of the Marshall

University researchers. '[Tamarack] enhances perceptions of the state's hospitality and its creative community'" (Tamarack Foundation 2009).

Getting the mountaineer all cleaned up and ready for polite company, though, comes at a cost. You must use good manners here, put your napkin in your lap when you eat your braised kale, and never, never talk about politics.

The Tamarack Foundation built this place to respond to a problem that it won't mention even as it tries to solve it: that folk life in the mountains is not robust, that musicianship and cooking and crafts are all under ongoing global cultural and economic pressure in a world where it is easier and cheaper for people to buy stuff rather than make stuff. Tamarack is not allowed to say that Walmart is the state's largest employer; that more often as not more local people will turn out to support the destruction of the mountains by the coal companies than will turn out to protest it; that meth labs are a much more thriving sector of cottage industry than are craft studios.

Tamarack isn't a lie—West Virginia really is a place of amazing cultural production. But it isn't just that, any more than it's just a place where everybody has Mountain Dew mouth. In building a cozy, appealing context for an upper-middlebrow-friendly rendition of Appalachia, Tamarack disconnects the work from the landscape. Part of the cultural history of the mountain South is how the crises that have repeatedly faced inhabitants of the region seem almost to catalyze remarkable and enduring folk arts. But the crucible this state has been, and the way the conflicts and costs of the American Dream have played out here, a look at actually existing West Virginia, why, that's a bit impolite for the dinner table, isn't it? Especially since we've made it so convenient for you to be here.

But that may just be what you get in a partnership between a branding project and a highway department: a version of the region designed for people who are just passing through. Tamarack is a part of the larger whole that is the West Virginia Turnpike travel experience, wherein you are offered lovely vistas of actual West Virginia scenery but almost no visual evidence of the coal-mining industry, even though you pass within mere miles of massive current and former mountaintop removal sites.

What's most sad to say is that, while this Pygmalion project has succeeded in creating a more genteel Eliza Doolittle, not enough I-77 drivers are interested in taking a break to see My Fair Lady. What was supposed to be a revenue stream for the Parkways Authority has become a revenue *sink and a target of derision for small-government shouters who picked up on the class politics of the whole presentation: your highway dollars go to fund a nice store for out-of-town rich folks. The narrative practically writes itself. Ironically, the retail center intended as an image-builder for West Virginia has become something a certain segment of West Virginians on the political spectrum define themselves against.*

And as is so often the case these days, the populist strains of this argument are just a stalking horse for more corporate takeover. Former West Virginia governor Joe Manchin's solution to "the Tamarack problem" was to try to cut lease deals with chain restaurants and hotels on the one hundred acres of perfectly good land just sitting there around Clint Bryan's lovingly designed, carefully sited facility, doing nothing. "We'd still have Tamarack as the marquee," Manchin told the Charleston Daily Mail *back in 2009. "It can't make it on its own. If you want to keep the Tamarack as we know it, you've got to have money coming from somewhere else. We have the property to generate the resources to do that" (Stump 2009).*

But you know what? That idea didn't work any better. The Manchin administration called for proposals for use of that prime real estate, and no one, I mean no one, answered that call, leaving Manchin mouthing boilerplate bureaucratisms about the future of the facility: "Plan B is that we're going to operate Tamarack as efficiently as we possibly can," he told the Beckley Register-Herald *in March 2010. "We're going to leave it in that mode right now. Hopefully, there will be a little more direction, and oversight, if you will, to make it more efficient, more effective" (Porterfield 2010).*

More effective . . . To what effect?

At least if Tamarack dies it will leave behind a beautiful corpse. That steel-and-glass quilt star can be a monument to the perils of trying to make a living off your culture. It's a much finer revenant of development schemes gone by than the shattered mountaintops lurking out of sight nearby.

How to tell the story of the failed experiments? We need to look these examples dead in the face no matter how hard other sectors of our culture try to keep them safely out of view. The recent past, before it has had time to mature into history, always has a little something of the abject about it. Living memory means we have not yet had time to get over the embarrassment about our mistakes. The mess may be cleaned up, but the anxiety that the cleanup might not be complete, that the damage might still be visible beneath the plaster and primer, still hangs around.

We need to keep track of those scars, though—not just the wounds received in a noble cause but the ones got in more dubious undertakings. One thing it is important, it is necessary for Appalachian studies to do is to take account of these failed experiments with an eye toward the optative: What happened here that we can learn from? What valuable perspectives for the way to go in the future can be derived from studying the missteps of the past?

The last exemplar in this essay looks at the way that, even in some of our most iconic locations, multiple versions of the past are constantly competing for our attention, encoding their lessons into the landscapes we inhabit in complex landscape narratives. Appalachian studies scholarship should continue to preserve the diversity of Appalachian experience, with particular attention to those narratives that are most under threat of erasure. This final tale from my Appalachian travels illustrates what is at stake when one story tries to elbow out all the others.

Dateline: Cumberland Gap

The Cumberland Gap has long supplied American culture with a place where we can see multiple pasts and futures bumping up against each other: contested ground between the Shawnee and the Cherokee when Boone arrived, the vanguard of a march toward a new kind of society.

This pattern of worlds colliding is written deep into geology of the Gap's terrain. Powell (no relation) Valley, running through Tennessee and Virginia on the Gap's southern flanks, represents the contact zone between the Great Valley's petrified seafloor limestone and the coalfields' sedimentary shales. Just north of the Gap in Kentucky's Yellow Creek Valley, the town of Middlesboro is built in the crater of a three-hundred-million-year-old meteorite strike. From the Pinnacle, you can see the entirety of the three-mile-wide flat spot, an anomaly in the wrinkled topography of southeastern Kentucky.

But the story of the Cumberland Gap as it is typically told doesn't reach back quite that far. Instead it centers on two of the most canonically significant phenomena of American history: first, the conquest of the western frontier, then the Civil War. Daniel Boone's 1775 expedition through the Gap was the sociohistorical equivalent of a meteorite impact, the blow that breached the last remaining barrier between the inexorably, increasingly Anglo-European east coast and the North American interior. The next thirty years saw over a quarter-million migrants (including uncounted chattel slaves) pass through the Gap in his wake.

During the Civil War the Gap embodied the nation's strife, an em-
battled symbol of an embattled people, a space of turmoil that changed
hands four times in a region unstably divided in its loyalties. The Gap was
again the frontier, but here in its older sense of being a borderland among
separate nations, a landscape befitting the "brother versus brother" narra-
tive of the War between the States. Like much of the southern mountains,
the Gap was a place where both strategic positions and political loyalties
were very much up for grabs, a place that now, in hindsight, illustrates
the many dissonant strands that had to be overcome to restore the civili-
zation that, according to American mythology, Boone had delivered here
a century before.

In these respects, the Gap is a textbook Historic Site: buckskin, can-
nons, scenery, the works. Its very existence establishes the significance of
Appalachia in the Grand Narrative of America. But the Gap isn't just an-
other stoic monument to American exceptionalism. Its iconic significance
centers not on a person, event, or landmark but on the changeability, the
malleability of American landscape and culture, on the Gap's status as
a place where, as Frederick Jackson Turner memorably declared in his
1893 lecture on the "Frontier Thesis," you could "stand . . . and watch the
process of civilization, marching single file."

The visual equivalent of Turner's analysis is the Gap's most icono-
graphic portrayal, George Caleb Bingham's 1852 painting, Emigration
of Boone, *in which the orderly pyramidal composition of Boone and his*
compatriots draws light and order into the center of a painting whose
landscape is otherwise cast in a twisted and menacing twilight.

But as many historians since have argued, the realities of American
history never provide such an orderly spectacle. What American studies
scholar David Lubin has written about Bingham's Boone can be said of
the cultural geography of the Gap as well: "Stagy and static, seemingly
nothing more than a petrification of an official ideology, Boone is actually
much more a palimpsest of discourses, some more outdated than others,
but all, tragically or not, fluid and viable in our world today" (1994, 105).
National expansion and consolidation is one story that can be told by,
about, and in this space. But that traditional patriotic tale is only one of
many that inhabits the place.

At a site like this, you preserve "the" historical narrative at the peril of
neglecting the other significant stories, the ones that await the observer
who's careful, maybe a little cockeyed. Among many other ways that the
Gap has provided a national resource, it is also a reservoir of different

kinds of stories, stories about what this place and, more broadly, what Appalachia and what America are, could be, ought to be. It is a place where visitors can contemplate both our historical experiences and how we represent our historical experiences—not just our stories, but how we tell our stories.

In this sense the Cumberland Gap is a textbook example of what anthropologist Victor Turner (1967, 93–111) has enduringly termed a "liminal space," where unexpected combinations and recombinations of people and ideas seem to cluster. Just as in J. T. Trowbridge's literary imagination, the Cumberland Gap somehow commended itself to providing the backdrop for a politically and culturally hybrid community. The area has provided the physical basis for the projection of visions and models of other kinds of worlds. In other words, it's a frontier.

Caves, too, are archetypally liminal spaces—thresholds between darkness and light, inside and outside; between known and unknown, knowable and unknowable; between life and the grave. So it's not surprising to find that Gap Cave, just south of the Cumberland Gap proper and immediately adjacent to the Wilderness Road, is like the Cumberland Gap only more so: the fringes of the frontier, the threshold of the threshold.

Indeed, Gap Cave is the very incarnation of Lubin's "palimpsest of discourses" in its layers of graffiti from soldiers, tourists, students, local people, and travelers—no better emblem for the many people and kinds of people to shape this place. Documented as early as 1750 by Dr. Thomas Walker (in the popular narrative of wilderness exploration, he's Boone's opening act), Gap Cave served various people and purposes as a mine, a water supply, a shelter, and, curiously, a signature feature of the Gap's landscape, the subterranean complement to the Pinnacle's commanding overlook. Eventually, it came to be opened for paid admission as Cudjo's Cave from 1920 to 1992. Brochures proclaimed its "fantastic and bewitching beauty" and described a massive formation called the Pillar of Hercules, the "world's largest stalagmite" at sixty-five feet high and thirty-five feet around (see Matthews 2008).[4]

But if the cave sums up and underscores the Gap's mythological significance, it also embodies and intensifies the ironies of the way these liminal spaces have been physically and culturally reshaped. In recent years, certain layers of the palimpsest both inside and outside the cave have been given a good (literal and figurative) scrubbing, part of a larger effort to restore the entire landscape of the Gap to its "historic condition."

That's a term that sounds very definite and official, but on further inquiry, "historic condition" turns out to mean more like what it was back between, say, the late eighteenth to late nineteenth centuries. Or thereabouts. Precision work it isn't, but it has been an incredibly elaborate, ambitious project—on the frontiers, you might say, of public history in its effort to preserve a historic landscape by physically de- and reconstructing it.

First came the erasure of vehicular traffic via the rerouting of US-25 through a huge, modern, 240-million-dollar tunnel. Indeed, the tunnel is a cause, not an effect, of the reclamation project. By the late 1980s, the Gap, once celebrated for opening access to lands beyond, had become an impediment to the movement of people and freight across the Appalachians. The tunnel is a workaround for what was one of the most dangerous stretches of two-lane highway in the nation, diverting truck traffic from a winding mountainside roadbed originally laid out for traffic moving at the speed of pack animals. The tunnel's modernization of the infrastructure made available both the opportunity (an influx of federal development money) and the materials (clean fill dirt) for this peculiarly antimodern experiment.

Next, a four-million-dollar joint project of the National Park Service and the Federal Highway Administration removed the now-vestigial roadbed of the old highway, along with any and all billboards and roadside structures of any kind, including one of US-25's long-standing landmarks, the old Cudjo's Cave gift shop and ticket office. "We're more used to building roads than removing them," federal project engineer Jeff Schmidt told the press in 2001. "This is kind of a reverse cycle for us" (Simmons 2001).

Then, using eighteenth- and nineteenth-century illustrations of the southern approaches to the Gap, engineers used the excess fill dirt from the tunnel project to restore the shape of the hillside to some simulation of its pre-automobile-age topography, tracing a ten-foot-wide wagon road along the newly re-formed hillsides, which bury the highway roadbed to a depth of thirty feet in places.

Finally, students from nearby Lincoln Memorial University—the institution that owned the cave during the Cudjo's era—planted twenty thousand trees along the path of the deconstruction site—covering their tracks, as it were, through the very space they had helped commercialize by operating their roadside attraction.

Throughout the project, park officials stayed on message, asserting that "park visitors were walking the newly-restored Wilderness Road in the footsteps of Daniel Boone." "We're putting the pieces back together and re-creating as accurately as possible the first glimpse of the Promised Land," proclaimed park superintendent Mark Woods. "Past coming back to life at Cumberland Gap," declared the Knoxville News-Sentinel *(Simmons 2002).*

There are some problems with those ambitious (if ambiguous) declarations. Can you really "put those pieces back together" and historically regress a landscape? In many ways it's just an unrealistic claim on its face, starting with the problem that the ground beneath visitors' feet was until as recently as 1996 deep beneath the Gap itself. When you stand on the "restored" Wilderness Road today, there's a lot you have to train your senses to ignore to have even the vaguest sense of what life was like here in the past—most prominently, the sight and sound of busy traffic on the four-lane through the tunnel that made all this possible. All are symptomatic of the more conceptual conundrum of trying to reverse history through actions that themselves become a part of the history of the place. There were bound to be some internal contradictions.

The biggest of them all is that the attempt to make the past more available in many ways makes it less so. "History" appears to us as a narrowly defined zone that ended many generations ago, obscuring the fact that what we're seeing is actually a present-day definition of American heritage. Instead of reconstructing a meaningful, immediate, tangible past, the project constructs a comprehensible past, but one with no claims on the present: a remote and containable zone, organic yet carefully maintained. Static and stagy, you might say—not a revelation of the truth but an argument about what the truth of the Gap should be.

The case of Gap Cave, however, shows what a complex undertaking delimiting the truth can be. Though the above-ground property was incorporated into the National Historic Park in 1947, Lincoln Memorial University operated Cudjo's Cave as a tourist attraction until that aspect, too, was taken over by the Park Service in 1992. Then work began simultaneously to upgrade and downgrade the old show cave armature. The business had been in a long-term state of decline since the construction in the 1960s and 1970s of Interstate 75 some forty miles to the west. The old tourist infrastructure and the cave's geological finery were dilapidated and vandalized.

Park Service employees and volunteers from the Pine Mountain Grotto of the National Speleological Society (NSS), however, decided this was a part of the palimpsest of history that had to go. They spent years of steady work cleaning out trash, cleaning up (some, but not all) graffiti, and removing handrails, monuments, and wiring, inspiring author Larry Matthews to proclaim, in his NSS guidebook Caves of Knoxville and the Great Smoky Mountains, *"The cave now closely resembles its original condition" (2008, 79).*

But what is the "original condition" of a cave tens of millions of years old? Are we talking pre-Cudjo's? Precommercialization? Pre–white settlement? Pre–human arrival over ten thousand years ago? How would we know "original condition" when we saw it, if we could see it at all? Wouldn't its "original condition" be totally dark?

Truth be told, much of what's happened here is not restoration but redevelopment—a new version of the cave that's about the older versions of the cave. Lighting was removed, so visitors now carry flashlights, but pathways and stairs have been upgraded to newer, safer, more durable designs. The roadside show-cave landscape with its gift shop and signage is gone, but tourists still pay up to accompany a guide for the underground walk. Only now money changes hands not at the old roadside stand by the two-lane but at the park visitors' center, demurely out of view just the other side of the new tunnel.

Once in the cave, visitors receive a tour that hasn't changed all that much, though it's given these days by uniformed park personnel: true to the terms of the genre, it's a mix of history and lore, some scientific fact and some tall tales, woven together by the story of the development and redevelopment of the cavern itself as a tourist attraction. Though the tale of the historical restoration process is now a part of that story, guides also still tell the story of how Old Cudjo, the runaway slave, took shelter in the cave.

This "local legend," of course, is also the forgotten political fable of a Boston novelist, J. T. Trowbridge, whose 1864 best seller, Cudjo's Cave, *is set among runaway slaves hiding in a cave identified in the novel as being near the Cumberland Gap. In a story described as "a mixture of war-time propaganda, romance, and adventure," the cave becomes a meeting place of Quakers, Unionists, and other fringe types, a space where an alternative community could escape from and resist the region's politics and culture. Despite the fact that contemporary critics celebrated the "truth to nature" of his novel, there's no evidence that Trowbridge ever visited the area—rather, in his choice of setting he drew upon and intensified the popular geographical imagination of the Gap as a liminal, dynamic landscape.*[5]

But sure enough, though the master lighting system is long gone, at a stop late in the tour guides use flashlights to illuminate the formation known as Old Cudjo. When the beam strikes at a particular angle, shadows produce a wizened, bearded face in a calcite column—Cudjo himself, still safely hidden away. (Never mind that Gap Cave would be a terrible choice for a fugitive slave hideout, much less a seditious meeting place, frequented as it was by Confederate soldiers between 1861 and 1863, when the novel is set, and also when the Gap was occupied by the Confederate army.) Through such transformations and accretions has Trowbridge's fictional creation become a part of the cave itself, etched into the cultural bedrock of the Cumberland Gap by a beam of light.

That's perhaps not what the Park Service meant when it said "historic condition," but it's appropriate that Cudjo, the fictional creation of an author who never even set foot here, retains a place in the local collective memory. The Gap is an area whose actual material history has been shaped and reshaped by mythology, by literature, by culture. To have a figure—a kind of spectre, almost, a shadow-puppet—physically representing the presence of that myth is, in its way, an historical accuracy of a different order.

What's more, Cudjo's persistence is a clue to remind us of what the big restoration project leaves out, what lies beyond the boundaries of the authorized historic meanings of this place. The Gap became known far and wide as a crossroads of people and ideas—a reputation that Cudjo's Cave both drew upon and then widely reinforced. The transmogrification of Trowbridge's fiction into the Gap's historical landscape suggests that maybe the name "Cudjo's Cave" should be restored in the name of adding a bit more history to the deconstructed, reconstructed landscape's "historic condition"—history of a sort that can't be modeled out of clean fill dirt, but history that has shaped the landscape here nevertheless.

Tellingly, one very important aspect of the Gap's history that the restoration project leaves out by setting the wayback machine to the end of the Civil War is a story of the American Dream gone weirdly, ridiculously awry. The story, at least according to Robert Kincaid's 1947 book, The Wilderness Road, begins in Gap Cave (1992, 315). On a summer night in 1886, a Canadian speculator named Alexander Alan Arthur camped at the Gap with his mineral surveying team, witnessed the damage inside the cave resulting from an earthquake centered far away in Charleston, and seems to have taken it as a divine sign to begin another seismic transformation of the area.

Arthur was a flamboyant figure given to elaborate whiskers and Eng-lish riding costumes whose rise and fall as the impresario behind the development of Newport, Tennessee, as a model timber industry town forms an entertaining chapter in Wilma Dykeman's 1955 The French Broad. He pitched a romantic vision of the region filtered through a Brit-ish imperial sensitivity to drum up foreign investment in Middlesboro, Kentucky, "the Magic City," which was to be a center of iron and coal. On the other side of the Gap, Harrogate, Tennessee, supplied the latest in tourist technology with a luxury hotel and attractions including the H. Rider Haggard–themed "King Solomon's Cave," a kind of first draft of the experiment of combining literary fictions with the Gap's subterranean topography.

But this ambitious vision of the region's economic potential, appro-priately enough for its setting, cratered. The grand hotel went bankrupt within a year, the model industrial town burned, the global capital dried up in the collapse of Barings Bank, an event that shook the global economy and foreshadowed the bursting of the railroad bubble and the vast finan-cial collapse of 1893. Arthur himself, ever the living symbol, was seriously injured when the first train to the Gap on his newly opened railway line derailed, killing many of the investors and local gentry who had joined the grand-opening excursion (Kincaid 1992, 325).

The truth-is-stranger-than-fiction coincidences and almost operatic trappings of the narrative make this a story worth telling just for its enter-tainment value, but I also can't help but wonder if maybe the American public in the early part of the twenty-first century could have had some benefit from hearing a story of the social consequences of real-estate specu-lation and the hard lesson that markets don't always expand. This story is familiar to the Appalachian studies community from John Gaventa's pathbreaking work in Power and Powerlessness: Quiescence and Rebel-lion in an Appalachian Valley *(1980), which carefully anatomizes both the economic base and the cultural superstructure of Arthur's predatory capitalist project, and it's Gaventa's story that is surgically removed by the National Park Service restoration project in favor of one more friendly to Manifest Destiny. So one key question for those of us dedicated to having the public record report a truer account of the Appalachian experience is, How could this site give Gaventa a voice alongside Frederick Jackson Turner?*

There's another, better lesson to learn there, too. Out of the literally smoldering ruins of Arthur's experiment came a different kind of social experiment in response. The financial devastation left in Arthur's wake stirred the conscience of mountain missionaries, whose local school suddenly became something much more ambitious when Union general and philanthropist O. O. Howard took the reins. In short order, Arthur's former resort in Harrogate became the campus of Lincoln Memorial University. King Solomon's Cave became Lincoln Memorial's water supply and revenue stream, with Trowbridge's Cudjo helping paint the area in a more progressive light—no doubt making General Howard's fund raising in the Northeast a little more productive.

Whatever the ethical and political shortcomings of the nineteenth-century mission movement, its noblesse oblige and cultural imperialism,[6] having Lincoln Memorial University succeed Arthur's oligarchical resort community represents at the very least the replacement of an institution celebrating exclusivity with one devoted to access—a step in the right direction at least. It's fitting that this site, so profoundly shaped by different imaginative interpretations of the region, gave rise to significant Appalachian authors Jesse Stuart, James Still, Don West, and George Scarborough—all English majors at Lincoln Memorial University. Between the Appalachian writers passing through the Cumberland Gap and the body of significant work in the history of Appalachian studies about the Cumberland Gap, few sites on the map have constituted such an epicenter of regionalist writing. Maybe there's something in the water?

This part of the story, which is written into the bedrock of the Gap in the face of Old Cudjo, needs telling, too, not just for the native drama of it but because it demonstrates something important: that alternatives are possible, even in the very site of crisis, that some experiments can succeed and endure even if they always only work toward the best possible versions of themselves.

The archaeological survey work that accompanied the Gap restoration project discovered something interesting: the Wilderness Road was not really one thing, a pair of wagon ruts leading into destiny, but something more like a braid. Time and traffic and the collective impact of everybody's best guess about how to get the wagon up and down the hills meant the Wilderness Road was more of a zone than a highway. The compact, crushed-limestone trail slabbing its way across today's restored hillside is really a composite. Based on a true story, you might say.

How could this restoration project, such a rich, ambitious, and visionary public project dedicated to understanding the past, include some of those strands of the story? How much richer and more eminently useful would the history of the Gap be for the region, for the nation, if we didn't try mentally and physically to erase the parts of the story that follow its more traditional, triumphalist period?

If the pattern holds, someday this Park Service restoration will be another layer on the palimpsest, another attempt to rewrite the story of the Gap. Who knows what other fictions might shape the Gap? What new stories will we use it to tell? Examples are already emerging: some clever literary detective work has determined that Cormac McCarthy's novel The Road *(2006) begins its grueling postapocalyptic journey at the Gap. Landmarks in McCarthy's text and on the road map correlate neatly to describe a route on Highway 25 south, down the mountain from the Gap to McCarthy's hometown, Knoxville (Morgan 2007). In a direct inversion of Turner's idea that you can witness the panoply of American Progress at the Gap, McCarthy takes it as a vantage point on the disintegration of society.*

The novel opens with the father asleep in the woods, awakening from a dream of wandering in a cave (Gap Cave, surely?) with his son, "like pilgrims in a fable swallowed up and lost among the inward parts of some granitic beast" (McCarthy 2006, 3). This cold, foreboding space is emblematic of the menacing, mysterious isolation facing the man and his son in McCarthy's vision of a place beyond our contemporary dream of plenty, looking back down the way we came and finding little but ashes. Finding, in other words, a new, no-longer triumphal frontier, defined not by the absence of civilization but by its failure. But the Gap—and most especially its namesake cave—has always been a place of multiple, competing narratives, all in motion on the Appalachian landscape. Perhaps the Cumberland Gap can also help us see a way to avoid that fate.

Every now and then an opportunity appears to put forward in a public way a version of the region that includes a vision of the region: both what it is and what it could be. One thing that makes Appalachia what it is is the unusual concentration of deliberate experiments in shaping the land, and the lives of the people who inhabit it, to achieve some larger social purpose. That is a category that includes company towns and Civilian Conservation Corps campgrounds, communes and strip mines and strip malls. Appalachia is a space in which folks are constantly trying out new ideas in how we are going to work out our relationships with each other on a particular patch of earth and period in time.

Spaces like these give us the opportunity simultaneously to examine the failed experiments of the past and make arguments for a better version to come. That is where the academics with their slow-moving reflection and dedication to accuracy and completeness come in. For many in the Appalachian studies community, one thing to offer in return is the special resources our institutions still make available in whatever attenuated form: access to information and technology, dedication to getting the facts right, responsibility for maintaining spaces of thoughtful deliberation and intellectual honesty (most people just call them classrooms).

We need to be alert to situations in which we can deploy that knowledge in ways that both enrich the present and offer the opportunity to plan for a more decent future. We need to remember that Appalachian studies itself grew in part out of Alexander Alan Arthur's great mistake; the school that rose from the ruins of the resort trained writers whose works have become historical and cultural underpinnings of the field. It is fitting that Appalachian studies can trace its own genealogy in part to this place that is such a complex physical manifestation of the cultural imagination of Appalachia. I hope we never lose this tradition of arguing for this region, whatever its past, to become a better place.

We need to find the places in which we can publicly set the record straight about what this place is and how it got that way. But we should never lose sight of what it could be and bring our resources to bear on making arguments for how to get it that way.

Notes

1. This proposed volume would be the sequel to Jeff Biggers (2006).

2. The tale of the Scottsboro Boys cuts a wide swath across culture, including, but by no means limited to, a 2010 Broadway musical (*The Scottsboro Boys*, songs by John Kander and Fred Ebb, book by David Thompson); a 2000 PBS documentary (*Scottsboro: An American Tragedy*); a 1994 oral history (Goodman); a 1970 scholarly history (Carter); and a 2009 cultural history (Miller).

3. The video I originally viewed is no longer available on the city of Scottsboro website (http://www.cityofscottsboro.com), but the latest promotional videos available there and on the Jackson County, Alabama, Chamber of Commerce site (http://www.jacksoncountyal.com) make no mention of the Scottsboro Boys' trial or the museum.

4. Primary materials can be found in the archives of the Cumberland Gap National Historical Park, Middlesboro, Kentucky; the East Tennessee Historical Society, Knoxville; and the Small Library of the University of Virginia.

5. The reprint edition of Trowbridge's novel is generally available in the Cumberland Gap National Historic Site gift shop.

6. In Gaventa's words, "Whether by 'moulding' in the socialization institutions, or by 'choice' from amongst the alternatives presented to him by the power situation, the effect upon the mountaineer was the same: a shaping and influencing away from his 'stock' to participation in the ways and values of the new order" (1980, 68).

Works Cited

Biggers, Jeff. 2006. *The United States of Appalachia: How Southern Mountaineers Brought Independence, Culture, and Enlightenment to America*. Emeryville, Calif.: Shoemaker and Hoard.

Carter, Dan T. 1970. *Scottsboro: A Tragedy of the American South*. Baton Rouge: Louisiana State University Press.

Casto, James E. 2010. "Tamarack." *e-WV: The West Virginia Encyclopedia*. November 5. http://www.wvencyclopedia.org/articles/681. Accessed May 23, 2014.

Dykeman, Wilma. 1955. *The French Broad*. New York: Holt, Rinehart and Winston.

Gaventa, John. 1980. *Power and Powerlessness: Quiescence and Rebellion in an Appalachian Valley*. Urbana: University of Illinois Press.

Goodman, James. 1994. *Stories of Scottsboro*. New York: Random House.

Kincaid, Robert. 1992. *The Wilderness Road*. Kingsport: Arcata Graphics. Originally published in 1947.

Lubin, David. 1994. *Picturing a Nation: Art and Social Change in Nineteenth-Century America*. New Haven, Conn.: Yale University Press.

Matthews, Larry. 2008. *Caves of Knoxville and the Great Smoky Mountains*. Huntsville, Ala.: National Speleological Society.

McCarthy, Cormac. 2006. *The Road*. New York: Vintage.

Miller, James A. 2009. *Remembering Scottsboro: The Legacy of an Infamous Trial*. Princeton, N.J.: Princeton University Press.

Morgan, Wes. 2007. "The Route and the Roots of *The Road*." http://web.utk.edu/~wmorgan/TR/route.htm. Accessed May 23, 2014.

Patterson, Dewayne. 2010. "Museum Will Remain at Joyce Chapel." *Scottsboro Daily Sentinel*, April 13.

Porterfield, Mannix. 2010. "Tamarack Property Development Put on Hold." *Beckley Register-Herald*, March 29.

Ross, Andrew. 1998. *Real Love: In Pursuit of Cultural Justice*. New York: NYU Press.

Simmons, Morgan. 2001. "Cumberland Gap Getting Facelift." *Knoxville News-Sentinel*, August 26. Vertical File: Cumberland Gap, 1998-present. East Tennessee Historical Society, Knoxville.

———. 2002. "Past Coming Back to Life at Cumberland Gap." *Knoxville News-Sentinel*, February 3. Vertical File: Cumberland Gap, 1998-present. East Tennessee Historical Society, Knoxville.

Stump, Jake. 2009. "Manchin Has Plan to Help Tamarack." *Charleston Daily Mail*, March 31.

Tamarack Foundation. 2009. "Tamarack Foundation Study Details Economic Impact of Tamarack: Artisans and State See Employment, Revenue Benefits." February 24. http://www.tamarackwv.com/foundation. Accessed May 23, 2014.

Trowbridge, J. T. 1864. *Cudjo's Cave.* Reprint, Tuscaloosa: University of Alabama Press, 2001.

Turner, Victor. 1967. *The Forest of Symbols: Aspects of Ndembu Ritual.* Ithaca, N.Y.: Cornell University Press.

8

Reconsidering Appalachian Studies

SHAUNNA L. SCOTT, PHILLIP J. OBERMILLER,

AND CHAD BERRY

The road to Appalachian studies is long. It begins with the rise of the university and academic disciplines in Europe from the Middle Ages through the Enlightenment and continues with the establishment of higher education in the United States, owing a special debt to the settlement school movement and Progressive Era reforms. Finally, Appalachian studies emerges in the 1970s in response to the War on Poverty and movements for social justice that began in the 1960s. For readers particularly interested in the broad intellectual and institutional foundations of Appalachian studies, this last chapter, we hope, provides a brief overview of the field's "prehistorical" era, attempting to answer the question: How might institutions of higher education avoid disciplinary rigidity and blind spots in order to encourage interdisciplinary area studies? It concludes with a discussion of the pros and cons of interdisciplinarity with a special emphasis on its effects on Appalachian studies.

The Emergence of Disciplines

Contemporary academic disciplines trace their roots to medieval European universities, whose purpose was the "pursuit of divine learning" (Chaplin 1977, 3208). The early university curriculum consisted of logic, grammar, and rhetoric, which were then supplemented by arithmetic, geometry, music, and astronomy (Scott 2006). Chartered by the Roman Catholic Church and European monarchies in the West, early universities trained men to serve God and king. The demand for "learned men" increased throughout the

High Middle Ages, and by the eleventh century, professional colleges had emerged to teach medicine, law, and business (Scott 2006). The shift from "divine learning" to worldly application occurred in the context of larger global transformations, including the transition from feudal land tenure to capitalism, the emergence of a global colonial capitalist system, urbanization, political revolution, the emergence of the nation-state, and religious schisms. Not surprisingly, the mission of the university also changed in this period, from learning "in service to God" to learning by individuals and "in service to the nation."

Meanwhile, within the university, new academic disciplines, such as physics, chemistry, biology, anthropology, sociology, economics, political science, geography, literature, and linguistics, were created throughout the Enlightenment, early modern, and modern periods. As part of this process, academic disciplines over time would become increasingly specialized and fragmented (Reid and Taylor 2010, 177), decontextualized, and displaced—that is, lacking any concrete spatial, temporal, or social referent. This transition in higher education expresses an internal "logic of fungibility" through which individuals and places are viewed as interchangeable "general equivalents" much like commodities in a market (Reid and Taylor 2010). Put more simply, disciplines and universities often teach us that specific places and specific people are not as interesting or important to study as are abstract forces, such as the logic of capital, forces of modernization, and the profit motive. Places, in other words, are neutral, flat backdrops for the "real" action: the interplay of abstract forces. People are merely the products of the interplay of such forces. Appalachian studies works in tension with these propositions.

Historian Robert H. Wiebe (1966) chronicled how disciplines in the United States were institutionalized through the creation of professional associations, journals, university departments with credentialing (degree-awarding) capacities, and budgeting mechanisms throughout the nineteenth and early twentieth centuries. Disciplines were created through a struggle for legitimation as competing claims were made about the nature of reality, what can be known, how we can know it, and who counts as a legitimate producer of such knowledge. Expertise was largely assumed to be the province of white, privileged males, because women, new immigrants, Native Americans, and racial/ethnic minorities did not have full citizenship rights in the United States through much of the nineteenth century.

Reform movements in the mid-nineteenth century began to chip away at this new order, particularly movements to end slavery and promote enfranchisement of African Americans and women. As oppressed and marginal groups pushed for citizenship rights, democratization increasingly became a common mission of U.S. universities, reflected in part by the 1862 creation of land-grant colleges, which aimed to bring higher education to the sons and daughters of farmers, craftsmen, and other families of modest means. Even though the land-grant college initiative included educational institutions to serve African American citizens, and even as women's colleges expanded in this era, it took another century for American democratization to progress so far as to integrate racial and ethnic minorities and women into institutions of higher learning.

By the twentieth century, higher education in the United States had made public service a central part of its institutional mission statements (Scott 2006). But what public does it serve? How do we account for differing and conflicting interests among publics? What is higher education's relationship to power and authority? Does it legitimize and reinforce the status quo or raise questions about it? Does it soothe or stir?

Higher education always had its critics, and Kentuckian Wendell Berry addressed these questions in a provocative 1983 essay titled "Higher Education and Home Defense." In it, he argued that U.S. higher education had become a commodified form of career preparation; as such, it educated students to become displaced professionals who leave the communities in which they were raised and invest their identities in occupations rather than places. Because they place no value upon specific places or communities, these professionals pursue profit and career advancement (1987, 49–53). Institutions of higher learning, he writes, "uproot the best brains and talents . . . and make them predators of communities and homelands . . . [with] no reliable way to distinguish between the public interest and their own" (54–55).

Social movements, such as the civil rights, women's, peace/antiwar movement, and various environmental movements, also questioned the content, nature, and purpose of higher education. As a result of these movements, new area studies were created in the university—women's studies, African American studies, Appalachian studies, peace studies, and environmental studies, to name but a few—and sent the newly credentialed into many institutions big and small. Such social and intellectual movements decentered the universalism, ethnocentrism, and false objectivism of traditional academic disciplines, whose theories and questions have been historically premised upon a number of assumptions (white, male, heterosexual, middle class, etc.). Events of the late twentieth century—the dissolution of the Soviet Union, the erosion of the welfare state, and the consolidation of a neoliberal global capitalist system—challenged the political relevance of the nation-state (Strange 1996). In response, universities positioned themselves as international institutions and, like transnational corporations, defined and extended their missions beyond the borders of the nation-state (Readings 1996; Scott 2006). Such global focus, however, has further complicated traditional conceptions of the "public interest" and opened up new terrains for research, debate, and deliberation—not the least of which are the shifts to despatialize capital and deterritorialize politics, an intellectual maneuver that often works to the disadvantage of the poor and working classes and those residing in "marginal," "underdeveloped" places, such as Appalachia.

Interdisciplinarity

Here, we discuss the benefits of interdisciplinary area studies, along with the costs and barriers to creating and sustaining these programs in contemporary social, political, and economic contexts. By providing histories of the actors, institutions, venues, and funders who collaborated to create area studies, we illuminate the institutionalization of interdisciplinary fields and the social construction of knowledge.

There is a strong argument to be made that interdisciplinary area studies have the potential to counter damaging trends in disciplinary-based scholarship. These include hyperspecialization of expertise, the production of knowledge that is inaccessible to the public and fails to inform public deliberation, the socialization of students in narrow and alienating ways, and complicity in oppressive forms of power (whether of class, race, gender, ethnicity, or region). To counter these trends, interdisciplinary endeavors provide pathways to integrate disciplines and specialties to produce multidimensional inquiry about complicated, place-based questions while, at the same time, encouraging scholarship that is more publicly accessible and accountable.

Forces from within and without the university have pushed the institution toward interdisciplinary innovation, although the transformation of higher learning has not been uniform or fast. There is inertia in the structure and culture of institutions of higher learning due to the "dual institutionalization" (Abbott 2001) of the disciplinary-based departmental structure in the academic labor market and at the individual institutional level, with universities acting as both producers and consumers of PhDs from traditional disciplinary-based departments. A number of routine procedures within the university and in the disciplines interact to reinforce disciplinary legitimacy and rigidity. Accrediting agencies, for example, require that instructors earn a minimum number of graduate hours from within a discipline in order to teach in that discipline, reducing the job prospects of interdisciplinary PhDs who may be knowledgeable enough to teach within an allied discipline but do not meet the minimum number of disciplinary hours. So unless the newly minted PhD is fortunate enough to find a college or university with the same interdisciplinary program from which she graduated, she may not be able to find a job.

Another way that disciplines are reproduced is through departmental control over faculty appointment, promotion, and tenure decisions. When departments need letters of recommendation for hiring, promotion, and tenure, they often solicit them from practitioners from within the discipline, thereby aligning the campus with disciplinary norms, values, and perspectives (Sá 2008). Furthermore, higher educational institutions earn recognition and prestige through the collective achievement of their departments as assessed by discipline-based evaluators and disciplinary professional associations (Sá 2008). Ranking and rating systems generally rely on peer assessments that reward disciplinary achievements and departmental reputations, once again making an institution's status dependent upon disciplinary support and judgment (Feller 2002). Finally, it is a taken-for-granted assumption that discipline-based departments function as the guarantor of quality control for both faculty and students (Sá 2008). The fact that such institutionalized processes are seen as inevitable, natural, and efficient highlights what institutional theorists have dubbed the "path dependency" of institutions. Once an organization starts down a path, it fails to consider alternative routes. In fact, it sometimes cannot imagine that there is an alternate way forward, and, if there is, the cost of changing often seems too high. Both the title and purpose of this volume urge us to rethink and possibly resist path dependency—in other words, to evaluate our current path and continually be open to alternate intellectual and political pathways.

It is useful to identify key factors or conditions to facilitate alternative ways of thinking. First, structural change is required to transform an educational institution characterized by disciplinary reification into one that encourages innovative interdisciplinary collaboration—change in the organization of work, budgetary flow, and physical space allocation.[1] Cultural change is also necessary. An institution must test its assumptions, review its mission and objectives, engage in strategic planning and evaluation, and adjust its language, communication strategies, and self-image to reflect new institutional goals and identities centered more upon interdisciplinary, place- or problem-based inquiry (Holley 2009). The organizational culture must be ready for change and collaboration, and key stakeholders must be involved in addressing the cognitive blinders that prevent faculty and administrators from viewing work from a different perspective. Leaders who are willing to experiment with new ways of teaching and doing research are needed, and these leaders must identify and facilitate a critical mass of like-minded faculty who are willing to pursue this change (Ginsburg and Tregunno 2005). Such a major transition requires repeated communication and education about the benefits of interdisciplinary programs. Minds and ingrained habits cannot be changed overnight; the message must be reinforced, and faculty must be involved in envisioning, planning, and implementing interdisciplinary programs. It is essential to provide incentives to change, including but not restricted to financial ones (Ginsburg and Tregunno 2005); these are necessary to compensate for the costs and discomfort that a major change engenders. The power and interests of dominant coalitions who oppose such change must also be contested and countered, a task not easy to pursue. Also, many believe that the construction of new buildings or at least the provision of new spaces for interdisciplinary programs and collaboration are necessary but perhaps not sufficient to create interdisciplinary collaboration (Sherren et al. 2009).

Moreover, there are always costs to organizational change, even though the benefits often outweigh them. Interdisciplinary research has all the challenges of collaborative work generally: communicating clearly, managing and supervising teams, and agreeing on the methods, theories, and approaches involved in research and writing. In addition, universities typically do not allocate resources or credit to individuals and units who collaborate across colleges; evaluation, promotion, and tenure procedures do not properly evaluate and often undervalue collaborative and interdisciplinary work; and departmental cultures frequently seem indifferent or hostile to interdisciplinary work (Sá 2008).

Area Studies

All of this requires the investment of limited money, time, and energy. One might reasonably ask: Is it worth the effort?

It should come as no surprise that it is. Area studies are better positioned to contribute to the debates in which Wendell Berry and many others have engaged about the purpose of higher education: whether to create selfish, career-maximizing, displaced individual consumers or grounded, committed, caring, critical citizens; whether to continue the neoliberal paradigm that has resulted in corporate deregulation, environmental crisis, and increased social

200 · SCOTT, OBERMILLER, AND BERRY

stratification or to question that paradigm in the quest for sustainability, social and environmental justice, and democratic community building. Area studies constitute a means to combat the trend of displacement criticized by Berry (1987) and Reid and Taylor (2010) in part because such initiatives usually focus on marginalized places and oppressed groups, thus encouraging us to think and act outside of disciplinary "boxes." While traditional academic disciplines are mostly organized around the study of phenomena across space rather than the study of multiple intersecting phenomena in one area (Moseley 2009, B4), area studies such as Appalachian studies order phenomena differently, focusing upon the "particular" and the "actual" (Reid and Taylor 2010) rather than the abstract, disembodied, displaced "spectral" space created by "postcommunal" disciplinary experts. By focusing on the construction of a place, for instance, area studies resist the exclusionary universalism and specialization that has too often defined the narrower and overly specialized academic disciplines (Limerick 2001).

Area studies can transform not only how people *think* about the world but also how they *act* within it. Centering our inquiry on places, groups, or problems (Abbott 2001) rather than abstract forces creates relationships with those places, people, or problems that require deep *and* broad knowledge and engender durable commitments to actual people, places, and problems. Appalachian and other place-based or regional studies have the potential to correct the failure of American colleges and universities to fulfill their "mandate to serve localities or regions—to receive the sons and daughters of their regions, educate them, and send them home again to serve and strengthen their communities" (Berry 1987, 53). Because area studies build upon disciplinary knowledge while simultaneously challenging disciplinary boundaries and practices, interdisciplinary fields are potentially heterogeneous, critical, and disruptive of received knowledge and dominant ideology and assumptions.

Although area studies offer an alternative to disciplinary balkanization (Sherren et al. 2009), an interdisciplinary field is not an inherently superior "accuracy engine" (Bouchard, 2012, 86). The disciplines themselves are historical creations, "spun off" from integrated humanities because they promised to provide greater accuracy, detail, and insight into a complicated reality. There is no reason to assume that the reintegration of disciplines represented by twentieth- and twenty-first-century interdisciplinary movements will be permanent or that it will not in the future give way to another cycle of specialization in the name of accuracy. Even as we advocate for area studies, we recognize that oscillations between specialization and integration and between the general and the particular may be as useful as the movement between disciplines and across cultural borders for generating knowledge.

Final Thoughts

Let's face it, this book is written by Appalachian studies scholars for faculty and graduate students in our and other interdisciplinary fields. It may not be read by policy makers or staff at foundations and state and government agencies. For that matter, very few non-academicians inside or outside of the region will know or care that it has been published.

But that is OK, because Appalachian studies is the academic wing of a larger social movement. It is where public intellectuals gather (to paraphrase Doug Reichert Powell in the previous chapter) to provide the Appalachian movement with access to information and ideas, to get the facts right about the region and its people, and to maintain spaces for thoughtful deliberation and intellectual honesty.

By doing their jobs, Appalachian studies teachers and researchers have furthered the movement by educating generation after generation of students and have been doing so for nearly forty years. We have attained about ten graduating cohorts of undergrads so far. Indeed, Shaunna Scott is a member of that first cohort. This is not only expanding the pool of practicing Appalachianists but also sending more culturally aware and politically alert graduates into all sectors of society: government, education, business, non-profits, and churches. Whether they end up inside or outside of Appalachia, the region and its movement for social justice will surely benefit.

Our students are the vectors of a legacy of teaching, mentoring, research, writing, and creativity established by Appalachian studies. Those in the field need not worry that their hard-won insights will be lost or not attended to, because the next generation has absorbed them, is using them, and will build upon them.

In some places, social change comes in the volcanic eruption of revolution, while in academia change generally comes from the gradual shifting of intellectual tectonic plates. Clearly a necessary but difficult virtue in Appalachian studies is patience. But the tempo of patient, careful scholarship can be frustrating for others in the Appalachian movement. The field began in the tension and turmoil of activism vs. scholarship, but currently, if not a complete fusion, there seems to be mutual respect between the two points of view. And why shouldn't there be? Both are necessary components of the movement they share, both have a mutual goal of social justice, both believe in transformation, and both manifest the qualities of dedication and determination in moving toward that goal.

There are other challenges for Appalachian studies. It is difficult to stay current with the many intellectual strands of such a braided field. Communication across various disciplinary approaches is also hindered by differing vocabularies, theoretical assumptions, and methodological techniques. Ironically, the very richness of interdisciplinary work in Appalachian studies sometimes makes it hard to communicate within the field itself. Another challenge of interdisciplinarity is establishing standards for quality work. As hard as it may be for a field with widely varying scholarly norms and expectations, the field has to strive for the best understanding and interpretation of the region and people. Appalachia deserves no less.

Despite these problems, could it be that Appalachian studies isn't interdisciplinary enough? For instance, urban planners, demographers, and ethnographers (among others) are needed to understand urban Appalachia, immigration, housing, and employment. To be fully interdisciplinary, Appalachian studies needs to add disciplines both to broaden the field's perspective and to add depth to its understanding of regional realities. To be sure, that will be a challenging task that will add new tensions and pose even more communication problems, but it can also make the field more dynamic and relevant to the region.

Although most of the region's population lives in urban and suburban areas, Appalachian studies maintains a strong rural bias. There is relatively little research on the sizable metropolitan populations within the region. Does urbanization launder out culture? Does Appalachian culture flourish only when used as a tourism and commercial stimulus for the economic development of rural places? Why does the field seem uninterested in these questions?

Appalachian studies has pretty much ignored both the impact of and the need for migration into the region. Most current commentaries are on Hispanics, an important part of the Appalachian social and economic landscape to be sure, but Hispanics now run a distant second to Asians in the migration streams entering the region. This is an overlooked factor in the economic development of Appalachia: on average each foreign worker with an advanced degree creates 2.6 jobs for American workers. Asian immigrants frequently come with or earn advanced degrees. What are the policy implications of this phenomenon for the region? What does this blind spot tell us about Appalachian studies?

Appalachian studies overlooks the region's middle class by ignoring it or dismissing it as nonexistent or unimportant or "shrinking." On what evidence is the claim based that the class structure of the region consists only of poor/working-class people and elites? The field has produced no studies describing the size, nature, distribution, and impact of an Appalachian middle class. Is this because it doesn't exist, or does the myopia of the field obscure the entirety of the Appalachian class structure? How does Appalachia define its middle class, and what is its role in the region's institutions and economy? Or its future?

Why is Appalachian studies largely silent on other areas important to people in the region—housing and employment, for instance? What, if any, role should mobile homes play in the region's housing infrastructure? How can we support the construction of affordable, energy-efficient, healthy, sustainable housing in the region? How can policies be changed and incentives offered so that more land is available for housing and alternative economic development?

What are the actual employment/income outcomes of regional economic development schemes (whether they come from the top down or from grassroots efforts)? How can Appalachian studies take an active role in reimagining (and evaluating) new types of economic development, in creating alternative locally owned economic enterprises, and in exploring alternative organizational forms, such as cooperatives and employee-owned businesses? There are some examples out there—in the mountains and beyond—and these experiences must be shared more widely. Can the field reverse the trend in higher education of creating placeless, self-centered, career-minded professionals and, instead, educate and nurture civic-minded, responsible citizens of places?

The answer is yes, but we must get out of offices and classrooms and go to the community. One step in the right direction would be to follow Fickey and Samers's charge (and live up to the field's tradition): engaging students in experiential and high-quality service learning throughout the region, conducting participatory-action and community-based research, and ensuring the labor and resources of our higher education institutions serve the people and the region. Another would be to provide more paid internships to place our students in the region to learn while doing meaningful work, teaching them to network with local community members, leaders, and organizations (see, for example, University of Kentucky Appalachian Center's Tomorrow Corps, https://bluegrassblade.wordpress.com/2014/08/27/uk-tomorrow-corps). The STAY project (http://www.thestayproject.org/) is notable; it aims to make the region a more welcoming and diverse place and provide more reasons for young people to stay in, return to, or move to the region to make a life.

How can Appalachian studies take advantage of new technologies to teach and collaborate from a distance and to share its research, videos, and archives globally? How can more people access information and seek an education, even if they need (or just want) to live in a place that doesn't have a bricks-and-mortar college? Colleges and universities, Appalshop, Highlander, and other institutions throughout the region have a massive amount of information (documents, recordings of performances and interviews, photographs, films) in their archives that could be digitized and used for teaching and research. If it hopes to thrive in a digital age, Appalachian studies needs to figure out how to do this.

Appalachian studies should be exceedingly mindful of the "digital divide" and how technology often works to reproduce old forms of inequality and create new ones. Broadband access is spotty in the mountains and other rural places throughout the region, and it can be expensive. How can we work with our institutions to avoid creating a two- or three-tiered higher-education system where some people cannot access any kind of education, others can only afford to enroll in online education, and only the most privileged get a high-quality residential education?

Appalachian studies should collaborate and converse more with related interdisciplinary fields, such as women's, African American, New West, and Pacific Islands studies. Perhaps Appalachian studies could arrange joint conferences with other area studies or invite special panels to our conference. Appalachian studies journals could commission special issues with comparative scholarship and conversations with other area studies and disciplines. More Appalachian studies teachers could use technology to create partnered, collaborative classrooms, which would enable students to share their ideas, work, and experiences cross-regionally and interculturally.

Cross-field collaboration is especially needed in a globalized world. As has been maintained throughout this volume, Appalachia is neither isolated nor exceptional. It is connected to the rest of the world and is affected by many of the same forces and trends penetrating other regions. Appalachian studies, for example, faces funding cuts under an education regime that has seen declining public support for higher education, a greater reliance on tuition dollars to fund higher education, a view of higher education as career training, and corporatized "profit-center" budget models being implemented at many colleges and universities (Clark 1998; Pelan 2012; Rhoades and Slaughter 1997).

When universities and colleges conceive of interdisciplinary studies as primarily a way to generate external grant funding, fields such as Appalachian studies that have critical, transformative potential will paradoxically suffer because they are not likely to be governmental- or corporate-funding priorities. A frantic chase for grant funding in a context of decreased funding for higher education creates a competitive, cutthroat environment in education and further reinforces the status quo in capitalism: money drives research priorities and knowledge construction, just as it controls the electoral and legislative processes. In recent years, some Appalachian studies programs have been closed, reorganized, and combined with other programs. Some have faced extreme cuts to their budgets. If the 1970s saw the birth and growth of Appalachian studies in higher education, the 2010s have seen a reduction and withdrawal of support for them. The time has come to engage in more systematic cross-interdisciplinary collaboration if we hope to survive to build knowledge and transform society.

This is not a full list of questions, possible directions, biases, and blind spots, but it is, we hope, suggestive of some of the things that "need doing." Appalachian studies is up to the task, because the field, similar to other area studies, starts with a focus on the subject—whether it be an historically oppressed or marginalized group or a geographic area. When it's at its best, Appalachian studies keeps its connection with its community-based, activist side and follows up on questions and issues that are raised in the struggle to create a more just, meaningful, and sustainable world. Our interdisciplinary approach works because our topical areas are more complex and varied than a single discipline can encompass and our questions and issues are so clearly connected to people's everyday lives, dreams, and struggles.

Notes

1. Universities may produce PhDs, but they are not the only consumers of doctorally credentialed faculty. Interestingly, smaller colleges often have quite different academic organizational structures. In the Appalachian College Association, for example, almost half have organized academic areas in divisions as opposed to departments. Berea College, for example, in 2011 implemented a divisional restructuring, after two years of thinking and planning, in order to enhance interdisciplinarity, hire additional interdisciplinary-minded faculty, and promote new kinds of teaching and learning.

Works Cited

Abbott, Andrew. 2001. *The Chaos of Disciplines*. Chicago: University of Chicago Press.
Berry, Wendell. 1987. "Higher Education and Home Defense" (1983). In *Home Economics: Fourteen Essays*, 49–53. San Francisco: North Point Press.
Bouchard, Danielle. 2012. *A Community of Disagreement: Feminism in the University*. New York: Peter Lang.

Chaplin, M. 1977. "Philosophies of Higher Education, Historical, and Contemporary." *International Encyclopedia of Higher Education.* Vol. 7, 3204–20. San Francisco: Jossey-Bass.

Clark, Burton R. 1998. *Creating Entrepreneurial Universities: Organizational Pathways of Transformation.* Oxford: Pergamon Press.

Feller, Irwin. 2002. "New Organizations, Old Cultures: Strategy and Implementation of Interdisciplinary Programs." *Research Evaluation* 11:109–16.

Ginsburg, Liane, and Deborah Tregunno. 2005. "New Approaches to Interprofessional Education and Collaborative Practice: Lessons from the Organizational Change Literature." *Journal of Interprofessional Care* 19(1): 177–87.

Holley, Karri A. 2009. "Interdisciplinary Strategies as Transformative Change in Higher Education." *Innovative Higher Education* 34:331–44.

Limerick, Patricia Nelson. 2001. "Going West and Ending Up Global." *Western History Quarterly* 32(1): 4–23.

Moseley, William G. 2009. "Area Studies in a Global Context." *Chronicle Review,* December 4.

Pelan, Rebecca. 2012. "Practising Disobedience: Feminist Politics in the Academy." *Hecate* 38(1/2): 210–22, 234.

Pye, Lucian W. 1975. "The Confrontation between Discipline and Area Studies." In *Political Science and Area Studies: Rivals or Partners?,* edited by Lucian W. Pye, 3–22. Bloomington: Indiana University Press.

Readings, Bill. 1996. *The University in Ruins.* Minneapolis: University of Minneapolis Press.

Reid, Herbert, and Betsy Taylor. 2010. *Recovering the Commons: Democracy, Place, and Global Justice.* Urbana: University of Illinois Press.

Rhoades, Gary, and Sheila Slaughter. 1997. "Academic Capitalism, Managed Professionals, and Supply-Side Higher Education." *Social Text* 41:9–38.

Sá, Creso M. 2008. "'Interdisciplinary Strategies' in U.S. Research Universities." *Higher Education* 55:537–52.

Scott, John C. 2006. "The Mission of the University: Medieval to Postmodern Transformations." *Journal of Higher Education* 77 (1): 1–39.

Sherren, Kate, Alden S. Klovdahl, Libby Robin, Linda Butler, and Stephen Dovers. 2009. "Collaborative Research on Sustainability: Myths and Conundrums of Interdisciplinary Departments." *Journal of Research Practice* 5(1): 1–29.

Small, Mario L. 1999. "Departmental Conditions and the Emergence of New Disciplines: Two Cases in the Legitimation of African-American Studies." *Theory and Society* 28(5): 659–707.

STAY Project. http://www.thestayproject.org/. Accessed June 5, 2014.

Strange, Susan. 1996. *The Retreat of the State: The Diffusion of Power in the World Economy.* Cambridge: Cambridge University Press.

Wiebe, Robert H. 1966. *The Search for Order.* New York: Hill and Wang.

Contributors

CHRIS BAKER is a professor of sociology at Walters State Community College in Tennessee, where he works in rural development.

CHAD BERRY is Goode Professor of Appalachian Studies, professor of history, and academic vice president and dean of the faculty at Berea College. He is the author of *Southern Migrants, Northern Exiles* (University of Illinois Press, 2000) and the editor of *The Hayloft Gang: The Story of the National Barn Dance* (University of Illinois Press, 2008), and he was the 2006–7 president of the Appalachian Studies Association.

DONALD EDWARD DAVIS is an independent scholar and consultant and currently serves as the governmental affairs representative for the American Chestnut Foundation in Washington, D.C. He is the author of the award-winning *Where There Are Mountains: An Environmental History of the Southern Appalachians* and is presently completing a book on the environmental history of the American chestnut.

AMANDA L. FICKEY is an assistant professor of intercultural geography and coordinator of Appalachian studies at Union College. Her research interests include economic geography, political economy, regional economic development, diverse economies, and alternative economic spaces.

CHRIS GREEN is director of the Loyal Jones Appalachian Center at Berea College, where he is an associate professor of Appalachian studies. A poet, editor, and scholar, Green has edited or authored four books, and he coedits the Series in Race, Ethnicity, and Gender in Appalachia at Ohio University Press.

ERICA ABRAMS LOCKLEAR is an associate professor in the Literature and Language Department at the University of North Carolina in Asheville. She is the author of *Negotiating a Perilous Empowerment: Appalachian Women's Literacies* and has also published in *Appalachia in the Classroom: Teaching the Region*, the *Southern Literary Journal*, *North Carolina Literary Review*, *Appalachian Heritage*, and other publications related to Appalachia, literacy, and the South.

PHILLIP J. OBERMILLER is a senior visiting scholar in the School of Planning at the University of Cincinnati and a fellow at the University of Kentucky's Appalachian Center. A former president of the Appalachian Studies Association, he recently edited (with Robert Ludke) *Appalachian Health and Well-Being*.

DOUGLAS REICHERT POWELL is an associate professor of English at Columbia College Chicago and director of the First-Year Seminar. He is the author of *Critical Regionalism: Connecting Politics and Culture in the American Landscape* (2007) and coeditor (with John Paul Tassoni) of *Composing Other Spaces* (2009).

MICHAEL SAMERS received his doctorate from Oxford University and is currently associate professor of geography at the University of Kentucky, having previously taught at the Universities of Liverpool and Nottingham. His research focuses on immigration, labor markets, and the political economy of economic development.

SHAUNNA L. SCOTT is associate professor of sociology at the University of Kentucky, the editor of the *Journal of Appalachian Studies*, and a past president of the Appalachian Studies Association. She currently focuses on creating partnerships among students, faculty, and community members in transitioning to more diverse and sustainable postcoal economies.

BARBARA ELLEN SMITH is professor of women's and gender studies in the Department of Sociology at Virginia Tech. She recently coedited, with Steve Fisher, *Transforming Places: Lessons from Appalachia* (University of Illinois Press, 2012).

Index

Anglo and Celtic heritage: folk schools and, 16–17; folksong collection and, 26; "worthy" poverty thesis and, 28. *See also* whiteness (social construction of)

anthropology, 14

Appalachia: A Report by the President's Appalachian Commission (1964). *See* President's Appalachian Regional Commission

Appalachian Alliance, 19, 102

Appalachian centers, 21–22, 72, 134, 152–53, 161

Appalachian College Association (ACA), 21, 205n1

Appalachian Consortium, 67–69, 72

Appalachian Development Highway System (ADHS), 173–74

Appalachian Harvest Network (AHN), 108–10

Appalachian Heritage (serial): on Affrilachian writers, 76; Appalachian bibliographic profile and, 74; as Appalachian studies publication outlet, 21; bibliographic writings in, 73; central-Kentucky publishing outlets, 72; electronic access for, 161; founding of, 65–66

Appalachianists, 30–31

Appalachian Journal (serial), 20, 21, 65, 68, 161

Appalachian Land Ownership Study/ Appalachian Land Ownership Task Force, 19, 20

Appalachian Mountain Books (serial), 73

Appalachian Notes (serial), 74

Appalachian Regional Commission (ARC): Appalachian Land Ownership Study funding, 19; Appalachian Regional Development Act, 98–99, 121, 124, 128; Area Redevelopment Act, 96; contract research and, 22; critical perspective on development and, 158; emphasis on infrastructure, 162; founding of, 28–29; "growth center" developmental model, 25, 128–30; isolation thesis and, 131; "lagging" discourse and, 120, 124–25; overview, 98–101; SALS recognition by, 106; short-term "technical" problem solving and, 122, 124–25, 145; suburban sprawl and, 173–74; support for Appalachian activism, 21; transportation funding proportion, 136n1

Appalachian Renaissance, 65, 71–72

Appalachian Review (serial), 64

Appalachians and Race (Inscoe), 48–49

Appalachian State University, 21, 67, 68, 152

Appalachian studies: academics vs. activism tension, 72–73, 142–47, 155–56; Appalachianists, 30–31; as area study, 16; camaraderie in, 150–51; conferences and workshops, 20, 22–23; current challenges for, 52; definitive themes in, 5–6; history of, 16, 194; journals, 21; omissions and blind spots, 4–5, 142–43, 156–60, 194, 202–3; paradigm shifts in, 27, 43, 48–50, 56; place-neutral thinking and, 195; review works on, 1–2, 141–42; self-reflection in, 162–63; vertical/horizontal integration in, 5. *See also* diversity; education; higher education; interdisciplinarity; social change

Appalachian Studies Association (ASA): activist initiatives in, 72–73; Appalachian Studies Conference, 20, 22–23; camaraderie of scholarly community, 150–51; membership and organization, 163n1; minority Appalachians and, 75, 142–43, 151–52; as oppositional social space, 146–47; outsider knowledge of Appalachia and, 163; overview, 20; Wilma Dykeman fellowship, 143

Appalachian Studies Conference, 163n1, 163n6

Appalachian Studies Youth Conference, 32n2

Appalachian Sustainable Development (ASD), 108–11

Appalachian Voices, 123

Appalachian Volunteers (AVs), 17–18

Appalachian Writers Association, 20

Appalachian Writers' Workshop, 23, 66–68

Appal/ReD Legal Aid (formerly Appalachian Research and Defense Fund), 18

Appalshop, 19–20, 22, 152, 163

ARC. *See* Appalachian Regional Commission

Area Redevelopment Act, 96. *See also* Appalachian Regional Commission

area studies: alternative methodology for, 9–10; Appalachian studies isolation from, 153; colonization/decolonization and, 13, 14–15; comparative place-based

The University of Illinois Press
is a founding member of the
Association of American University Presses.

Composed in 10.5/13 Adobe Minion Pro
by Kirsten Dennison
at the University of Illinois Press
Manufactured by Cushing-Malloy, Inc.

University of Illinois Press
1325 South Oak Street
Champaign, IL 61820-6903
www.press.uillinois.edu